THE WAR ON WOMEN

THE WAR ON WOMEN

And the Brave Ones Who Fight Back

SUE LLOYD-ROBERTS

**SIMON &
SCHUSTER**

London · New York · Sydney · Toronto · New Delhi

A CBS COMPANY

First published in Great Britain by Simon & Schuster UK Ltd, 2016
A CBS COMPANY

3 5 7 9 10 8 6 4

Simon & Schuster UK Ltd
1st Floor
222 Gray's Inn Road
London WC1X 8HB

www.simonandschuster.co.uk

Simon & Schuster Australia, Sydney
Simon & Schuster India, New Delhi

A CIP catalogue record for this book
is available from the British Library

Hardback ISBN: 978-1-4711-5390-7
Trade paperback ISBN: 978-1-4711-5391-4
eBook ISBN 978-1-4711-5393-8

Typeset in the UK by M Rules
Printed and bound by CPI Group (UK) Ltd, Croydon, CR0 4YY

MIX
Paper from
responsible sources
FSC® C020471
www.fsc.org

Simon & Schuster UK Ltd are committed to sourcing paper that is made
from wood grown in sustainable forests and support the Forest Stewardship
Council, the leading international forest certification organisation. Our
books displaying the FSC logo are printed on FSC certified paper.

CONTENTS

ACKNOWLEDGEMENTS

Huge thanks to everyone involved in making this book, both to those behind the scenes at the BBC and to all the brave women who have fought and continue to fight for justice.

Particular thanks to Ian O'Reilly, Vivien Morgan, Lyse Doucet, Lynne Franks, Sue MacGregor, Katharine Hamnett, Yasmin Alibhai-Brown, Sam Smethers, Hibo Wardere, Nimco Ali, Matthew Sweet, Luke Mulhall and Tony Jolliffe.

Thank you to the team at Simon & Schuster for their support, especially Abigail Bergstrom, Harriet Dobson and Nicola Crossley, and thank you to Sue's agent, Caroline Michel.

From Sue's husband Nick Guthrie and her children, George Morris and Sarah Morris.

The publishers would like to give special thanks to Sue's family, for their support in finishing this book.

PREFACE

I was standing on a stage addressing an audience in Trafalgar Square on Valentine's Day when the idea of *The War on Women* came to me. I had been persuaded by the formidable Lynne Franks, PR person and activist extraordinaire, to join her cast of speakers for the One Billion Women Rising rally. The brainchild of Eve Ensler, of *Vagina Monologues* fame, the annual event aims to draw attention to violence against women worldwide.

Clearly, God is not a feminist. The day before and the day after the rally saw London sparkling in bright winter sunshine. On that day, it was pouring with rain, buckets of it. I looked out on a crowd of a couple of hundred brave, bedraggled women, and a few men, cowering under umbrellas. The absurdity of it all suddenly came to me – not the rain but the reason we were all there.

I remembered other rallies I had attended in Trafalgar Square on behalf of Tibetans, Kurds, Palestinians and the Bushmen of the Kalahari. Why is it, I asked myself, that women who make up 51 per cent of the world's population are still campaigning for fair and humane treatment in the twenty-first century, as if we are just another of the world's persecuted minorities?

My friends call me the BBC's 'Hopeless Cause Correspondent'. When I look back on thirty years of human rights reporting, the majority of my attempts to draw attention to injustice and suffering from Texas to Tajikistan via Ireland and Pakistan have involved women. Are women doomed to be just another hopeless cause and, if so, why?

I do not pretend that this is a comprehensive look at the problem or that I can provide an answer. The life of one woman reporter is too short for that. This sets out to be an anecdotal account of my personal experience of the problem, based on three decades as a foreign correspondent for ITN and the BBC, of meeting with women who deserve better and with the brave ones who fight back.

Sue Lloyd-Roberts
2015

Publisher's note:

Sue Lloyd-Roberts sadly died on 13 October 2015, before she was able to finalise the content of this book. The information contained on these pages was correct at the time of Sue's writing; Simon & Schuster UK will be happy to correct any omissions or errors in future editions.

INTRODUCTION

My flat looked like a florist's the week of Mum's death. I received hundreds of messages of condolence: cards, letters, emails, texts, Facebook messages and, of course, flowers. It was overwhelming but in retrospect wonderful because it was testament to how many people loved and admired my mother.

There was one message that stood out more than any other though; it was from a close family friend, and amidst the terrible sadness it gave me some hope and happiness.

Dear Sarah,

Question: Do we agonize over the raw deal that Sue and her family are, and will suffer in her not leading the fuller life that she truly deserved — or do we acknowledge and celebrate an amazing life lived that touched the minds and hearts of many, worldwide?

The answer: Surely, no, we don't agonize and yes we do celebrate. I've held on to that and that's what I'm going to try and do for you, and for her.

This book is a celebration of Mum's life. She left this world far too soon but before she died she left us with this amazing collection of her experiences. *The War on Women: And the Brave Ones Who Fight Back* is an opportunity for us to remember her, it's an opportunity for us to recognize her strength and bravery and to acknowledge how she championed and helped so many women who are suffering all over the world.

On top of being one of the best journalists of her generation, she was also brilliant at one of the hardest tasks women face: being a mother. My older brother, George, and I grew up in North London and our house was always full of fascinating people. We would often come home to Mum sitting on the sofa with a Tibetan monk or making a cup of tea for a Pakistani refugee. Our home was a haven for people she met through work and they would often stay the night or spend the weekend with us. I remember Mum's delight on seeing a Tibetan monk's face light up when we took him to the ballet at the Royal Opera House. He'd never seen anything like it.

There was always a party of some sort going on at our house, it was a hive of activity and new faces, and our home received a lot of attention from our neighbours in Muswell Hill. Mum loved nothing more than throwing dinners, lunches and parties. As teenagers, my brother George and I would often find ourselves sitting next to government ministers, journalists, activists or victims fleeing persecution from one war-torn country or other. There was always food in the fridge – usually Mum's lasagne and a few bottles of wine – and we'd sit around a big table in the kitchen and the world would be put to rights.

It was a great childhood. We were pretty much allowed to do whatever we liked except Mum wasn't keen on 'mindless television', as she called it. Whatever we were watching or reading had to be improving and cerebral. Growing up, George and I weren't really allowed to sleep in; weekend mornings would start with her stomping up and down the stairs, singing 'Oh What a Beautiful Mornin''. Never welcome after a hangover but what I wouldn't give to hear her sing that now. She'd always be up first, making waffles with bacon and maple syrup, and whoever happened to emerge from the house and join us at the kitchen table would be welcome for breakfast. She had boundless energy. I remember weekends when friends would wake up to Mum walking around the house, often naked with all the curtains open. She'd say of the neighbours: 'If they've got nothing better to do, then let them stare.' Not exhibitionism, just absolutely no shame about her body. It was a *great* body.

Our street in Muswell Hill was a real community, one that was very much built and nurtured by my mother. She famously held a street party to celebrate the Queen's Golden Jubilee; she organized the whole thing. There was a line of beautifully decorated trestle tables running down the middle of the closed road and food and drink was plentiful. We danced in the street until late that night. But, as a staunch republican, Mum came to the party dressed in black in mourning for Oliver Cromwell. She had a brilliant sense of humour, great wit and an eye for the ridiculous. She loved poking fun at any kind of pomp.

For my mother there was no problem – big or small – that couldn't be solved by a long walk. Come rain or shine George and I walked up mountains. We were incredibly lucky in so many ways because Mum took us all over the world with her. By the time I left home, George and I had already met the Dalai Lama in India, stayed in mud huts in tiny villages in Nepal and camped with Bushmen in the Kalahari Desert in Botswana and Aborigines in the Outback in Australia. We graduated from Snowdon in North Wales to Everest Base Camp (from the Tibetan side, of course), we summited Mount Kilimanjaro in Tanzania together and climbed the Singalila Ridge in northern India.

But as small children, all our holidays were in Snowdonia in North Wales with our Great-aunt Frances. Mum first took me up Snowdon aged eight, coaxing me up, ridge by ridge with sticks of KitKat. Her family's roots were in North Wales and our ancestral home was hugely important to her. So much so that George and I have another mountain to climb; she wanted her ashes to be left in the Pennant Valley in Snowdonia. My ancestors were given a title for building Belan Fort in North Wales. Gwendoline Wynn, my great-grandmother, was the last lady of the family. She married a doctor and lost the title. But I have a photograph of Mum as a debutante at Queen Charlotte's Ball, which was the height of the London season for the upper classes when Mum was a teenager. She was sent there to find a suitor . . . She didn't, thankfully. She went on to university and made her own career. Mum had a great sense of family history but coming from so much privilege, money and class turned her into a republican and a socialist. Despite accepting a CBE from the Queen, she hated authority and hated being deferential. Nobody told her what to do.

There wasn't an element of snobbery in her and she believed strongly in equality and fairness across gender, race and class. She taught George and me to be kind and inclusive and to always champion the underdog. She devoted her life to fighting for the rights of people less fortunate than herself. This book is a tribute to the underdogs in this world who refuse to accept their lot and be silenced; this book is for those who are brave enough to fight back.

My mother was a passionate feminist and she told me from a very young age never to rely on a man. I do very much rely on my wonderful husband, we got married in 2014 and Mum loved organizing the wedding. But I remember when I sent her a proof copy of the invitation which read: Luke Mulhall and Sarah Morris invite . . . her response was, 'Sarah, if your name is not first on the invitation, I'm not coming. It means he's won already.' It hadn't even occurred to me but I did swap the names and Mum did, of course, come to the wedding. She loved my husband but she hated patriarchy and fought hard against it.

Mum went into hospital at the end of July 2015 for a stem cell transplant as treatment for leukaemia and didn't come back out.

On her last day before going in, we spent the day together in Angel around Camden Passage, doing fun, girly things like having manicures and pedicures, trying to distract ourselves I suppose from what was happening the next day. We went to the Reiss sale and Mum bought herself a bright-red dress. She looked beautiful in it. She said it was to be her book-launch dress. She was determined to get this book out in time for the Women of the World Festival in March 2016 at the South Bank Centre.

We had a good dinner out that night, talked about travelling, where we'd most like to go in the world. She jokingly called it 'the last supper' but I had no idea at the time that it would be our last supper together.

Three months later we were making funeral arrangements and I had the horrible job of thinking about what she would wear in her coffin. It had to be that Reiss red dress. This book meant everything to her. She worked so hard to get it finished before she went into hospital, fearing the worst. Sadly she didn't get to finish it. Ninety-nine per cent is her writing and my brother George and I have been privileged enough to work with her brilliant editor Abigail Bergstrom to shape the book into what it is today. I'm so proud of Mum for writing this, for having the idea in the first place and for working so hard on it – particularly throughout her illness in the last year of her life. I hope she's reading this somewhere wearing her red book-launch dress, proud of herself and pleased with the final result.

THE CRUELLEST CUT

Female Genital Mutilation

Maimouna stirs in her sleep, her eyes flickering. Something doesn't make sense. She can see it is still dark through the open window that gives out onto the communal yard and yet she can hear the distinct sound of her neighbour crushing peanuts in a metal bowl preparing to make *domodah*, the traditional peanut stew of the Gambia. She feels her insides tighten and quickly opens her eyes wide as she remembers – it is cutting day.

Her mother, Mama Mouna, is the village circumciser. The family is held in respect by their fellow villagers and the extra money that the cutting brings them is welcome. Apart from that one role, her parents are too old to work. Her mother has turned sixty and has told Maimouna that she is the chosen one of the two daughters – she is to be the next village cutter. Her mother admits that she is now too weak to restrain the girls as they struggle and fight her during the circumcision ceremony. Maimouna has helped her mother on several occasions in the past and at the next ceremony she will be in charge of the cutting.

As Maimouna lies in bed contemplating the day ahead and her future, she knows that the responsibility for taking over this duty in her village will be a considerable one. The village boasts a prosperous community of some two thousand people, the overwhelming majority of whom believe in the tradition of female circumcision. All the women in her community are convinced that it would be impossible to get their daughters married unless they are cut. They would be considered dirty or impure.

She hears her daughter, Ami, roll off the mattress next to hers and drawing near. 'Mum, is this the day?'

Maimouna nods. Five-year-old Ami doesn't know what the day actually means. She only knows what her mother and aunts have told her, that once every two years the girls in the village have to dress in their best clothes and, accompanied by villagers beating drums and waving branches, they will be led into the special house where they will 'become women'.

Maimouna reaches for her best *grandmuba*, a voluminous dress that reaches to the floor and covers the arms, which she had laid out the night before, and a matching headdress. Ami carefully puts on the shift that she had been given several weeks ago for this special day. There is fish and rice stew left over from the night before but neither mother nor daughter feel hungry; one is too nervous and the other too excited. It is now light and they could hear the drummers approaching, beating on their *tamas*.

The neighbour's daughter rushes in and grabs Ami by the wrist. 'Quick! We'll be late,' she says as she heads to the door. Ami follows, forgetting to say goodbye to her mother. Maimouna is in no hurry. The procession will circle the village several times, collecting the girls before ending up at the main family compound where her mother lives. She has already prepared the mattresses on the floor in the room where the girls will spend several days recovering and she has made the tomato paste she will use to treat their open wounds. She shudders as she remembers the girls who have bled to death in the room.

She walks slowly to her mother's house. Mama is already in the courtyard where the cutting will take place with her sister, Maimouna's aunt. They are preparing the razors and cloths to mop up the blood. Maimouna drags one of the mattresses from the recovery room into the courtyard, waiting for the first girl to arrive. The girl will be led through to the courtyard blindfolded and then laid on the floor so that Mama can make quick and effective cuts. 'Watch me closely,' she reminds her daughter. 'Next time, you will have to do it.'

Maimouna hears the drums and shouting as the procession approaches the family compound. 'There is always lots of playing of drums,' Maimouna explains. 'They take drums and pans and make a lot of noise so that, if the girls are screaming, people won't hear the screaming of the girls they are cutting. The girls waiting to be cut know something is going on but, because of the beating pans and clapping and shouting, they don't know what.'

Maimouna waits nervously for the first girl to be pushed down a long narrow corridor and through the curtain which hangs between the house and the courtyard. Her mother is ready with the razor while her aunt has prepared rags to stuff into the girls' mouths if their screaming gets too loud. Mama instructs her sister to pin down the girls' arms and Maimouna is told to hold down their legs. 'If the girl is big,' Mama says, 'you will have to sit on her chest.'

By midday, Maimouna has held four girls as they spat, bit, struggled and fought. She is exhausted, physically and emotionally. The first child to arrive in the courtyard is excited and happy. She is expecting a present or maybe some special food to celebrate her maturity. Her aunt has suggested that maybe she will get a glimpse of the boy who has been chosen to marry her one day.

But instead, she is told to lie down, her legs are forced open and then there is the searing pain as first her clitoris and then her labia are cut off with a razor. She has never experienced such agony. She screams and screams but still the cutting goes on. She hears Mama shout at Maimouna: 'Hold her, hold her. I can't do it unless you keep her still.' When at last the cutting stops, another woman carries her to the windowless recovery room and lays her on a mattress. She is crying and blood is pouring down her legs. She thinks she is going to die.

All the time, the men in the courtyard outside keep beating on the *tamas*, attempting to outdo the chilling shrieks of the girls. But, as the next girl is pushed past the soiled red curtain into the courtyard, her expression has grown more frightened and panicked. Despite the drumming and shouting, she hears the desperate cries of her friend and knows that there is something not right about this special day.

The girl is Ami. Maimouna lays her blindfolded daughter on the mattress, now drenched in blood, and pins down her arms. The child's grandmother makes the first swipe with the razor. Ami screamed: 'Mum, Mum, where are you? Help me! Help me!' Ami has no idea that it is her great-aunt who is pinning her arms to the ground while her mother forces open her legs.

Maimouna says:

Can you imagine holding down your five-year-old daughter, and they are cutting her and she is screaming and calling out 'Mum' and Mum is the one who is holding down your legs and there is nothing Mum can do? So, I was shaking my head and tears were coming to my eyes and I said to my mind that, whatever happens, I will never do this, I will never do the cutting but I cannot tell it to anyone. If I say it to the people, by this time I would not be here. So I just keep it in my mind. This is when I regretted having a daughter.

This was an extraordinary, revolutionary moment for this 36-year-old woman, which can only have been prompted by a resource of humanity and compassion deep within her which defies everything that she has been taught and has been brought up to expect. Maimouna's destiny is to cut. Her mother, grand-mother and generations before them had done their duty for the local community. And yet this woman, with no education and well before anti-female genital mutilation activists arrive in her village to tell her so, realizes that to inflict so much pain and to mutilate a young girl is wrong.

After she makes up her mind to break with the family tradition, she knows she has to flee the village. When her mother dies in 2009, the situation becomes critical. She starts making excuses, saying she needs more time and has to collect the appropriate 'juju' artefacts befitting a circumciser. One year, two years pass and the village elders come to her house to ask her when she is going to assume her responsibilities.

'I told them that I needed to find the jujus to protect the girls. Because when the cutting takes place, witches come to bewitch the girls who are cut and this can cause them to die. I said I needed time to find the right jujus. In fact, I was buying time. I was play-ing with them, saying that I cannot just do the cutting when my mother died, it takes time.'

But the elders get impatient. They bring her juju necklaces, leather belts and ornaments which, they say, are sufficient for the task ahead. Just as they are beginning to threaten her, she gets the chance to escape from the village and the job that repels her. Her brother emigrated to the UK a few years earlier and has written with the news that he is to get married to an English woman. Maimouna persuades the family that she is the one who should go to the wedding.

She obtains a visa from the British High Commission in the capital, Banjul, and flies to the UK to attend the ceremony in Derby. Her brother refuses to look after her when she tells him that she has no intention of returning to their village. She is alone and hungry when a Pakistani family she met at the local mosque take pity on her. They give her a bed and advise her to go to the

Home Office reception area in Crawley and apply for asylum. She is sent to the high-security prison for women asylum seekers, Yarl's Wood, where she is told she will probably be deported.

Maimouna is given a judicial hearing before a judge who, after hearing her case but without calling any expert witnesses, rules against her. Her error was in lying on her visa application, claiming that she wanted to come to the UK for a wedding and for not appealing for asylum as soon as she arrived. He accuses her of deception. He claims to be familiar with the customs of West Africa and observes that the way she ties her headdress suggests that she comes from a wealthy, educated family and that she would easily be able to go back to the Gambia and fend for herself.

She did not dare answer back at the time but later tells me that she did not know whether to laugh or cry at the judge's alleged authority on the subject of headdresses. 'The way we tie the cloths around our heads has nothing to do with tribe or class,' she says indignantly. 'We tie the cloth around our heads the way we want to. It's fashion!' She laughs but a moment later she is crying. Ami is one of five children. In order to avoid cutting she has abandoned them all.

Maimouna tells me her story in a bedsit in Hounslow, West London where she is waiting to be deported. The room is on the third floor of two handsome nineteenth-century houses with white stucco facades that have been knocked together by the local council to provide holding areas for asylum seekers. As I make my way past the chaotic pile of bikes and prams parked in the hallway, a black teenager darts out of one of the doors, the son of a Somali family living in a room on the ground floor.

On the first floor, there is an Albanian family living opposite two young Afghan males. The world's refugee population is well represented here. Some had travelled thousands of miles and hidden in the backs of lorries for the last stage of the journey across the Channel. All are waiting to hear whether the Home Office will believe their stories of persecution and whether they will be allowed to stay. Maimouna shares her room with a professional Iranian woman, in her forties, who fled Tehran after participating in the Green Revolution in 2009. She had tried, unsuccessfully, to challenge the rule of the Ayatollahs.

With tears flowing down her cheeks, Maimouna tells me how much she misses her daughter and four sons. 'But I am in the middle. Because if I go home now and start cutting those girls so that I can return to my kids I am selfish. Sometimes I think I am not fair to my kids and I have to go back to do the cutting but when I think that, I say to myself: because of my kids how many girls am I going to cut? How many girls am I going to affect? How many girls am I going to put in the position I am in today?'

FGM is being tackled in the Gambia. An NGO (non-governmental organization) called GAMCOTRAP has approached about a third of the villages to persuade them to stop. Unfortunately for Maimouna they have not yet reached her village. GAMCOTRAP ask the male village leaders to let them present their arguments at a village meeting. Once they get permission, they explain the dangers of FGM and how the deaths of so many girls after the cutting and of so many women and babies in childbirth are in fact due to FGM and not due to the evil spirits which are so routinely and conveniently blamed.

Once they get the villagers to agree to stop cutting, they hold elaborate 'Dropping the Knife' ceremonies. I attend one such ceremony in a village outside Serekunda. The women dance and sing the songs that they once sang while they accompanied the girls to the cutting ceremony, hastily followed by songs which celebrate their new knowledge and their decision to 'drop the knife'. I end up dancing with the women and I become very emotional when I think of what has been achieved. All the women I am linking arms and dancing with have been cut. Their granddaughters, who dart between us squealing with delight at the music and the joy of the event, have not. It is an uplifting, inspirational moment.

The next morning I am given a reality check. GAMCOTRAP face an uphill struggle. I am taken to a meeting of cutters in a region of the country the NGO is only beginning to approach. Sitting on plastic chairs in a circle in the yard of a compound belonging to a village elder, one of them holds a frightened-looking eight-year-old girl on her lap. She boasts to me: 'I cut forty children this year, including my granddaughter and look how well she looks on it!' Another says, 'I earned $3 per child cut AND a bag of rice and some clothes!' They all tell me how much they enjoy the respect they get from the local community.

Dr Isa Touray, the charismatic and brave executive director of GAMCOTRAP, is a realist. A formidable woman who has been imprisoned for her anti-FGM advocacy, she is resplendent in her traditional yellow, floor-length dress, matching headdress and bold jewellery. She tells me that she needs more funds to reach more communities and to carry out follow-up visits to check whether, after all the parties and celebrations, communities are really adhering to the NGO's teachings. Why does she think it is so difficult to challenge the tradition?

'FGM is about control over female sexuality,' she says. 'That is, about controlling the pleasure women get from the erogenous zones. We all know that it is about enjoying sex. It is about the bodily dignity and integrity of the women, which is something very powerful. In essence, it is about control over women's bodies, control over women's pleasure. If women don't get pleasure, they are more easily controlled. And too many men in Africa want to keep that control.'

The Gambia's eccentric president, Yahya Jammeh, who is said to have boasted that he could cure HIV/Aids with his herbal remedy, has declared that FGM is part of Gambian culture. In 2013, a month after the BBC broadcast my film about FGM in the Gambia, he withdrew his country from the Commonwealth claiming he no longer wants his country to be subjected to neo-colonial influences.[1] His decision will make it much harder for anti-FGM activists in the country to campaign against what the president celebrates as a traditional practice.*

President Jammeh refuses my request for an interview. The nearest I get to a member of the governing elite is an exchange with the country's most senior imam, Muhammed Alhaijie Lamin Touray, president of the Supreme Islamic Council. It is pouring with rain when we arrive at his mosque in Gunjur village in Kombo South for Friday prayers. The men are inside the mosque building and the women in the anterooms and corridors outside where inadequate roofing give them little respite from the rainy season. I sit among the women while waiting for the imam to finish his sermon.

The imam invites me and my cameraman into his home where the men sit on chairs against the walls of the room; apart from me, there is not a woman in sight. In his sermon that day, he preached that FGM is part of Islamic law and that genital mutilation is good for women. Why? 'It is a beautiful thing. It is a good thing,' he tells me. 'This is the reason why it is accepted in Islam, why we practise it and why there is nothing wrong with it.'

'FGM has many benefits for women,' the imam continues as he warms to the subject with his all-male audience nodding in agreement. 'The thing they remove when they cut the girl is very itchy. It is so itchy that women even have to resort to using a wire scourer to relieve the itching. And, on other occasions, a woman who has not been cut has a watery discharge. When she gets up from a chair, her clothes are all wet and this causes embarrassment to her if she is in a public place.'

---

* President Jammeh announced in November 2015 that FGM would in fact be banned in the Gambia. The Gambian government approved a bill outlawing the practice on 31 December 2015. The new law states that anyone found engaging in female circumcision could face up to three years in prison or a fine of 50,000 delasi (US$1,250).

At this stage, as the only woman present, I have to intervene with some indignation. 'I have had a clitoris for sixty years,' I say, 'and this has never happened to me!'

'Well you are an exception among women,' he says and bursts out laughing, his wicked eyes gleaming.

It is not the absurdity of his argument but it is the laughing that makes me most angry. If he truly believes that the mutilation of young girls is approved by God and that it is good for women, he would not laugh. He knows what he was saying is preposterous and this clearly amuses him. It is as if he is admitting that genital mutilation is all about control. Nonetheless, through gritted teeth, I thank him sincerely for the interview. At least he had agreed to talk to me and, for the purposes of my report, he confirms the chronic misogyny that lies behind the custom.

So where did the mutilation of little girls, the agonizing pain, the premature deaths, the denial of pleasure and the incomprehensible logic of this misogynistic act begin? There are illustrations of both girls and boys being circumcised in Pharaonic tombs, well before either Christianity or Islam arrived on the African continent. The belief that a woman's sexuality has to be controlled is deeply entrenched in the history of humankind. Ever since Eve stole the forbidden fruit, the early Christian fathers warned that a woman is not to be trusted. The ethos of Christianity is determinedly patriarchal, from the doctrine of the Holy Trinity to the male-dominated ecclesiastical hierarchies of today. 'The Bible in its teachings degrades women from Genesis to Revelation,' wrote the suffragette Elizabeth Cady Stanton; and 'a woman's role is to submit.'[2]

Even the revolutionary scientific thinkers of the nineteenth century who debunked the story of the creation of the world as laid out in the Bible succumbed to this view. With his theory of evolution, Charles Darwin may have rejected the myth of Adam and Eve, but his theory of natural selection favoured the male of our species. Weak, less-intelligent women, he believed, were less affected and less worthy of selective pressures. Likening the mind of a woman to that of a child when considering marriage and deliberating over the advantages of a wife, he wrote of 'a constant companion (friend in old age) who will feel interested in one, an object to be beloved and played with – better than a dog anyhow – and someone to take care of the house'.[3]

In the early twentieth century, the French anthropologist Gustave Le Bon announced that 'there are a large number of women whose brains are closer in size to gorillas than to the most developed male brains' and that 'they excel in fickleness, inconstancy, absence of thought and logic, and incapacity to reason.'[4] He concluded that it would be dangerous to provide the same education for girls as boys. A woman's inability to think straight and behave in a responsible way is a theme that permeates Western, Christian thought and Islam alike. It underlines the need for a women's subordination to men and, above all, the need to control her.

In the Koran, the chapter on The Women and her role as homemaker under strict supervision comes after the chapter on The Cow. We learn that a woman lacks judgement and cannot be trusted. In the Islamic legal code, the testimony of two women is equal to one of a man. Furthermore, she is a temptress with dangerous sexual attractions. 'When the woman comes towards you', Mohammed said, 'it is Satan who is approaching. When one of you sees a woman and he feels attracted to her, he should hurry to his wife.' Women, he warned, are the source of *fitna*, disagreement and division among people.[5]

Neither the Bible nor the Koran advocate female genital mutilation but the inference is there – that a woman is inferior and, in her sexual appetites, she is a threat. A woman who feels no sexual pleasure is more likely to be faithful and obedient. It is as if all that matters for a woman are the three Vs: her vagina, her virginity and her virtue. A woman is fulfilled by the reproductive role of the vagina and her virginity and virtue are essential to maintain social order. From these beliefs, it is possible to see how the idea of FGM evolved to ensure a woman's passive sexual behaviour, guaranteeing her virginity before marriage and fidelity once a wife. Her clitoris is, therefore, utterly superfluous.

My favourite descriptions of the clitoris comes from *New York Times* science journalist and author Natalie Angier: 'The clitoris is pure in purpose. It is the only organ in the body designed purely for pleasure. The clitoris is simply a bundle of nerves: 8,000 fibres, to be precise. That's a higher concentration of nerve fibres than is found anywhere else in the body, including the fingertips, lips and tongue and twice the number in the penis. Who needs a handgun when you've got a semiautomatic?'[6] No wonder the enemy of women find the clitoris so dangerous.

The World Health Organization defines FGM as 'all procedures that involve partial or total removal of the external female genitalia or other injury to the female genital organs for non-medical reasons' and specifies four types. Type 1 is clitoridectomy, the partial or total removal of the clitoris. Type 2 is excision, partial or total removal of the clitoris and the labia minora, with or without excision of the labia majora. Type 3 is infibulation, narrowing the vaginal opening through the creation of a covering seal. The seal is formed by cutting and repositioning the inner, or outer, labia, with or without removal of the clitoris. Type 4 includes all other harmful procedures to the female genitalia for non-medical purposes, for example pricking, piercing, incising, scraping and cauterizing the genital area.[7]

Maimouna's mother carried out Type 3 where the clitoris is removed and the labia is sewn up, leaving only a small opening for urine and menstruation. The village cutter will open the gap on her wedding night. Only then is penetration possible. Sometimes the gap is so small that it can take six agonizing months to achieve penetration. No wonder some women have told me that intercourse can be as excruciating as childbirth. What is believed to be a woman's natural inclination to enjoy illicit sex, is thus effectively and painfully curbed.

'This FGM thing,' Maimouna says, 'means that you receive pain all the time and you receive horrible, horrible pain three times. You feel that pain the day they cut you and it will last for two or three months afterwards. When you are going to marry, they have to open you before you have sex with your husband and so that is another pain. When you have your child, they have to open you again for the baby. It is horrible. And so, it is a lot of pain that we go through.'

Egypt, the country that boasts the first evidence of FGM some four thousand years ago, today offers the highest incidence of the practice. Egypt is a country of around 90 million people and, according to UNICEF figures in 2013, has the highest number of women who have been mutilated of any country in the world, nearly 30 million, or 91 per cent of the female population.[8] This figure is nearer 100 per cent in the villages of the Upper Nile, where the river cuts a deep, wide passage through the desert plateau. Camels and donkeys pull carts along dusty paths, egrets strut along the muddy banks and hoopoes make their distinctive 'oo, oo' screech as they soar above the palm trees.

There is none of the bustle here of the villages of the Gambia where women walk freely through the streets in their garish, colourful dresses with matching headdresses and faces uncovered. In the villages of the Nile, life takes place behind closed doors in mud-bricked compounds. The men go to work and do the shopping while the women stay out of sight. If they need to leave their houses, women cover their heads. In the villages I visit, I find Muslims and Christians living side by side; both communities practice FGM.

My guide, a member of a Cairo-based NGO fighting FGM, takes me first to a house where a Christian woman invites me to sit on a bed with her and her teenage daughters, under a painting of the Madonna and child. Nawara is unembarrassed as she tells me how her mutilation has caused her a lot of problems in her marriage and how thankful she was when the anti-FGM activist came to the door a few years ago and told her that FGM is now illegal in Egypt. 'I won't have my daughters circumcised,' she says, smiling. 'They won't have the pain and problems I had.'

We call on her Muslim neighbour next door. The mother here, Fatima, introduces me to her family of four sons and five daughters. She points to the youngest, eleven-year-old Aysha, who is the only one who has not yet been circumcised. 'I will remove that part of my daughter,' she says. 'Otherwise, she may play with it or she might ask a boy to touch that part and she might enjoy it. It might be a stranger or even one of her male cousins. So the cutting will protect her and, when she feels the pain of it, she will be more careful about this part of her body.' Aysha looks bewildered by the conversation going on and I look at her anxiously and wish that she were the daughter of the mother next door.

The village midwife who is due to cut Aysha in a few weeks' time, is delighted when she is told there is a journalist in the village who is asking about FGM and is eager to meet me. A large, imposing woman dressed in long green and black flowing robes, she brings her face to within inches of mine and wags her finger at me as she declares, 'I am telling you purified girls grow taller and receive marriage proposals. But unpurified girls stay short and single!' She bursts out laughing and slaps me on the knee with glee. I recoil from her in horror but manage one more question. Does she enjoy her work I ask? 'I love it. I love it more than my own eyes. It makes me so much money. How can I not love it?'

The anti-FGM campaigners, who carry their message from village to village with varying success, tell me that the Christian church leaders are much more responsive to their message than the imams. The Reverend Yacoub Eyad shows me around the

Assembly of God Church in the village of Akaka and reminds me that Abraham circumcised his son but nowhere in the Bible do we find an instance of female circumcision. 'We pray that, with God's help, we shall be able to teach people the truth,' he says with feeling.

I wait outside the mosque in the same village to catch the imam before Friday prayers. I am modestly dressed in loose slacks and a long-sleeved shirt, but my head is uncovered and when the imam arrives with a large entourage, he refuses to look at me. I ask my translator to ask him what he is doing to help stop FGM and he says, 'The Prophet did it, peace be with Him, and so this is legalized by Islamic Law.'

What he says is in blatant disregard to the known history of the Prophet Mohammed and to the Koran, which make no mention of FGM. Furthermore it contradicts Egypt's former grand mufti, Ali Gomaa, who announced in 2007 that FGM is against Islam.[9] The Egyptian government subsequently banned the practice. The imam sweeps off without acknowledging me. People bow and scuttle out of his way. He is clearly a feared and respected man.

What difference does a ban on FGM by the government in Cairo make, especially to remote villages along the Nile? Very little, says the Egyptian novelist and anti-FGM campaigner Nawal El Saadawi. El Saadawi was sacked from her government job in the Health Ministry for speaking out against FGM in the 1970s. Things have changed since then she concedes but 'you cannot eradicate such historical, rooted habits by law only. We need the education of mothers and fathers. There is a lot of misinformation that says that cutting girls is good, but it is all lies.'[10] If the main source of information for the average Muslim family comes from the likes of the imam of Akaka, there is little hope of real change.

FGM, says El Saadawi, is explained by the obsession with the hymen. 'Arab society still considers that the fine membrane that covers the aperture of the external genital organs is the most cherished and most important part of a girl's body, and is much more valuable than one of her eyes, or an arm, or a lower limb. An Arab family does not grieve as much at the loss of a girl's eye as it does if she happens to lose her virginity. In fact if the girl lost her life, it would be considered less of a catastrophe than if she lost her hymen.'[11]

The World Health Organization estimates that up to 130 million women worldwide have been subjected to FGM in over thirty different countries, the majority of them Muslim.[12] The anti-FGM campaigners are doing their best but the challenge is huge. FGM is practised in Europe, the Middle East and in twenty African countries, in a band that stretches from Senegal in West Africa to Ethiopia on the east coast; from Egypt in the north to Tanzania in the south. Like Egypt, the prevalence in Guinea, Somalia and Sierra Leone is believed to be over 90 per cent of the female population.

The films I made for the BBC in 2012 and 2013 were among the first on FGM to be shown on British TV. I reported from Egypt, France, the UK and the Gambia. In the film I made in Paris, I showed how the French have taken a pragmatic, no-nonsense approach as FGM became a growing problem as the numbers of immigrants from Africa increased. In 1983, a law banning FGM was passed. One hundred circumcisers and complicit parents have been sent to prison for the crime. The message from the French government is unequivocal: the mutilation of children will not be tolerated and perpetrators will be severely punished.

'The trouble with England is that you are very respectful about the traditions of every community that comes to live in your country,' said Isabelle Gillette-Faye, the head of an NGO that campaigns against gender-based violence called GAMS (Group for the Abolition of Female Genital Mutilation). 'In our country, it is totally different. We expect our migrants to integrate and obey our laws and traditions.' We meet at the Eurostar terminal in Gard de Nord in Paris. She is angry with the British not least because GAMS has just intercepted two girls who were on their way to London to be cut.

'We are doing so much with our high-profile trials to eliminate FGM from France,' says Gillette-Faye, 'and then we find that parents can pop across the Channel to get their children cut in England. Someone from the community contacted our organization to say that a family had tickets for the Eurostar to go to London to get two six-year-old girls mutilated. The call came on Friday and they planned to leave on a train on Saturday and so we had to move very quickly.' The parents were educated and well off and Gillette-Faye thinks they had organized a private clinic in London for the task.

The French system is more intrusive. Between birth and the age of six, every French child receives free medical checks-ups and treatment at special mother and baby clinics. The genitalia of all French children of this age are examined regardless of their ethnic origin. Beyond six years old, doctors, teachers and school health visitors are taught to be extra vigilant with children whose background puts them at risk. Parents who want to take their children out of school and to countries where cutting is rife are warned that they will be prosecuted if the child returns with anything missing. 'We have not seen anyone cut in France for a while,' says Gillette-Faye.

In Britain, our tradition is to respect local customs and not to insist on integration. We respect tolerance and accept cultural differences but it allows abuse to take place behind closed doors. It took an immigrant from Ghana, Efua Dorkenoo, who worked for the NHS, to launch her campaigning organization Forward and create the momentum to bring about the Prohibition of Female Circumcision Act in 1985. Efua was awarded an OBE and worked tirelessly on the campaign until her untimely death in October 2014. She was frustrated by the lack of prosecutions and would often say, 'There is no time to rest while children are being abused.'[13]

It is the source of endless speculation why the people of two countries, the French and the British, separated by some twenty miles of water should take such different stands on so many issues. The idea of doctors routinely examining the genitalia of children would be anathema in the UK. It would lead to the most indignant and noisy outburst yet in the ongoing debate about the loss of personal freedoms versus the greater good, in this case to protect tens of thousands of British girls from being mutilated. It doesn't stand a chance. A senior child protection officer at the Metropolitan Police told me that 'inspections, in our terms, could be considered a form of abuse in itself'.

Like France, the numbers of women who have been genitally mutilated in the UK has risen with the number of immigrants entering the country from those parts of the world that practise FGM. The figures prepared by the City of London University and Efua Dorkenoo before her death suggest that in England and Wales there are over 100,000 women who have suffered FGM and every year there are 20,000 children at risk of being cut.[14]

There is little doubt that illegal mutilations are taking place in the UK. I remember standing with a Ghanaian woman on the sixteenth floor of the 'Red Road' tower blocks, home to hundreds of refugees in Glasgow, as the wind and rain lashed at the windows. Ayanna, a 23-year-old mother, fled Ghana a year ago and applied for asylum in the UK to escape an abusive husband and prevent her six-month-old baby girl from being genitally mutilated. 'My husband would have insisted,' she explains. 'All the women in my community have been cut.'

Looking out onto the bleak townscape she says, 'I am so happy to be here in Britain, but I am also afraid.' She tries to avoid contact with the African community. 'They'll tell me that my daughter should be cut. It's being done here,' she says, pointing through the window at the other tower blocks which make up the Red Road housing estate. 'The older women do it – the grandmothers,' she explains. 'I know that just last week one three-year-old and a two-week-old baby were cut.' What do they use? I ask? 'Razors and scissors,' she replies.

And what about the prosecutions? Why have we failed so lamentably here compared to the French and their one hundred convictions? The only FGM case to be heard in a British court looked like a panic move to protect the reputation of the Crown Prosecution Service. Days before the director of public prosecutions, Alison Saunders, was due to appear in front of the House of Commons Home Affairs Committee to answer the question 'Why have there been no successful prosecutions?', a 32-year-old obstetrician at the Whittington Hospital in north London, Dr Dhanuson Dharmasena, was charged with performing FGM. Senior police officers said that the charge against the doctor was 'good news' that sent out a strong message that 'the people who carry out FGM will be caught and charged'.[15]

The jury took thirty minutes to dismiss the case against Dr Dharmasena. During the trial it emerged that hospital staff had failed to warn the doctor that the patient had been mutilated when she was a child in Somalia and that her labia were sewn tightly together. Dharmasena made a quick cut to get the baby out and save its life and then, in order to stem the blood that was gushing from the wound, sewed it up again. A member of the hospital team accused him of performing FGM, of re-infibulating her. Dharmasena argued that the 1.5 centimetre, figure-of-eight stitch was vital to stop the bleeding. He thanked the colleagues who supported him and told the jury that, 'I have always maintained that FGM is an abhorrent practice that has no medical justification.'[16] Thus ended the UK's first, much-anticipated trial for FGM.

Obstetricians in the UK were horrified when mutilated

women first presented themselves at Accident and Emergency departments in the advanced stages of childbirth. They had to learn urgent new procedures in the delivery rooms. The birth channel was sometimes so well sealed that the babies could not get out, resulting in prolonged and obstructed labour. The incidence of post-partum haemorrhage is increased as is the need for caesarean sections. If sophisticated medical attention is not available, the incidence of high death rates during childbirth increases.

Women from Africa are presenting themselves in gynaecological departments with abscesses and genital ulcers. Comfort Momoh, a senior midwife at St Thomas's Hospital in London, shows me pictures of cysts the size of a baby's head on the edges of a woman's vulva, the like of which she has encountered on several occasions while dealing with the life-endangering consequences of FGM. Women who come to the hospital complaining of chronic back and pelvic pain and kidney infections are often found to be victims of FGM. As Momoh shows me slide after slide of her patients, we share a mutual horror at the evidence of unnecessary pain in the name of a baseless tradition.

We need to challenge the communities here in the UK who remain loyal to this horrific procedure. While I was in Glasgow, I asked for directions to a working man's cafe frequented by Somalis in order to ask the men for their views on FGM. 'It's a woman thing,' one man told me, 'the mothers and grandmothers do it because it is the tradition.' 'It's up to the woman,' says another, 'some might like to be cut and others may not.' The impression they gave me is that they did not care much either way. And yet the women I meet say that they fear that their daughters will not get married unless they are cut. Surely it is time for someone to get the two sexes to sit down and talk about the issue.

The only glimmer of hope I found while investigating FGM in the UK came from Bristol where an enlightened sixth form teacher, Lisa Zimmerman, has encouraged her pupils from FGM-affected communities at the City Academy Bristol to take the initiative. They have made a film, *The Silent Scream*, which highlights the tensions in a migrant family when an older daughter tries to persuade her parents not to cut her younger sister. After making music videos and attending public events all over the UK, Zimmerman and eighteen-year-old Fahma Mohamed were invited to meet UN Secretary General Ban Ki Moon. He told Fahma, 'You are the hope of our future.'

I have seldom met a feistier, more well-informed and determined group of fourteen- to seventeen-year-old teenagers. Amina speaks chillingly of 'cutting parties' that take place in the Bristol area. 'They get all the girls together because it is cheaper to do it that way. An older woman, a grandmother, will normally do it.' What do they think that the prime minister should do about FGM? 'I would like to ask him what would be happening if the little girls at risk had blonde hair and blue eyes?' answers Muna Hassan. 'I would like to tell David Cameron to grow a pair and do something about FGM and, if he can't, then there's no point in him being in his job.'

The girls want to be protected from their own parents. In their film *The Silent Scream* they skilfully and movingly point out how difficult it is for a child to challenge the firmly held beliefs of the people they love and trust. Many potential prosecutions in the UK fail because children do not want to criminalize their parents. They want education on FGM to become part of the school curriculum. 'We need help in arguing and persuading our parents,' says Fahma. 'If all girls had access to facts about the dangers of FGM and how it has no basis in our religion, it would make things easier for us.'

At the Girl Summit, hosted by the UK government and UNICEF in 2014, who met for the first gathering of its kind in the UK, David Cameron said to the hundreds of women and representatives of NGOs fighting FGM: 'it is absolutely clear about what we are trying to achieve, it is such a simple but noble and good ambition, and that is to outlaw the practices of female genital mutilation (FGM) and childhood and early forced marriage, to outlaw them everywhere, for everyone within this generation. That is the aim. That is the ambition.'[17] The prime minister's words are bold but they are disingenuous and have not been backed up by action. Real political will and significant resources need to be made available to reach out to the thousands of immigrants who arrive in this country with the centuries'-held belief in their right to mutilate their daughters.

Naana Otoo-Oyortey, the new executive director of Forward, points out that religious leaders were in short supply at the Summit. These men should be challenged over the misinterpretation of religion that justifies FGM. Respect for tradition and culture appear to prevail over the need for head on confrontation. Following the Summit, the government allocated a mere £1.4 million for an FGM prevention programme in the UK which Otoo-Oyortey dismisses as 'insulting ... the Government is sending a message that this issue is not important enough.'[18]

On the positive side, a new law now makes it mandatory for workers in the health, education and social sectors to report incidents of FGM they come across to the police, which could help bring about more prosecutions. And the government has promised to step up border controls, to stop girls being taken back to the country of their family's origin to be cut during school holidays. In 2003, the Female Genital Mutilation Act was updated making it illegal for FGM to be performed on UK nationals outside the UK.[19] Once again, there have been no prosecutions under the Act.

In the Gambia, I meet Aja, a village circumciser who admits that she has cut young British girls, members of her family who are living in the UK. It was easy enough for Aja's daughters to bring the girls to the Gambia to be cut during the school summer holidays. 'I have one daughter married to an Englishman. Her daughters don't get circumcised. But the other three who are in England are married to Gambian men and they brought them back here to be cut.'

DFID, the UK's Department for International Development, has pledged £35 million to help combat FGM in countries outside the UK and, indirectly, this will help British girls who are threatened with the risk of being cut in the countries of their parents' origin. But, having spent some three years researching FGM in the UK and abroad, I get the firm impression that the UK government is more enthusiastic about combating the problem overseas than at home. The lack of prosecutions compared to France remains inexplicable. The routine examination of children's genitalia is a non-starter. There has been no real debate about the far easier option, the introduction of education about FGM into the school curriculum.

And then there is Maimouna, who fled the Gambia in order to avoid mutilating girls in her village. Why has her claim for asylum been denied? She has now been living in the UK for five years, she has been interned at Yarl's Wood detention centre for six months, has had one judicial hearing and has been turned down on her appeal. The GAMCOTRAP team have yet to ask permission for a meeting in her village. If she is forced to return, she will be forced to cut.

Sitting on her bed in Hounslow, Maimouna tells me, 'They would kill me if I said no to cutting. I would receive a family beating and I would be dead.' Two weeks later, I sit with her sister on a metal bed frame that has been dragged into the courtyard of her house in the Gambia for the purpose of our meeting. Kombeh is nearly blind, which is why their mother chose Maimouna to take over her job. I ask Kombeh what would happen if her sister, Maimouna, returned and refused to become the village circumciser?

She looks at me through her rheumy eyes and says with emphatic menace, 'Everywhere among black people, we have our traditions and, if you don't obey that tradition, something bad will happen to you. She is the village cutter and she has to cut. There will be a curse which she will be powerless to resist. I am telling you, anything could happen to her.'

I go to visit Maimouna's five children, who are being looked after by a neighbour, a few miles away. Their father has remarried and has nothing to do with them and it is considered too dangerous for Maimouna's children to stay in the village. I am not told what the financial arrangements are for the upkeep of the children. The neighbour lives on a big farm but the five teenagers appeared to inhabit one dark room outside the main house.

Their eyes light up when I tell them that I had recently seen their mother and that she is missing them but otherwise they come across as a sad, neglected little group. The neighbour explains their listlessness, 'They are really suffering. They are sad all the time. I try to comfort them by saying that maybe their mother will come back. The girl, without her mum, is badly affected, especially at school. She can't do anything because she is always thinking about her mum.'

I look at Ami and think of the five-year-old writhing in agony and calling for her mother as Maimouna held down her legs while her grandmother cut her. It was that moment that drove Maimouna from her children. I think back to how the tears coursed down Maimouna's cheeks as she spoke of her children. 'I miss my kids so much,' she told me, 'and I know they miss me. But if I go back to look after them, I am not true to what I believe in my heart to be wrong.'

And, incredibly, the village is still waiting for Maimouna. Her sister tells me that no one has been cut since their mother died and Maimouna ran away. The village elders insist that it is only that one family who can do the job. 'It is only our family who can do this,' says Kombeh. 'Maimouna must come back.' But because she is not there, dozens of children have been spared from mutilation.

The Home Office confirm that no British official has visited Maimouna's home to test the truth of her story. The decision to refuse her asylum was taken, a spokesman tells me, 'based on the belief that it would be safe for her to return'. After all the judge had concluded that the way she ties her headdress proved that she is wealthy and educated and could rebuild her life elsewhere in the Gambia and 'socialise amongst educated groups'.

I call on Maimouna again, two years after that first interview, in her bedsit in Hounslow. She is in the same house but now has a room of her own. She watches TV all day, makes calls to her children in the Gambia and once a month goes to the local Home Office asylum agency to collect her food vouchers where, on each visit, she is reminded that she could be deported any day. She is not allowed to work, has no money and relies on her brother to send her the odd £10 note so that she can talk to her children.

She is in despair at losing her appeal. 'If they send me back, I have no choice. I shall go back and I shall do my work on cutting day. If I don't, they will kill me and I have nowhere to hide.' Tears stream down her face. 'It is the only way I will be able to see my children again. I have lost the battle. I shall have to cut.'

2

THE GRANDMOTHERS OF THE PLAZA DE MAYO

Women in Argentina's Dirty Wars

It was my son's twenty-fourth birthday party and we'd gone to dinner at his house to celebrate. We had eaten the cake, sung 'Happy Birthday' and we were playing cards. It was just after midnight when three men, dressed as civilians, knocked on the door. They came in and asked what we were doing. I explained that we were celebrating my son's birthday. They said that they wanted to look at the books in the house. My daughter opened the cupboard where they kept their books.

They looked through the books, some of them were political, and then bundled my son and daughter-in-law into the police car. They said that they wanted to question them and that they would bring them back in a couple of hours. I started to scream and cry and my husband asked me why, saying that they would be back soon. I told them that he did not know what was going on in Argentina and that we would never see Andres and Liliana again. I was right.

I arrange to meet Raquel Radío de Marizcurrena at the office of the Grandmothers of the Plaza de Mayo in an elegant street in the centre of Buenos Aires close to the Jewish quarter. The brass plaques on the doors advertise the firms of lawyers, architects and accountants. Push open the heavy wooden door and an elderly porter in uniform directs you to the old-fashioned lift, pulls open the iron gates and obligingly pushes the button for the fourth floor.

The office itself could belong to a busy law firm. A receptionist is on the phone, someone bustles by carrying a pile of files and, through open doors, I can see people in meetings, sitting at computers and making cups of tea just like in any other office. But what is remarkable here is that everyone is a white- or grey-haired woman in her seventies or eighties.

I have asked to meet with three grandmothers: Raquel, Delia Giovanola de Califano and Rosa Tarlovsky de Roisinblit. There is a strict protocol to be observed. They expect all visitors to bring a good supply of Argentinian cakes when they come and I have not disappointed them. I bring bags filled with locally made sweet almond cakes, doughnuts and a ricotta tart. They provide the coffee and tea and we sit in an office, in front of a wall filled with the photos of young, smiling couples.

Raquel's son disappeared on 24 April 1976, a month after the coup that installed the military dictatorship and what became known as the 'Dirty Wars' in Argentina. The socialist government of Isabel Perón had been overthrown by the army under the leadership of General Videla. Anyone loyal to the previous government was considered a socialist and a subversive for whom there was no place in the new era of militarism and right-wing, Christian family values.

The generals may have been deeply Catholic but they were vengeful and murderous. The preferred time for rounding up subversives was the middle of the night when the roads could be cordoned off by soldiers and neighbours preferred to cower under bedclothes rather than challenge the gun-toting, plain-clothed policemen as they prowled the streets. Anyone with Perónist, socialist sympathies learned to dread the knock on the door. Delia says:

> It was 2.00 a.m. on October 16th, 1976 when they came for my son and daughter-in-law, Jorge and Estela. They took them in the night, leaving my three-year-old granddaughter alone, sleeping in her cot. As they left, they knocked on the neighbour's door and said, 'Don't open, this is the Army. There is a baby alone in the flat next door.' She looked through her keyhole and saw the couple being taken away, handcuffed and hooded, Estela in an advanced state of pregnancy and obviously in distress at being forced to abandon her daughter.
>
> When they left the building, the neighbour walked into the apartment because they had left the door open and she picked up my granddaughter, Virginia, and took her to her place.

Delia was working as a teacher at a primary school when the neighbour called her the next morning and asked her to collect her granddaughter. 'I had no idea what was going on. I asked her, what do you mean they have taken away Jorge and Estela? Why? Who took them? Where?'

No one seemed able to provide an answer but as mothers began to gather at the gates of army barracks and outside police stations asking for the whereabouts of their children, it became clear that they were not alone. Similar kidnappings were being repeated throughout Buenos Aires and all over the country. Mothers began to compare notes and meet. Their activity was little short of a social revolution in Argentina of the time; women were supposed to be in the background while men took decisions and asked questions. 'Motherhood allowed them to build a bond and shape a movement without men,' says Rita Arditti in her book *Searching for Life*.

At first they trod cautiously and asked their priests and journalists to help them search for their children. The Catholic Church supported the regime and most journalists were too afraid. The press was encouraged by Argentina's fascists to reinforce the image of a woman as mother and homemaker, rather like the German Nazi ideal of the woman devoted to her 'kinder, kuche, kirche', children, kitchen and church. Women's magazines warned women to keep their children away from the views of the 'subversives'.

Only the English-speaking newspaper the *Buenos Aires Herald* dared to tell their story. Censorship was strictly and widely applied in Argentina during military rule but because the *Herald* was published only in English, the generals did not bother to silence it. Uki Goni was a young journalist at the time when frantic, tearful women arrived at the newspaper door asking to speak to anyone who would listen to them. As the newsroom rookie, he was told to go down to reception to deal with them. Soon even the editor realized that they had an important story and news of the *desaparecidos*, the 'disappeared', began to make the front page.

When I meet Goni at his elegant flat in Buenos Aires he says:

One thing that really stands out in my mind in my days reporting about it for the *Herald* was that I often found women came up those steps to the *Herald* to report the kidnapping of their kids but I seldom saw a man. If ever I saw a husband coming up the staircase, he would be being dragged up the stairs by his wife. And when they sat down to talk about it, the man would say, 'Shut up! Don't talk about this. I might lose my job. This is dangerous. They'll probably come back anyway.'

I think it says something about motherhood or womanhood. I was only twenty-three or twenty-four at the time but I noted their response to their husbands. They would say, 'Shut up! I don't care whether they kill me or whether they kill you, I want to know where my child is.' The mothers would meet one another at the paper or outside police stations and that's how they got organized.

It was an extraordinary achievement. Many of the women had barely finished secondary school, they had been stay-at-home mothers with little contact with the outside world. Few of them shared or even understood the idealistic, left-wing politics of their children and the beliefs that saw them dragged from their homes in the middle of the night. It is hard for us in the twenty-first century to appreciate the risk that these women, steeped in the patriarchal traditions of South America in the 1970s, were taking.

A climate of fear prevailed. If the children of one couple were detained, then even their closest family would avoid them through fear of guilt by association. Raquel remembers that 'after my son and his wife disappeared, my six sisters and my brother would have nothing to do with us. They were terrified that the same thing would happen to them.' Nonetheless, emboldened and empowered by their anger and their union, the Grandmothers put together twelve case histories and contacted the *Herald* and human rights organizations all over the world. Delia explains:

Mothers don't wait to fight. My son, my beloved son, Jorge, was my only son. As a mother, I couldn't not look for him. I was not going to abandon him. I think we found courage in our pain. Looking back on it, I don't know how we did it. After all, there was no precedent for women doing this kind of thing in our country. It was all improvised but, once we had established ourselves, we were well organized and well managed.

To me, it was an obligation. I owed it to my son, my daughter-in-law and to my granddaughter, Virginia, who was now living with me. I knew my daughter-in-law, Estela, when she was small. She was one of my pupils and I taught her to read and write. At fifteen, she started dating my son. I knew and loved her since she was little. The last time I saw her, she said to me 'we are so happy'. That was a week before they were taken.

There was an extra dimension to the panic felt by the three women sitting in front of me. Delia's daughter-in-law, Estela, was more than eight months pregnant when she was taken away. Raquel's daughter-in-law was five months and Rosa's daughter was three months pregnant when they disappeared. At first, their concerns were those of any mother whose daughter or daughter-in-law is expecting a baby – were the young women receiving enough food, rest and medical attention? Would they be allowed to come home before the birth of their babies?

A year after the coup and with no answers forthcoming, the women decided to demonstrate their concerns in public. They would meet every Thursday afternoon and walk around the square that faces the presidential palace. They had to walk so as to avoid being arrested for 'illegal assembly'. Meetings of more than a handful of people were forbidden by the junta. More and more mothers joined in the weekly circumambulation. They wore white headscarves, carried placards with photos of their children and became known as the Mothers of the Plaza de Mayo.

The authorities did everything possible to stop them. 'The police were terrible,' Raquel remembers. 'They threw us to the ground. We were hit with long weapons and attacked with tear gas. We used to put lemons in our mouths to lessen the effect of the gas. But the policemen on horses were the worst. They didn't care what they did. They just rode all over us. We would run like crazy.'

The attacks got worse as the generals tried to whip the Argentinian people into a nationalist frenzy in preparation for the Falklands War. Families of subversives were likened to traitors and were fair game. 'The worst day was one week before General Galtieri declared war on the Malvinas,' Raquel continues. 'That Thursday, the Thursday before the invasion, they became very aggressive with us. They used everything. It was terrible. They hit us with batons and fired at us with rubber bullets. They did everything possible to kick us out of the square but we stood our ground.'

It was the defeat of the Argentinian army by British forces in 1982 that put an end to Galtieri and the military regime. After the deaths of 650 Argentinian soldiers and 255 British servicemen, Argentina surrendered and the junta collapsed. The generals went but the missing children did not come back. Between 10,000 and 30,000 'subversives' were killed or had disappeared, their whereabouts unknown.[1] Around this time, the Mothers of the Plaza de Mayo were told some devastating news by the editor at the *Buenos Aires Herald*.

'Guillermo Cook told me that the fate of the kidnapped pregnant women was sealed the day they disappeared,' Delia explains. 'The pregnant women were never coming back. We learned that there were lists of couples from all divisions of the armed forces who were waiting for the birth of our grandchildren.' As soon as the young women gave birth they were killed and their babies were given to the waiting couples. The Mothers of the Plaza de Mayo became the Grandmothers of the Plaza de Mayo. Their children were dead but they began searching for their grandchildren.

By now it is late afternoon in the office of the Grandmothers and rays of sunlight are streaming through the window and highlighting the silver hair and tired faces of the three elderly women. An uncomfortable silence descends. Raquel and Delia look at Rosa. Thirty years on, she is the only one of them who has found her grandchild. They look to her to take up the story from here.

They came for her daughter, Patricia, and son-in-law at midnight in October 1978. Patricia was eight months pregnant. 'She was an idealist,' says her mother, Rosa. 'She wanted the best for our country, for her children and for the generation to come. She was fighting a cruel dictatorship and she gave her life for this cause.' Like Raquel, the soldiers who arrested Patricia and her husband left behind a toddler in her cot, two-year-old Mayane.

Twenty-two years later, Rosa asked her granddaughter Mayane to help out one afternoon at the Grandmothers' office. Rosa says:

My granddaughter was working as a volunteer one afternoon here and she received an anonymous call about a baby who was born at ESMA, the Army's Mechanical School, that was being used as a prison at the time. The caller said the baby was born on 15th of November 1978, which was about the time that my daughter was due to give birth and that the mother was a 26-year-old medical student, which is also true of my daughter.

We grandmothers are cautious and careful when we get such calls but Mayane was filled with the eagerness of youth and, without telling anyone, she rushed to the address which the anonymous caller had given her, the address where my supposed grandson was working. She went to the place and introduced herself to the man she found working there. 'What do you want?' he asked. 'I think we might be brother and sister,' she replied.

She was to be proved correct.

A number of grandchildren have been found through such anonymous phone calls and letters. The Grandmothers suspect that they might be former members of the armed forces who, growing old, feel guilty and want to make amends. But such tip-offs are treated with caution. The Grandmothers need proof. They were fortunate in that their search for their children and grandchildren coincided with perhaps the most remarkable scientific advance in the field of molecular biology – the discovery of DNA and its practical use for the purposes of human identification.

All the Grandmothers have sent their blood to be stored in a blood bank in Seattle. Rosa says: 'That afternoon, Guillermo came to our office and offered his arm for us to take a sample because he wanted to know if the girl was his sister. Mayane had shown him pictures of his parents and he had seen a distinct resemblance to the man whom she said was his father. My blood had been waiting for this moment, stored in a laboratory in Seattle for a long time.'

Rosa was not sure how long it would take for the results and so she went ahead with an engagement in America. 'I was in Boston,' she remembers 'because they were giving me an honorary degree at the University of Massachusetts when they told me there was a call for me. I picked up the phone and it was the geneticist saying, "Rosa, he is your grandson!"' Her eyes light up as she tells the story and recalls the celebration that followed. American academics who scarcely knew her joined in the rejoicing, 'We danced, we sang, we laughed, we cried and we jumped up and down with excitement.'

For a moment she is lost in the memory of the happiest day of her life since the disappearance of her daughter and she laughs and then looks guiltily at Delia and Raquel. They have no such story to tell. Even grandmothers who have found their grandchildren still turn up for the shifts at the Office of the Grandmothers, for the sake of the others. After all, they are all still united by that earlier catastrophe in which they all lost children, the tragedy which brought them all together.

Rosa refuses to acknowledge that her daughter, Patricia, is dead until the state admits what happened. 'I want to know who took her, why, who judged her and who condemned her? I will never say that my daughter is dead until they tell me what happened to her. I am so proud of her. She was a militant, yes, but she was fighting against state terrorism.'

Rosa cannot bring herself to visit the infamous ESMA, the Army's Mechanical School, in the suburbs of Buenos Aires, where Patricia gave birth. Instead I ask her grandson, Patricia's son, Guillermo, to take me. We queue up to get in through the forbidding metal gates on a sunny spring afternoon along with dozens of tourists who have come to visit the erstwhile labour camp, torture chamber and prison maternity ward. It has become a popular tourist destination for Argentinians wanting to know more about their recent past.

The general public are not allowed to go into the former prison. Only Guillermo, as a survivor, has permission to go inside and he shows me around. We walk up the concrete steps to where the young prisoners were held incarcerated on the top floor, under sloping roofs. The windows are small, the floors are made of wood and the heat in summer must have been unbearable. Guillermo takes me into a small cell and tells me what he knows about his birth, learned from a fellow prisoner who was ordered to help.

'I was born here,' he tells me. 'My mother was tied to a table, just a regular table and not a hospital one, to give birth. There was an army doctor and two other women prisoners, who had had some experience, to help. She asked the doctor if she could hold me. She named me Guillermo Fernando. She spoke to me and told me she was my mum.' The doctor then took the baby from her and they never saw one another again. He was given to an army officer and his wife.

Of the thousands of young women who were arrested during the military dictatorship, several hundred must have been

42

pregnant. The Catholic Church supported the junta but baulked at endorsing the killing of pregnant women and babies and so the army drew up lists of couples eager to adopt. Once the women had delivered, they had outlived their usefulness and were killed. The babies were given to military couples and to those who were considered politically sound.

While Rosa refuses to speculate about how her daughter might have died, Guillermo has done the research and is certain that his mother was among those who 'were drugged and thrown from planes on the now notorious death flights'. He speaks angrily as we walk down the dark corridors which his mother once knew. 'Their crime was to fight against the dictatorship. They wanted change, equality, freedom and democracy. The majority of women who gave birth here have never been found. We assume they were put on the death flights.'

It became a routine method of murder. The planes would take off from a military airport close to what is now a Memory Park on an estuary of the River Plate, just outside the city. The pilots were instructed to throw their human cargo out to sea but the bodies started washing up on the shores of the River Plate, close to Buenos Aires. So the pilots were told to dump the bodies further out as people began to suspect what was really happening to the *desaparecidos*.[2]

On the day I interview the three Grandmothers, Guillermo turns up at the office to fetch his grandmother, Rosa. She is coming to supper at his home with his wife and two children. They greet one another with hugs and affection. I watch them walk down the Calle Argentina together. They make an odd-looking couple – a tall, good-looking man in his late thirties, with dark hair and tanned skin bending almost double to talk to the tiny, red-headed, fair-skinned woman looking up at him with a broad smile that conveys all the pride, joy, relief and love she feels in his presence.

I return to talk with Raquel and Delia. It had been comparatively easy to bring about the reunion between Rosa and
Guillermo. One anonymous phone call had done the trick. Others
have not been so lucky but not for lack of trying. Delia explains
that back in the mid-1980s, once they knew that their grandchildren could be alive, there was a frightening sense of urgency,
'time was running out and our grandchildren were growing up
with strangers and without us'. They were each allocated tasks.
Some would beg for information from the guards at places like
ESMA while others, clutching photographs of their children,
would simply search the streets looking for children who might
resemble them.

'I covered La Lucila, in the north of Buenos Aires,' says Raquel.
'It was my area. We had found a granddaughter and I took with
me her grandmother and she and I would stand at the corner of
the street and watch the little girl leave for school in the morning and return home in the afternoon. Her grandmother would
spend hours just watching her. She was content to do that, until
we could draw blood.' But they had to get permission from the
courts to do that and it was not always forthcoming.

Delia remembers doing her share of spying. 'I even rang the
doorbell of a house, following a lead we were given by someone
who phoned the office. When the owner opened the door, I told
him that his son could be my grandson. He kicked me out but I
carried on investigating.' She discovered that the information on
his birth certificate was false and the court allowed a blood test.
It turned out that he was a missing grandson, although not Delia's
grandson, and he has been restored to his real family. 'I feel as if
he is my grandson because I helped in his search. All the recovered
grandchildren are very affectionate. They look after us as if we
were all their grandmothers.'

I ask Delia how she set out to find her grandson. 'After I lost my
son, I raised my granddaughter, Virginia, as my own daughter. I

never had any problems with her. She used to come to the Plaza de Mayo with me while I was still looking for her parents and her brother. She was still little and she did not understand. She enjoyed playing with the pigeons in the square.'

When she was eighteen, Virginia was given a job at the Provincia Bank. In effect, she was given her father's old job at the bank. A number of enlightened companies in Argentina, like the Provincia Bank, did that for the children of the *desaparecidos*. Two years later, she got married. 'This is when she started looking for her brother,' Delia continues. 'She appeared on TV, in a programme called *People Looking for People*, and the bank supported her in her search because there was another case of missing people among the bank's employees. The twins, the Tolosa twins, were found but my grandson was still missing. The bank sponsored the search.

'Two years ago, my granddaughter had some sort of crisis and started seeing a psychiatrist. She took leave from the bank and in August she committed suicide.' I am listening to Delia's comforting story of corporate responsibility and sibling love when I hear the words 'su suicidio'. Amidst the cups of tea and the cake plates, I can scarcely believe my ears. She says it in such a matter-of-fact way and I am shocked to the core. I start crying and reach for my handbag and a tissue to wipe away the tears. How much is a woman expected to bear? I ask myself.

Delia takes my hand as if to comfort me. I feel self-conscious and embarrassed. I am the one who should be comforting her. 'I know, I know,' she says shaking her head, 'my life has been a series of blows. Virginia left two children who are now the fourth generation to be affected by what happened. This coup d'état affected my generation, the generation of mothers, the generation of our children, the ones who are missing, the grandchildren, who are the children of the disappeared, and now, in my case, my great-grandchildren who have been left motherless.' She told me that

Virginia's husband blames her for his wife's death and does not allow her to see her great-grandchildren.

I turn to Raquel, whose son disappeared on the night they were celebrating his twenty-fourth birthday. She is also in tears and the two old ladies hold one another's hands. 'I am still looking,' Raquel says, 'and I hope it ends soon because of my age. I am eighty-one already but I want to see my grandson. I want to get to know him and I beg God to help me find him as soon as possible.'

Where were God's servants on earth when they were needed? The military junta ruled with the blessing of the Church. The Grandmothers feel badly let down. 'The Church always ignored us,' says Delia. 'I stopped going to church because I couldn't find the comfort I was looking for. I never stepped into a church again.' One of the Grandmothers got so enraged by her local priest refusing to listen to her account of her missing daughter she screamed and grabbed his arm. 'Madam, calm down,' she remembers the priest telling her, 'don't scream or something may happen to you too.'

The Grandmothers made several trips to Rome to petition Pope Paul VI. Chica Mariani, whose son and daughter-in-law were murdered and whose granddaughter was kidnapped, recalls asking for an audience with the Pope. 'They told us to place ourselves in the first row so that the Pope would see us. We prepared a poster with the name of our group for the Pope to see. When the Pope appeared, the men in black who followed him told him something and he skipped us. He saluted those before us and shook the hands of those after us. It was a terrible blow.' She says that they left the information about the children with Vatican officials but 'he [the Pope] never did anything, he never spoke up on behalf of the children. It was a big disappointment.'

The scandal of the Catholic Church's indifference to the mothers' campaign scars even the present incumbent of the See of Rome. During the military regime, Pope Francis was a Jesuit priest known as Father Jorge Mario Bergoglio. In October 1977, he was approached by the father of five months pregnant Elena de la Cuadra who had disappeared earlier in the year. Father Bergoglio obliged by sending a letter to the Archbishop of La Plata in which he wrote: 'I am going to the trouble of introducing Mr Roberto Luis de la Cuadra, with whom I had a conversation . . . He will explain to you what it is about.'

Elena's sister, Estela de la Cuadra, who lost five members of her family in the 'Dirty Wars', says she remembers her mother urging her father to go to Bergoglio in order to tell him about Elena's disappearance and their concerns because she was pregnant. Her mother was afraid that the priest would not listen to her if she went. The archbishop later told Roberto de la Cuadra that 'a family is raising the baby well'. They have never found the girl who, they were told, was christened Ana Libertad.

In 2010, Bergoglio was summoned as a witness in a tribunal about the excesses of the military regime and he admitted that he knew that Elena de la Cuadra had been kidnapped but did not know she was pregnant. When asked whether he knew about the missing children of the detained, he said that he did not know about them until the first trial of the military junta in the mid-1980s.[3] This is incomprehensible.

The Mothers of the Plaza de Mayo had been demonstrating about the missing children in the centre of Buenos Aires for years. They had been brutally attacked by the police and accounts of their efforts and suffering had been published in the international press. For an educated priest and member of the international Society of Jesus to say he knew nothing of the missing children is disingenuous in the extreme.

After my report on the Grandmothers of Argentina was broadcast on *Newsnight* in March 2013, Jeremy Paxman interviewed me in the studio about Father Jorge Bergoglio's role in the story of the *desaparecidos*. Cardinal Bergoglio had just been elected Pope.

I had brought back from Buenos Aires a copy of the letter he had written to the archbishop and transcripts of the tribunal in which he denied knowledge of the missing children, which we used to illustrate the interview. The next day, I received several furious complaints from British Catholics accusing me of bias against the Roman Catholic Church and dishonesty as a journalist.

In the 1990s, the bishops of Argentina promised to 'examine their conscience' about the role of the Church during the dictatorship.[4] However, they have since shown little enthusiasm to fulfil this promise. The election of Bergoglio as Pope Francis I has been welcomed as a breath of fresh air in the Catholic Church and his commitment to the poor and excluded are deservedly praised but he will always be dogged by questions of what he did or, rather, what he did not do during Argentina's Dirty Wars.

It is thanks to the courage and determination of the Grandmothers working alone that over one hundred children of the *desaparecidos* have been found. Those whom I met in Argentina have clearly inherited the strength of their parents who, forty years ago, were bold enough to defy the military. They have had to survive extraordinary circumstances. They were brought up by army officers or by those deemed politically correct by the military. In some cases, their abductors had been directly responsible for the murder of their real parents. They were brought up to accept the values and beliefs of their abductors, which were totally inimical to those of their biological parents.

They were accustomed to a world of privilege and wealth and, understandably, some were angry and reluctant when they were told the truth about their origins. I met Victoria Montenegro at the Memorial to the Victims of State Terrorism, on the shores of the River Plate just outside Buenos Aires. The names of the approximately thirty thousand who were murdered by the junta are inscribed on walls of granite. We find the names of her parents – Roque Orlando Montenegro and Hilda Romana Torres, who was eighteen when she disappeared ten days after her daughter was born.

Standing with her back to the memorial, Victoria admits that she was furious when the Grandmothers found her.

I really didn't want to know the truth or anything about my real family. I was very angry with the Mothers and with the Grandmothers. I hated them profoundly. I was convinced that I was the biological daughter of my abductors. For me, it was a political thing. I believed that they were just using me to get revenge on the colonel, the man I believed was my father.

I had been brought up to believe that our country had gone through a war and that my father, the colonel, had had to fight in that war and that was the reason that they wanted their revenge on him. I was brought up in an army barracks and subjected to a lot of ideological pressure as a small child.

She says this almost defensively. We walk to a bench and spend some minutes looking at the people who have come to spend their Sunday in the Memorial Park – the elderly, couples strolling hand in hand and young children dodging among the huge slabs of granite, each one containing names of the murdered. Modern Argentina has proved itself ready and able to face its past. Senior army officers and even clergymen have been put on trial and are serving prison sentences. '*Nunca más*', never again, is a slogan generally agreed upon.

But victims of the terror, like Victoria, still find themselves confused. After the Grandmothers contacted her, she agreed to have a blood test and discovered that she was in fact Victoria Montenegro, daughter of two left-wing activists who died for their beliefs, and not María Sol Tetzlaff, the privileged and pampered daughter of a colonel. She admits that she cannot entirely escape her education, 'I see myself as very distant from my real uncles, cousins and grandparents. I was brought up to have very strong beliefs which are hard to get rid of.'

Just as she hated the Grandmothers when they first contacted her, she now feels similar anger against the parents who deceived her. 'I can now see that what tied me to them was nothing to do with love. We were like a spoil of war to them. I now see that my life must be what I can salvage from the past and I can only do this by acknowledging my true identity.' As more of the story emerges, Victoria has learned that not only was her supposed father a child abductor but he also gave the order for her parents' arrest and eventual murder.

Victoria's husband and three teenage sons wave to her from the entrance of the Memorial Park. They have arranged to meet her here, on their weekly visit. 'It is important for them to try and understand,' she says. 'It was a shock for them too to learn that their grandfather was a fraud.' She refuses my request to talk with her sons. 'No. I have to protect them,' she says firmly. 'We have to take things slowly.'

The Grandmothers believe there are still hundreds of children out there who are yet to be found. Today, TV and radio stations regularly broadcast news of the Grandmothers' campaign with details of forthcoming trials. The radio presenters, who are often members of the families of *desaparecidos*, urge those with doubts to get in touch.

'When I saw the ad on TV, it was like a bolt out of the blue,' says Catalina de Sanctis. 'I had been confused all my life. I always doubted who I was. At the age of seven or eight, I looked at myself in the mirror and said to myself that I look like no one I know. I asked my mother, why don't I look like you or Papa? She said I looked like an uncle of hers but I did not believe her. I looked different, I did not fit in at the Catholic school they sent me to and I could never agree with my adoptive father. He was a soldier and we had a different way of thinking.'

After seeing the TV ad, she confronted her parents again. 'I plucked up courage and said to the woman who abducted me, "I am the daughter of one of the *desaparecidos*, aren't I?" She burst into tears and admitted that I was but she said that the families of those kind of people – the terrorists – wanted nothing to do with their babies. She said that the Grandmothers were lying and were snatching children from the families who loved them. She said this was the truth.'

Like Victoria, Catalina was torn with conflicting emotions. She started off by trying to protect her abductors and says: 'I felt that I shared the guilt of my abductors. I did not want them to get arrested because of me.' Like Victoria, she also shared some of their beliefs: 'It was childlike, but they had led me to believe that the Grandmothers were bad. I was afraid of them, I even hated them.' Confused, she fled to Paraguay with her boyfriend for a few months. When she returned, her abductors turned nasty and threatened her. Her alleged father, an alcoholic, became violent; her supposed mother became depressed.

By this time, a neighbour who knew the family and who shared Catalina's suspicions, contacted the Grandmothers. The Grandmothers offered Catalina a blood test. She had the test and discovered that she was the daughter of Myriam Ovando and Raúl René de Sanctis and was welcomed into their families. They told her that, in 1977, her mother Myriam had been studying psychology and her father Raúl was a student of anthropology. They were both members of the 'Perónist Youth'. Myriam was twenty-one and was five months pregnant when they both disappeared in April that year.

It turned out that at about the same time as Catalina's parents disappeared in 1977, her abductors approached the Christian Family Movement, an organization that played a key part in selecting babies born of 'subversive' mothers in order for them to be given to respectable families, loyal to the dictatorship. The woman who would later pretend to be Catalina's mother, María Francisca Morilla, had been trying to conceive for many years and had failed. In April 1977, she turned to the Movement for help and wrote excitedly to her soldier husband, who was serving away from home at the time, to tell him that she had met with the official in charge of baby allocation. 'She told me,' she wrote, 'that she had worked for many years with the Movement and she had never come across a case of health problems or malformations with these babies and that they are all very healthy and their deliveries are usually quite normal.'

Although, according to the hospital records, the birth was not quite normal. In the records of the military hospital of Campo de Mayo in Buenos Aires, it claims that María Francisca Morilla gave birth to a girl at 5 p.m. in the afternoon of 17 August 1977. Six days earlier, the record says that Myriam Ovando, Catalina's real mother, had a dead foetus removed from her womb at 10 a.m. on the morning of 11 August. The records had apparently been deliberately falsified to provide alibis for the baby snatchers.

All these details came out in the fourteen days of court hearings in which María Francisca Morilla and Carlos Hidalgo Garzón were charged with abduction. Garzón had tried to persuade the prosecutor that he had suffered a mental breakdown and could not endure the trial. The judge decided otherwise. Catalina attended every day, sitting just metres away from the man and woman she had once called father and mother.

I meet Catalina a week before the court was to be recalled for the sentences on the abductors to be pronounced. She does not want me to come to her house and she cancels our appointment twice before she agrees to meet me in the office of the Grandmothers for an hour in her lunch break. She is an attractive woman but nervous, agitated and clearly damaged by all she has been through. The strain of the trial is taking its toll, she explains. Every day brought a new and painful revelation.

She learned from letters and witnesses produced in court that her mother had christened her Laura Catalina and, after the baby was taken from her, she believed that her daughter was being looked after by her own family. Knowing that she was likely to be killed, she had written a letter to her mother asking her to 'remember me and love me through my daughter'. She wrote, 'although she doesn't know it, my blood runs through her little veins'. Twenty-one-year-old Myriam Ovando was never heard from again.

We are allowed into the court to film the proceedings on the day of the sentencing, 12 March 2013. Morilla, a large, stern-looking woman looks implacable and emotionless as she stares at the judge throughout the proceedings. Her husband, Garzón, sits with his head bowed. Neither reacts when the sentences are read out – twelve years for Morilla and fifteen years for Garzón. The courtroom bursts into applause.

Catalina punches the air with excitement. She embraces her boyfriend and then stands, looking defiantly at the guilty couple as they are led away to begin their prison sentences. Outside the court, human rights activists and journalists have been gathering all morning to hear the result. Smiling happily, Catalina tells me that she is very happy; she no longer has any doubts.

'For me, the most important thing and what made me change my attitude towards my abductors was the realization that they had made it necessary to murder my parents. Myriam and Raúl were murdered in order for them to be able to keep me and that makes my adoptive parents accomplices in my parents' deaths.'

There is a group of Grandmothers also waiting for the news outside the court that day. I am surprised to see Delia among them, 81-year-old Delia who has lost her daughter, her grandson, her granddaughter and her great-grandchildren because of Argentina's 'Dirty Wars'. She is linking arms and laughing with the other Grandmothers and with Catalina, rejoicing in her victory. She catches my eye and smiles as if to say: 'You see? I haven't given up hope.'

3

IRELAND'S FALLEN WOMEN

A Story of Religious Persecution

We got up at six in the morning and went to Mass. You were allocated a drawer with a loaf of bread and half a pound of butter for a week. That was breakfast. If you didn't go to Mass, they would take your drawer away from you. After breakfast, you went straight down to the laundry. It was heavy, heavy work. There was a break at twelve for dinner, potatoes and cabbage and fish, and then back to work until six. Then porridge and then you went back to the laundry until half past eight.

One night, 24-year-old Mary Merritt decided that she could stand it no more. She had been working unpaid, imprisoned in the Magdalene High Park Laundry in Dublin for eight years. As she made her way back to the dormitory that she shared with twenty other young women, she noticed a ground-floor window had been left open. She waited until her room-mates and the nuns who supervised them were asleep, crept downstairs and climbed out of the window.

'I had never been out in the world in my life. The only world I knew was one of nuns and priests.' Finding herself in a road in the middle of the night, she asked the way to the priest's house.

She knocked on the door and when he invited her to come in and sit down, she told him.

> I've ran out of the High Park Laundry and I need help. Then he came over and sat on the chair beside me and started rubbing my knee, then he pulled down his trousers and raped me.
>
> I had no idea what was going on. I knew nothing about such things. I was crying my eyes out and I said, 'You're hurting me.' Then when he was finished he said, 'Now, this is between us. I'm going to give you sixpence. Don't tell anybody. I'm only trying to help you,' he said. He gave me sixpence and he opened the door and let me out. There was a police car waiting and it took me back to the laundry.

Mary's crime for being cut off from the world, sexually abused and institutionalized for thirty years of her life was to have been born illegitimate. She was born in 1931, in a Mother and Baby Home where pregnant, single women were taken by irate parents or the censorious village priest. After the birth, the mothers would spend a few months with their babies before they were forcibly removed from them and were either adopted or put in an orphanage. Mary's mother would have been told that she had sinned and that Mary was proof of that sin and that they had no right to a future together.

Mary was born nine years after Ireland's independence when a cash-strapped government was happy to delegate welfare responsibilities to the religious orders. They ran the schools, hospitals, orphanages and Mother and Baby Homes. Who better than priests and nuns to deal with women who had flouted the holy sacrament of marriage and indulged in illicit sex? Unmarried mothers and their unfortunate offspring were handed over to those deemed best able to supervise and punish them.

According to the law, Mary would have been expected to stay in the care of the nuns until she was sixteen. Orphanages were aptly called 'industrial schools' at the time; although the government paid for the children's keep, the religious orders also put them to work. Official checks were random and few and the nuns were able to shuttle the girls from the orphanages to work unpaid in the laundries on the most spurious of pretexts.

For the first six years Mary was allowed to go to the local school. 'I remember that they always arrived ten minutes after us and they left ten minutes later than us so that we would not be able to mingle with them,' recalls Catherine Corless, a local historian in Galway. 'They were segregated and made to sit at the back of the class. To this day, I can remember the sound of their hobnail boots as they walked in pairs to and from the school. You could hear them well before you saw them. The townspeople would call them "whores" droppings.'

Mary remembers that she was taken out of school at eleven and made to 'scrub three long corridors every morning and then I was sent to work on the nuns' farm'. Any lapse at work or any sign of rebellion was harshly punished. 'A nun came down one day and I can't remember what she said but I cheeked her back. She took off her thick leather belt and just belted me across the back and the hips. They left the wound open, left me bleeding for two weeks and I still have the scars on my hip today.

'One day, when I was sixteen, I was so hungry after working on the farm that I took some apples from the orchard. They took me to the High Park Convent in Drumcondra in Dublin and they left me there and they said now you stay there until you learn to stop stealing.' And how long were you there? I ask her. 'Fourteen years,' she replies and adds, 'you get less for murder these days.' Did you ever ask why you were sent to a laundry for fourteen years for stealing some apples? 'Yes, I did ask them, and I asked was I ever going to get out of here, am I going to die here? I had no family, nobody, not a sinner in the world who was going to help me get out.'

The regime was harsh and designed to depersonalize the new recruits. Mary remembers arriving at the laundry and being taken to the clothes depot. ' "You have to get into these clothes," a nun told me. It was a big, long serge skirt and white apron and a cap. Then she said, "From now on, your name is not Mary O'Connor. Your name is going to be Attracta and you have to answer to that name." I refused to answer to that name for three weeks. My name was Mary, I told them, and that was the end of it.' But, after a spell in the punishment cell, she had no choice but to comply and to conform.

It has taken a number of phone calls to persuade Mary Merritt to leave her home in Kent and return to Ireland to be interviewed about her experiences. She tells me she now hates the country but she is committed to getting her story heard and agrees to cross the Irish Sea. We meet at Glasnevin Cemetery in Dublin, the final resting place for Irish national heroes like Michael Collins and Éamon de Valera and hundreds of girls and women who never had the chance to realize their potential. Mary has had her hair newly dyed, dark brown, and cut in a bob for the filming. She has also invested in a new pair of black patent-leather shoes for the occasion, which trouble her a bit as she wanders through the graveyard.

With her jacket done up tightly against a September squall, Mary leads me solemnly up to a mass grave and lays down a bunch of flowers. There are 160 names on the giant headstone, all of them former workers at the High Park Magdalene Laundry in Drumcondra in Dublin. 'One of my jobs was to lay out the bodies when they died,' she says. 'I was happy to do that work because I would say to myself, "At least they've got away from the nuns now and their sufferings were over."' She touches the name Mary Brehany engraved on the headstone and turns to me. 'Sue, this was my friend. They kept her in the laundry for fifty-six years. I don't think I would have survived if she hadn't been there with me.'

The mass grave in the Dublin cemetery was not the first resting place for the former workers at the High Park Laundry. Mary and I drive down the road and walk through the gates of what was once the vast convent estate.

'The vans would draw up here,' she explains pointing to the forecourt of an abandoned grey stone building, which was once the laundry where she was forced to work. 'The nuns would hand out the packages of washing done up in brown paper. We weren't allowed anywhere near the people who came to collect them.' She points to a corner of the building with a bricked-up window. 'That was the place we called "The Hole". It was like a cell, where they would put us as punishment.'

We walk around to the back of the estate, past the cranes and mechanical excavators working on what is now one of the prime development sites in Dublin, to a hotel car park. In the early 1990s, when the Sisters of Our Lady of Charity wanted to raise some cash, they sold the plot of land on which cars belonging to travelling salesmen and tourists are now parked in neat rows. The site, which was a green field back in 1993, was filled with the bodies of former laundry workers.

I leave Mary in the hotel where we are staying to rest. At eighty-three years old, she finds the experience of revisiting the scene emotionally exhausting. My cameraman Ian O'Reilly and I drive an hour out of Dublin to County Kildare to meet Barney Curran, the gravedigger employed by the nuns to exhume the women's bodies. He is now retired and lives alone in a row of small, whitewashed terraced houses. He comes to the door, a little unsteady on his legs, and does not appear at all surprised that I want to hear about events that took place more than twenty years ago. It was, he says, the most disturbing thing that happened to him in a lifetime of gravedigging.

I sit with him at the kitchen table where he clears a space through piles of old newspapers for two mugs of tea. 'Well, the nuns were trying to sell the place and there was big money involved,' he starts. 'So they didn't want anyone to know what was going on and they wanted to keep it hush-hush. We had to put big screens up as we worked and we were supposed to tell no one about it.'

The nuns told him there were 133 bodies buried in unmarked graves in the field. 'I could see pretty soon that there were more but when I told them this they said, "No, there are only 133." So we kept digging and we found 22 more bodies which they said they did not even know were there.' Barney also found something else in the mass grave. 'A lot of plaster of Paris, on their wrists, their arms, their legs, their feet, their ankles. There were broken arms and legs. It seems to me that the women were too small and frail for the kind of work they were doing.'

So what was going on in the network of laundries run by the religious orders in Ireland? The laundries were operational for more than two hundred years; the first was opened in 1767 and the last closed in 1996. Tens of thousands of 'fallen women' were sent to them by their embarrassed families and hypocritical priests and to save local communities from moral contagion. They were named after Mary Magdalene, a follower of Christ who, some say, was a reformed prostitute.

Men have been obsessed by the idea of the fallen woman ever since the Virgin Mary set impossibly high standards for our sex. 'Woman is the root of all evil,' St Jerome, one of the early Christian sages, wrote in the fourth century.[1] Canon laws issued in the thirteenth century legitimized the idea of their incarceration: 'Those women, who having abandoned the marriage bed have fallen away due to the sinfulness of the flesh, should, for the sake of God . . . be placed in convents with religious women, so that there they may perform perpetual penance.'[2] The idea gained popularity in Ireland in the nineteenth century when the majority of the vast laundries were built.

They were found across the water in England too where pre-occupation with the fallen woman consumed Victorian society. 'There are more entries in Gladstone's diaries about prostitutes than there are about political hostesses,' Anne Isba notes in *Gladstone and Women*, 'more recorded visits to the fallen women on the streets of London than recorded attendances at the balls and soirées of the *grandes dames* of polite Victorian society.'[3]

Charles Dickens, who despised his wife and kept a mistress, was involved in running a home to look after such women. Urania Cottage for the Redemption of Women, Dickens said, should uphold the virtues of 'order and punctuality, cleanliness and the whole routine of household duties – washing, mending, cooking' and would ensure the path to redemption.[4] In both Ireland and England, frenetic washing was apparently seen as the approved route for the cleansing of the soul. No such energy was employed in finding or chastizing the men involved in the forbidden couplings.

In Ireland, the 'fallen woman' label was conveniently allowed to embrace any women who appeared to challenge the traditional notions of Irish morality. Not only prostitutes but unmarried mothers fell into the category, whether pregnant because of incest, rape or accident. Some women were even sent to the laundries for prophylactic reasons. Girls considered too pretty for their own good by the nuns who taught them at school were sent to the laundries to prevent them from 'falling'. Mary Merritt was condemned to a laundry perhaps because she showed too much spirit, which might have become her undoing.

The justification behind the laundries was a toxic mix of the need to maintain moral order in a strict, patriarchal society along with the eagerness of the religious orders to profit from a free workforce. As James Smith points out in his history of the laundries, they shared 'overriding characteristics, including a regime of prayer, silence, work in a laundry, and a preference for permanent inmates' which 'contradicts the religious congregations' stated mission to protect, reform, and rehabilitate'.[5]

One of the best descriptions of the inside of the laundry comes from the Irish poet and playwright Patricia Burke Brogan, who became a novice nun in 1963. She was ordered to work as a supervisor in the laundry run by the Sisters of Mercy in Galway. 'This is the richest branch-house of our Order,' said the nun who accompanied her on her first day.

> She opens a heavy double-locked door. A deafening noise hits us. We're in a room with huge machines from which the steam hisses. Prison bars pattern the roof-windows. The grey walls are sweating. There's a stench of soiled clothing. Bleach fumes sting my throat. I gasp for air. Gradually I see that the room is full of women. Elderly women, middle-aged women and young girls all seem to merge with the grey of womb like washing machines. Have I slipped down into Dante's Inferno?[6]

'Why are the women here?' asked the nervous novitiate. She is told: 'These women are penitents. They're weak. They have no control. They have broken the sixth and ninth commandments. No one wants these women. We protect them from their passions. We give them food, shelter and clothing. We look after their spiritual needs.' A few weeks later, Burke Brogan decided she no longer had a vocation and she left the Order and wrote the play *Eclipsed*, in which she tells the story of the laundry.

The few pictures of the laundries that survive show rows of women and girls, in uniforms, washing and ironing, under the supervision of the nuns. There are the huge mangles which the gravedigger Barney Curran says were responsible for the injuries.

He tells me that when he sneaked a look inside the laundry at High Park, where Mary worked, he reckoned that the mangles would have required five or six of the undernourished inmates to operate them. A few of the women in the photographs have shaved heads, a regular form of humiliation and punishment. Mary Merritt's hair was shaved.

After she had been raped by the priest, the nuns refused to believe her story and put her in the punishment cell for running away. 'One of the nuns came down to "The Hole" and she cut my hair to the bone and then I was taken upstairs and I was made to kneel in a room with all the women there, kneel down, kiss the floor and say I was sorry for what I did and promise not to do it again which I didn't promise, of course. "No, I'm not promising to do anything," I said, "because I want to get out of here," and I might do it again.'

Mary did get out again, a few months later. She was pregnant as a result of the rape and the nuns sent her to a Mother and Baby Home in Dublin to have the baby. Just like her mother, history was repeating itself. Mary called her baby girl Frances Cristina but was not allowed to attend the baptism and so didn't know that the nuns christened the child Carmel.

She was allowed to breastfeed the baby for a year and 'then they said to me, "You've got to go back to the High Park Laundry because that is where you came from." I was in a terrible state. I did not want to leave my daughter. "This is the only thing I have in my life," I told them. But the nuns said they would look after the baby and told me not to try and look for her.' Mary closes her eyes for a few seconds and tears trickle down through her lashes onto her cheeks. For an eighty-three-year old, her memory and stamina are remarkable but for today the interview is over.

I meet several survivors of the laundries during the course of filming and wonder how they survived and remain apparently strong and apparently sane, after all they have been through. On the surface, they appear remarkably resilient and they have seemingly unlimited energy to cooperate with the press and badger their government and even the UN to listen to their stories and demands for compensation. They all say that it is anger and a continuing sense of injustice that keeps them going.

But the more I communicate with them, the more the insecurities, the hypersensitivity and the low self-esteem become evident. Some are jealous of each other and fear that one survivor's story might appear more important than another's. If we promise two nights in a hotel for Mary in Dublin while we are filming, another will demand the same treatment or more. They argue with one another if they feel slighted or gang up on me if they felt exploited. A psychiatrist might identify this behaviour as the classic legacy of neglect and abandonment.

I meet 64-year-old Elizabeth Coppin at the former laundry where she was interned in Waterford, in the south-east of Ireland. The old convent building is now an adult education college, but the long, tiled corridors with religious paintings and sculptures of Christ on the cross remain as does the convent's huge church. Elizabeth shudders as we push open the doors. 'We had to come here to Mass every morning,' she says. 'The laundry workers on one side, the children from the industrial school on the other and the nuns in the middle.' She grimaces as we pass the confessional box. 'We had to come to confession every Sunday. But what did we have to confess? They were the sinners, not us.'

Like Mary, Elizabeth was transferred to the laundry from an industrial school. Like Mary, the nuns shaved her hair, put her in a uniform and changed her name when she arrived. 'So straight away your identity is taken because my name is changed, my hair is cut and I'm not wearing my own clothes,' she says. 'I'm stuck in there at fourteen years old and I have to answer to the name Enda, which is a man's name in Ireland. How do you cope with that at that age?' I ask Elizabeth why she thought they did it? 'Just to dehumanize me,' she says, 'to make me feel nothing in society.'

Time and again the women tell me that the nuns told them that they were worthless and, if you hear that often enough, you begin to believe it. Like Mary, Elizabeth fled to the UK to escape the stigma and to reinvent herself. But both women are still scarred by the physical and psychological abuse of their childhood. They have tried hard to rebuild their lives but are still haunted by nightmares. Mary and Elizabeth's husbands, both English, tell me that they have had to cope with their wives screaming aloud during their nightmares, even decades after they left the care of the nuns.

So what is going through the minds of these women who force a child to work for fourteen years to punish her for taking an apple, chastise her for being raped by a priest and then steal her baby? What we are dealing with here in Ireland is a 'War on Women' by women. It was women who shaved the heads of the inmates and locked them in 'The Hole' for minor misdemeanours. On the current website for those applying to be a Sister of Our Lady of Charity, it says that women are expected to take vows of poverty, chastity and obedience.[7] I cannot find the words 'care' or 'compassion' in the job specification. It speaks of a life devoted to the spiritual life and to God but nothing about service to the local community.

But for more than two hundred years, the nuns did provide service of a kind to the communites of Ireland. They took the vulnerable and society's rejects into their 'care'. Some of them may have responded to the challenge with sympathy but many nuns abused the trust placed in them. Irish Catholic families were traditionally large and a fifth or sixth daughter would be encouraged to join one of the religious orders. It meant fewer mouths to feed and the chance of winning respect in the local community. But it also meant that many nuns had no actual vocation. These women may well have felt cheated by their exclusion from what went on outside convent walls. A sense of moral superiority, jealousy, anger and frustration are all I can think of by way of explanation to account for the treatment meted out to Mary and Elizabeth by the nuns.

The Roman Catholic Church is determinedly patriarchal. The Pope sets the rules, the bishops announce them from the pulpit and the priests enforce them on the ground. The idea of a female priesthood is not even debated by Rome. It was the priest who invariably brought the pregnant girls to the gates of the convent. The nuns were, for all intents and purposes, the prison officers, answerable to the men in authority.

Burke Brogan writes of how the nuns sought to win favour with the priests and how the local bishop seemed almost to usurp God in their estimation.[8]

The Mother Superior calls me to her office. She sits on a throne-like chair. On her desk an ornate silver frame holds a picture of his Lordship, His ruby-ringed hand emerging from crimson robes, edged with delicate lace, is raised in blessing.

'On your knees, Sister,' the Mother Superior orders the novice as she enters, 'and remember to keep your eyes downcast, custody of the eyes at all times, Sister!' The phone rings. Mother Superior lifts the receiver. Her stylish shoes shift under the rosewood desk. 'Yes, yes, Father, I'll hold on. Oh good morning, my Lord.' She softens her voice as she speaks to the Bishop. 'Yes, My Lord. I'm working on the ledgers now. I should have them finished tomorrow, my Lord. Yes, I'll send the cheque. Thank you, my Lord.' I'm amazed by her change in attitude.[9]

The account given by Burke Brogan of the simpering Mother Superior reminds me of women in a similar position I met in Iran. I interviewed the head of the Sisters of Zeinab, who are charged with enforcing the strict Iranian morality rules on women and acting as a brute force during demonstrations. Although she was over sixty and very stout, she went to exaggerated lengths to conform to the official dress code, including robust leather boots and long gloves, to ensure that Ian, my cameraman, had no chance of catching a glimpse of tempting flesh.

She took a call from President Ahmadinejad's office about a forthcoming 'Death to America! Death to Israel' demonstration in Tehran. She too gushed and simpered as she took the call and promised to order hundreds of women to attend the demonstration in their black abayas. What is it about such women who have apparently rejected close contact with men in their private lives but who are nonetheless desperate for their approval? They carry out the orders to obey religious rules laid down by men and to punish other women into submission with unquestioning zeal. Denied real power themselves, they abuse the women under their control in a desperate attempt to win praise from the men who in turn control them.

Why did more of the so-called 'fallen women' not stand up to the priests? How could they bear to hand over their babies to the nuns so routinely? I call on Lindsay Earner-Byrne in her office in the School of History at University College Dublin. She reminds me that it is hard to understand the powerlessness felt by these women.

> The culture was so hostile that many of these women felt they had no choice, first of all to go into these homes and secondly to do whatever was required of them when they were there. And if that meant walking away from their baby and never seeing their baby again, they felt that had absolutely no choice.
>
> I have heard a lot of oral testimonies from women who tell me that they know they signed adoption forms in the 1950s and 1960s but they have no memory of signing them

because they were so traumatized and because they had no free choice. There was no financial support for women who had children outside marriage until 1972. Society considered their behaviour a crime. They referred to women as 'first-time offenders' when they had one baby and 'repeat offenders' after they had had two. So there was this language of criminality and the phrases are still being used as late as the 1970s.

I meet Earner-Byrne just a few weeks after the revelations that some eight hundred babies and young children had died in a Mother and Baby Home in Tuam in Galway in western Ireland between 1925 and 1960 and that their bodies had been buried in unmarked mass graves and some had even been deposited in a former cesspit. Journalists and TV crews from around the world descended on the town of Tuam, trampled on the former convent grounds where the babies' bodies are believed to be buried and published reports about the massacre of the innocents.

'The shock seemed to emanate from ignorance that this happened,' says Earner-Byrne who was surprised by the headlines that greeted the news of the Tuam deaths. According to her research, the death rate of babies born in the Mother and Baby Homes was routinely some five times that of babies born outside the convent walls. The babies were kept in long rows of cots, she explains, sometimes two to a cot and they died of infections, malnutrition and neglect. 'What conclusion do you draw,' asks Earner-Byrne, 'other than that this was a price Irish society was willing to pay for an illusion of moral superiority?'

Earner-Byrne says that mothers were often told not to grieve if their babies died because, after all, they had gone to a better place. 'It was said constantly that these poor children carry the crimes of their parents. So that if they are baptized and they die, they go straight to heaven where at least they are absolved of carrying that sin. This idea fed into the inertia when it came to dealing with their deaths. The acceptance of that high death rate was part of the moral picture.'

And the death of babies was commonplace. Laura Mann worked in Dublin as a midwife in the 1940s and 1950s. She remembers 'terrible, terrible poverty, families with ten children living in two rooms, fighting for survival'. Contraception was illegal and sterilization unobtainable. Children died, mothers weakened and pleaded with their priests for permission for a break and not to sleep with their husbands. 'But the priests told them that they would not get absolution if they did not do what they had to do,' says Mann, which entailed submitting to their husbands and having more and more babies, even if it killed them. 'The big thing was to have children,' says Mann, 'even if you were crippled or dropped dead in the process, and many did.' In 1931, a papal encyclical decreed that women who died in childbirth were martyrs.[10]

While researching my film on the Magdalene Laundry survivors, which I called *Ireland's Hidden Bodies, Hidden Secrets*, I came across so many aspects of the abuse and contempt shown to women and their babies in Ireland that there simply was not the space for them all in the half-hour documentary I was making.

The bodies of babies who died in the Mother and Baby Homes were used by medical students for dissection. Children like Elizabeth Coppin were used for drug trials and to this day her medical records for the period are redacted. But of everything I learned, the practice of symphysiotomy is the most shocking and bewildering.

It was a procedure that was introduced in Ireland in 1944 by doctors, influenced by religious leaders who were wary of caesarean sections (CS) on the grounds that most doctors recommended that a woman should be sterilized after her third CS for health

THE WAR ON WOMEN

reasons. But sterilization would mean that a woman would not be able to do 'what she had to do'. Devout Catholic doctors feared that it might be used as a covert form of contraception.

Doctors in Ireland came up with a novel idea. If a woman's pelvis was too small to allow for a normal birth, then the accepted procedure should be to break the pelvic bone. 'I saw the doctor go over and get a hacksaw,' Nora Clarke remembers. 'I know it was a hacksaw because I had seen one in the butcher's where he used it to cut up animals. He started to cut through my bone. The blood spurted out like a fountain. It went everywhere. The nurses were being physically sick. The doctor was angry because the blood splashed his glasses.'[11]

This procedure was carried out on hundreds of women in Ireland until 1983. In 1968, Pope Paul published his *Humanae Vitae*,[12] in which he reinforced the Catholic Church's opposition to any form of contraception and sterilization. Marie O'Connor, a contemporary writer who campaigned against symphysiotomy, accuses the Catholic Church of promoting 'medicine from the Dark Ages, encouraged by senior clerics who were obsessed by sexuality and utterly opposed to the crime of birth prevention. The driving forces were control, ambition and religion.'[13]

In 2012, some one hundred survivors of symphysiotomy travelled from all over Ireland to Dublin to tell their stories and demand compensation. They gathered in the Lighthouse Cinema in the Smithfield area. Rita McCann, eighty-six, came from Co. Kerry and, unfamiliar with Dublin, couldn't find the venue. 'Then I spotted two women limping and said to myself, "I'm sure they are heading for it." When you see the limps, you get the message.'[14] Many women arrived in wheelchairs and complained of difficulty in walking, chronic back pain and incontinence. Another survivor, Claire Kavanagh, said, 'Put fifty of us in a room and you'll get different stories but the same ending. We are all cripples.'[15]

Not a single member of SOS, as the survivors of symphysiotomy call themselves, say that they gave permission for the butchery carried out on them. Back at University College Dublin, Earner-Byrne reminds us that: 'You have to understand the position of women in society. They had no say and no voice. They were constantly reminded that they had duties and responsibilities. They had no rights in a society that was profoundly influenced by faith.' A married woman was expected to give birth, by whatever means possible, until she died just as a woman who gave birth without the sacrament of marriage would be punished and her baby taken from her.[16]

It is the film industry that has to be thanked for moving the subject of institutionalized abuse in Ireland from stories told at gatherings of survivors and in university studies to a national platform where the Irish public has been forced to confront what had been going on in their name. *Mothers Against the Odds*, a film on symphysiotomy by Anne Daly and Ronan Tynan, led to debates in the Irish Parliament, new support groups, the involvement of lawyers and calls for compensation.

The Magdalene Sisters, a feature film about the Magdalene Laundries and based on Patricia Burke Brogan's play *Eclipsed*, was produced by Peter Mullan in 2002. It shocked all who saw it. For years, it had been generally accepted that the laundries were doing important welfare work for women and girls who had no other options. My sister-in-law, who was brought up in Cork, remembers taking laundry down the road to their local Magdalene Laundry with her mother. Her mother told her that they were doing their bit to help the nuns look after homeless, desperate women.

The publicity produced by Mullan's film, which tells of the lives of four women incarcerated in a laundry in Dublin in the 1960s, caused controversy and raised questions. It emboldened survivors, including Mary Merritt, to submit accounts of their experiences to the committee of UNCAT (The United Nations Convention Against Torture), which in turn put pressure on the Irish government to investigate. The government responded but there was surprise when, in 2011, the then prime minister, Enda Kenny, called on Senator Martin McAleese, a devout Roman Catholic, to research the issue and report back.

Only a man loyal to the Catholic Church and sympathetic to the religious orders could have written in the introduction to his report into the Magdalene Laundries (published in February 2013) 'that many of the Sisters of the four Religious Congregations which operated these institutions . . . have experienced a profound hurt in recent years as the debate on the Magdalen Laundries gained increasing public prominence. Their position is that they responded in practical ways as best they could . . . to the fraught situations of the sometimes marginalised girls and women sent to them, by providing them with shelter, board and work.'[17]

The publication of the McAleese report in early 2013 coincided with the film *Philomena*, directed by Stephen Frears. Judi Dench was nominated for an Oscar for the film, which tells the true story of Philomena Lee and the fifty-year search for her son who was taken from her and sent for adoption in America. Philomena goes to America only to discover that her son had died the year before. He had been told by the nuns that his mother had willingly abandoned him.

Philomena reignited the outrage at the unnecessary suffering of so many women in Ireland at the hands of the servants of the Roman Catholic Church. Philomena Lee was invited to meet Pope Francis, an encounter she says that she found cathartic. 'Those nuns would be so jealous of me now,' she said as she left her audience in the Vatican.[18] Meanwhile, Senator McAleese continued to defend the nuns. In his report, he writes: 'ill-treatment, physical punishment and abuse . . . was not something experienced in the Magdalen Laundries.'[19]

The McAleese report was widely criticised by the Irish press. The *Irish Independent* said 'It is too shameful' and accused the government of a cover-up.[20] Amnesty International called it 'an abject example of how not to carry out investigations into allegations of past human rights abuses'.[21] The UN Committee Against Torture said the report 'lacked many elements of a prompt, independent and thorough investigation' and asked, 'Was survivor testimony given a lesser rank or status in this inquiry than records of the State and the religious orders?'[22]

I read the over 1,000-page McAleese report with astonishment and asked for an interview with the senator but was refused. He now lives in Rome and, his spokeswoman told me, stands by his findings. I wanted to ask him why he skims over the personal stories of those who were held in the laundries, showing a contempt for the thousands who suffered within their walls. The report plays with statistics and is misleading with the truth. For example, in the Executive Summary, which is often all that is read in a report of such length, it says the median duration of stay for women in the laundries was 27.6 weeks, in other words approximately seven months. Yet 150 pages later, in the 'Statistical analysis', the average stay is calculated at three and a half years. Since many of the records are lost or were never kept by the Orders, we shall never know the real figure.

Mary Merritt spent fourteen years in a laundry and should, she says, have been given an appropriate hearing. Her eyes light up with fury as she remembers her interview with Senator McAleese. The senator interviewed over a hundred women for the purposes of his investigation and was sent submissions from many more. Lawyers working for the Justice for Magdalenes pressure group collected testimonies from several survivors telling of their brutal treatment but McAleese did not acknowledge their accounts in his report. Mary claims he ignored her too.

'I told him about the punishment cell and the rape. He

completely ignored the rape. He tried to move on to another subject but I said to him, "I'm telling you something that is very serious and you are passing it off as if it never happened to me and you don't believe me!'" After her unsatisfactory exchange with McAleese, Mary spoke to the Irish police, the Garda, about the assault but because of the number of years that have passed no action was taken. Mary admits it would be a waste of time; the priest was middle-aged at the time of the attack in 1955 and would by now be dead.

The official government report into the Magdalene Laundries glosses over the abuse and, to the astonishment of survivors, their lawyers and academics who have studied the history of Ireland's religious institutions, it concludes that the laundries did not make a profit. The nuns submitted audits of their commercial transactions to the inquiry, prepared by their own accountants, which were never made available to the public. McAleese, who trained as an accountant, concluded that the Magdalene Laundries operated on a 'subsistence or close to break-even basis, rather than on a commercial or highly profitable basis'.[23]

I meet up with another Magdalene Laundry survivor, Gabrielle North. When Gabrielle's mother learned that she was planning to run away to England with her boyfriend, she turned to the local priest for help. He obliged by sending Gabrielle to a Magdalene Laundry in Limerick. We meet at the entrance of the former convent buildings. 'This is the wall I tried to escape over,' she says pointing up to the three-metre-high walls that surround the former convent estate. 'In those days, there were jagged bits of glass on the top so, although I tried, I couldn't get over,' she explains. 'I remember falling off and I still have the scars on my leg to prove it.'

We walk over to the buildings where Gabrielle was interned, and peer through the iron gates at a yard. 'This is the exercise yard where we were allowed to walk around. That was the only exercise we were allowed, just walking around. I can't remember for how long. It was just like a prison. I remember eating most of my meals alone, at the punishment table. I was sent there most days for talking too much.'

Gabrielle did not work in the Laundry. She was put to work making the famous Limerick lace, so famous that she can remember the day that a call came from the White House in Washington. 'We were commissioned to make the christening dress for the third child of President Kennedy,' Gabrielle remembers, 'little Patrick who died. Lots of American tourists would come into the convent workshop and would watch us and place orders. We would sell lace collars, handkerchiefs and the like. The nuns were definitely making money. They would say that it wasn't commercial, but it was. They were very secretive about it.'

The nuns are famously secretive about their accounts. Nonetheless, their old ledgers turn up in the strangest places. I was tipped off about four huge, dusty leather-bound ledgers dating back to the 1950s in the White House pub in Limerick. The publican discovered them among a job lot of furniture he bought from the Laundry when it closed and he now keeps the ledgers as decoration on shelves above the bar.

He was good-natured enough about getting up on a ladder to bring them down to my level. 'Not many people ask to look at them,' he says. 'I think that most people are just glad that the Laundry and the nuns have gone.' The ledgers are filled with neat, handwritten entries. The client list includes private individuals, dozens of colleges and convents, a collection of restaurants and hotels, the railway station and regular entries for the Limerick Lawn Tennis Club. There was not much going on in Limerick where the nuns were not making money by doing the washing for them.

After lunch in the pub, Gabrielle and I walk to the modern housing estate now owned by the nuns, next to the old Laundry.

There is a large statue of 'Christ the Good Shepherd' on the lawn and neighbours point out the bungalow where the remaining elderly laundry workers still live with the nuns. There are CCTV cameras at the gates and the windows are open as we ring the bell. Curtains twitch, then the windows are firmly closed and nobody comes to the door. 'I know some of the nuns who knew me in the Laundry are still there,' Gabrielle says. 'I asked them when I was seventeen why they imprisoned me and I would like to ask them again now, but they won't say anything.'

The nuns won't say anything and won't pay anything. The Irish government has launched a compensation scheme for former laundry workers, which is running into tens of millions of euros. Although the nuns made money out of the survivors, the four religious orders concerned are refusing to contribute. They have expressed 'regret' for any pain they may have caused but they are not prepared to pay up. Irish government ministers have expressed 'disappointment' and say that 'negotiations are ongoing' with the nuns but no one is holding their breath.[24]

I call on Claire O'Sullivan at the *Irish Examiner* in Cork, one of the few newspapers in Ireland to have made use of the Freedom of Information Act to investigate the nuns' finances. She is outraged. 'The nuns are very canny businesswomen and they have been very clever with their money. The four orders are incredibly wealthy,' she says. 'They sold up to €300 million worth of property during the Irish economic boom. They owned assets, in 2012, of about €1.5 billion. They have put it into trusts, and they have point-blank refused to give one single penny towards the redress scheme [compensation] for the Magdalene Laundries.'*

Ireland likes to present an image today as a modern, secular country and yet it appears that the governing elite is still in the

---

* Two of the religious orders have claimed that they do not have the funds to contribute to the scheme.

thrall of the Roman Catholic Church. O'Sullivan points out that the McAleese report's conclusion that the nuns made no profit from the laundries meant there was less pressure on them to contribute to the compensation schemes. 'Since the foundation of the Irish state, the Catholic Church has operated in tandem with the government and the state,' she says. 'The separation of the two has not yet happened and there is no facility for a strong critique of the Church by the state.'

Instead, the Irish people are turning away from the Catholic Church. In May 2015, a referendum revealed 62 per cent of people in favour of gay marriage.[25] The Archbishop of Dublin, Diarmuid Martin, confessed himself bewildered by the result. 'I ask myself, most of these young people who voted yes are products of our Catholic school system for twelve years. I'm saying there's a big challenge there to see how we get across the message of the church.'[26] It is too late. The last few years have uncovered scandal after scandal involving the Catholic Church in Ireland, not only the treatment of unmarried mothers and their babies but horrific child sex abuse by priests and subsequent cover-up by the Church authorities. Today, fewer than 20 per cent of the population attend Mass.[27]

In 1922, when Ireland's social problems were handed over to the Catholic Church to deal with, 93 per cent of the population were practising Catholics.[28] Ireland has broken free from a theocracy in little more than a generation but it is taking time to reform the laws passed in more deferential times. As recently as 1983, two-thirds of the people voted against the legalization of abortion.[29] Women still do not have access to safe abortion in the republic of Ireland and nearly four thousand Irish women travel to the UK every year to exercise their right over their own bodies. With popular votes in support of divorce and gay marriage, abortion is the next hurdle.

Mary Merritt left the laundry after fourteen years, when she was twenty-seven. 'The work was getting less and less and they were letting some of the women out of the laundry.' Like thousands of former Magdalene Laundry workers, she fled Ireland for the UK where she worked in a dry cleaners in West London before setting up her own business with her husband, Bill.

Mary is receiving compensation from the government scheme but she is still angry. 'They took my life, they took my human rights, they took my hair, they took my clothes, they took my name and they also took my daughter which was the worst of all.' She went back several times to the Mother and Baby Home where she had been forced to abandon her daughter and begged them to tell her where she was. They refused.

In 1999, Mary received a letter from a social worker in the UK. Her daughter, Carmel, had traced her and wanted to meet. 'What was that about?' Mary says. 'I asked the nuns again and again to tell me where my daughter is and they refuse to answer me. They tell me they don't know. They get a letter from British social services and they give them the information they had all the time!' Mary flew back to Ireland to meet her daughter. She took her to the High Park Laundry and to the Mother and Baby Home in Dublin where she was born to try to explain her history.

While Mary is with us in Ireland, she arranges to meet Carmel for only the second time, at the cafe in Glasnevin Cemetery. Mary has a surprise for Carmel. She has found the photo taken of them by a sympathetic nurse at the home, before she was forced to go back the laundry and abandon her. Mary, a young mother of twenty-five, is cradling Carmel in her arms. 'You were a lovely baby,' says Mary. 'Mind you, though, I was jealous of your blonde hair!' Carmel is overwhelmed. 'I shall treasure this,' she says. 'As soon as I get home I'll frame it.' People on neighbouring tables strain forward to listen to the two women – one in her eighties and one in her sixties, as they talk and weep.

'You don't blame me, do you?' Mary asks Carmel, anxiously. 'Of course not, of course not,' says Carmel with tears running down her cheeks. Carmel now runs a shop in Dublin and is married for the second time. She discovered by chance that she was adopted and the hunt for her mother and the knowledge that she too is a victim of this tragic episode of Ireland's history has taken its toll. 'It hasn't been easy for any of us,' she tells me as she says goodbye to her mother.

Before we part, Mary and I go back into the cemetery. She wants to say goodbye once more to her friend Mary Brehany. As we approach, we hear the sound of mechanical excavators. Next to the mass grave where Brehany is buried, a new grave is being prepared to receive the latest former laundry worker to be buried the next day. Although the High Park Laundry closed in 1991, many of the women forced to work there had become so institutionalized that they could not leave the 'care' of the nuns when the laundry closed. The headstone above the grave marks several recent burials – Joan O'Reilly who died in 2012, Mary Ryan who died in 2013, Sally Doherty in 2014. No one knows how many never escaped the nuns.

Mary leaves the cemetery for the airport to go back to England. 'Not soon enough!' she says as she climbs into the taxi. Apart from seeing her daughter again, she hates returning. 'All I want,' she says, 'is an apology – from the nuns, the priests, the government, the Pope, anyone. I want an apology before I die.'

4

SAUDI ARABIA

The World's Largest Women's Prison

'Follow me. You are not going to believe this,' says Reem Asaad. She has recently stopped breastfeeding her daughter and she wants to buy a new bra but is unsure of her current size. She takes me to a lingerie shop in the centre of Riyadh and goes through the rails of bras, frowning. 'Now watch,' she says as a Pakistani male shop assistant comes up and asks if he can help. 'I need a female assistant,' she says to the man, 'because I want to be measured.' 'I am sorry, ma'am,' says the assistant, 'we have no female assistants.' She buys three bras and takes them up four escalators to the public toilets on the top floor to try them on. They don't fit. She returns the bras and buys three more. She carries out this procedure four times before she finds a bra that will fit her.

For her, the difficulty women have in buying a bra in Saudi Arabia sums up the craziness of attitudes towards women in the only country in the world where women cannot drive. Men and women are not allowed to mingle unless they are related. Women are therefore not allowed to work in shops and so the lingerie counters are manned by men. 'So how do we buy our underwear? We are expected to discuss size and physical details that I wouldn't even talk about to my friends let alone to a male stranger.'

Reem admits that bra-buying is an irritant rather than a major human rights issue but she is a feminist and a campaigner and, within the restrictions laid down for women in Saudi Arabia, she says, 'You have to start somewhere.' She is an investment analyst, writer on economics and lecturer in finance and management at Dar Al-Hekma University in Jeddah. She is married, has two daughters and, as she sweeps down the corridor of the mall to meet me wearing the mandatory black abaya that covers all but her face, I note that she is very confident and very beautiful.

The importance of keeping Saudi women out of sight of male Saudis who are not family members is more important, in the minds of the mad mullahs, than the prospect of women being measured by a male stranger in a shop. Perhaps because that male stranger is invariably from South East Asia, he is not considered a proper man. In fairness to the men serving behind the lingerie counters, they look as uncomfortable as the women shoppers. Welcome to the absurdity that is the kingdom of Saudi Arabia!

My shopping expedition with Reem takes place in March 2011, three years into her campaign. 'Things have to change. The concept is flawless,' she says. 'The idea of women selling women's underwear to other women is so natural that any other option is just invalid.' She has a Facebook campaign, a blog and a petition that calls for a boycott of Saudi lingerie stores by shoppers and support from international lingerie manufacturers.[1]

Thousands of Saudi women support the campaign, backed by foreign companies and activists outside the kingdom. There was opposition from Muslim clerics who warned that women working in shops would encourage them to defy their husbands and it would end up by corrupting the country's morals. In the end, reason prevailed. King Abdullah himself ordered a ban on male staff in 7,300 retail lingerie outlets, creating job opportunities for more than 40,000 Saudi women.[2]

I like Reem but I don't like shopping malls. In a normal country, we would have gone out to a cafe or a small restaurant and carried on chatting after the filming was over. Saudi Arabia is anything but normal. Two women walking down the street alone or eating in a restaurant would attract unwelcome attention. For a woman, going out means going to a shopping mall while their drivers wait for them outside. A woman's view of the world is confined to what she can glimpse through tinted windows on her way there.

We find Reem's car and driver and she invites me back to her home, a modest enough house by Saudi standards – a house on two floors with a lift. Her husband is a large, friendly man whose father is Saudi and mother Lebanese, which might account for his progressive approach to women. He is clearly proud of his wife and, unusually for a Saudi man, gladly looks after their two daughters while we carry on talking.

'You can see, we are not rich,' she says. She is an academic and her salary is modest; her husband is an accountant. So that they can pursue their separate careers she has to employ a driver, which takes up a good portion of her salary. 'This is another reason why women can't work. There is no public transport and a woman cannot drive. In effect, after her husband has left for work, she cannot leave the home unless she has a private driver.'

Reem admits that her success in getting women the right to work in lingerie shops will be of little practical use unless women from less wealthy backgrounds can take up the offer. The king's support may have created 40,000 job opportunities for women but, without radical changes in the infrastructure of the kingdom, women won't be able to apply. Her next campaign is to fight for a safe public transport system so that women are not dependent on a personal driver. After that she will fight for daycare facilities for children of women who want to work. Reem is determined that work is the only way to release millions of women from a home environment that, in most cases, resembles a prison.

The average Saudi male argues that a woman is 'more comfortable' and 'privileged' sitting in her luxurious home waited on by the Filipina maid and driven to the shopping mall by the Pakistani chauffeur. 'Why would a woman want to work?' they ask. Work only brings a woman self-esteem, intellectual stimulation, the company of adults and financial independence – all anathema to the Saudi male whose job it is to control the female members of his family. Reem is right. Saudi Arabia needs the infrastructure to send the woman to work but first she has to break free from the shackles of tradition and education.

Daughters take their lead from their mothers. I lose count of the number of times I've told my daughter that women are equal to men and that she can achieve anything in life. The Saudi girl child sees her mother treated as a child, obeying orders from male family members and restricted in everything she does. Her sense of worth and self-esteem is damaged at birth. It makes the courage of women like Reem Asaad and the other Saudi female activists all the more impressive. They have broken the mould but millions more women do not dare and their daughters, sadly, will imitate them.

Defenders of gender segregation in Saudi Arabia claim that the system is based on the correct interpretation of the Koran and the teachings of the Prophet, the Sunna. Opponents argue that this is a false interpretation and point at the life of Mohammed to back them up. His first wife, Khadija, was a strong, older woman who employed him and then asked him to marry her. Another wife, Aisha, commanded an army at the Battle of Bassorah in 656. They quote the Prophet as saying that, 'You have rights over your women and your women have rights over you.'[3]

But the rights of women are in short supply in Saudi Arabia where the Prophet's words are interpreted to suit a misogynistic clergy. The Wahhabis, the dominant minority in Saudi Arabia, claim that their mission is to restore the Muslim faith back to their version of its original, purest form in which women are regarded as the embodiment of sin. These ultra-conservative Wahhabi clerics hold a time-honoured influence on the rulers of the House of Saud and the women of Saudi Arabia are the victims.

It began with a pact in the eighteenth century made between the cleric Muhammad ibn Abd al-Wahhab who promised to support the founder of the Saud dynasty, Muhammad ibn Saud, as he set about conquering land. The Saudi leader was expected to endorse their austere and puritanical beliefs. For more than two hundred and fifty years, that pact has spelled disaster for women living in the land that, at the turn of the twentieth century, became known as Saudi Arabia.[4]

Wahhabism treats women as perpetual minors and as mentally defective. A woman needs a male guardian at all times whose permission must be given before she can leave the house, undergo medical treatment, open a bank account and enrol for further education or travel. She can be married off at any age by her guardians. If she is divorced and has no father or brother, she may find herself asking permission for these privileges from her teenage son.

A woman's exclusion and subordination makes her dangerously vulnerable to abuse. The Saudi government recently introduced progressive laws to ban domestic violence but offered no guidance as to how a woman might get access to this law. She cannot go to the police station by herself. A woman who has been knocked about by her husband would have to ask her husband to drive her to the police station to report him. It is not going to happen.

The custom of segregation is strictly enforced. Senior Wahhabi clerics argue that it is based on two concepts, the need to shield the woman from potential corruption and a woman's alleged 'lack of capacity', that is, left to her own, lustful devices, a woman is certain to misbehave.[5] The Committee for the Promotion of

Virtue and the Prevention of Vice, the Mutaween, is responsible for enforcing segregation, dress codes and sobriety on women. Such is the enthusiasm for their task that their activities can be fatal.

In 2002, members of these morality police prevented fifteen schoolgirls from fleeing a fire because they were inappropriately dressed. With flames and smoke reaching up to the windows of their dormitory, the girls did not have time to grab their abayas before rushing for the doors. They were turned back in order to observe a dress code and they all died. To the Mutaween, a girl's modesty is more important than her life. Nonetheless, a year later, King Abdullah increased the budget for the Mutaween to some $400 million a year.[6]

The Mutaween are also responsible for enforcing the ban on women driving. There are no laws in Saudi Arabia against women driving, just religious edicts. Because there exists some confusion between the secular and religious laws in this respect, fifty women activists drove cars into Riyadh in June 1991 to test the water. They were arrested. To clarify the issue, the late grand mufti Sheikh Abdulazia issued a fatwa banning women from driving, justifying his move by saying that he feared that allowing women to drive would make it easier for the two sexes to mix and would therefore bring about chaos in society.

A further reason was added by the Saudi cleric Sheikh Saleh Al-Lohaiden in 2013 who warned that if a woman drives a car, it could have negative physical results 'as functional and physiological medical studies show that it automatically affects the ovaries and pushes the pelvis upwards. That is why we find those who regularly drive have children with clinical problems of varying degrees.'[7] If it wasn't so stupid, it would be hilarious. Like the imam I met in the Gambia, it might be a good idea if these men stuck to what they might be good at – the study of religious texts.

It was Wajeha al-Huwaider, a journalist and campaigner for the right of women to work and drive, who coined the description of Saudi Arabia as 'the world's largest women's prison'.[8] She compares the women in Arab states with prisoners in Guantánamo. At least, she argues, the latter can see the light of day and have a chance of release but the women of Saudi Arabia 'who have never joined any terrorist organization and have never harmed anyone, but they nevertheless live as prisoners all their lives'.[9] In 2008, she posted pictures of herself driving on YouTube. A year earlier, she wrote to King Abdullah pleading with him to lift restrictions on women and to allow them to drive and work. She has been harassed by the authorities ever since.

In 2011, al-Huwaider received a text from a woman saying that her husband had locked her and her children in the house and they had no food. She drove with a fellow campaigner to the house but they were intercepted by the police and arrested. It is now thought that the call was a deliberate hoax. She was charged with 'supporting a wife without her husband's knowledge, thereby undermining the marriage' and, when the case came to trial in 2013, she was imprisoned for ten months.[10]

Ever since reading al-Huwaider's description of Saudi Arabia as a huge prison for women, I wanted to go. When I report on a country with appalling human rights records – and therefore hostile to media attention – my normal practice is to go undercover. I have travelled as a tourist and mere 'North London mother of two' to many nasty regimes: the former Soviet Union, Ceauşescu's Romania, Burma under military rule, Chinese-occupied Tibet and, most recently, during the civil war in Syria.

I find being a woman helps hugely. My apologies to those who expect more robust behaviour from someone purporting to be a feminist, but I have no inhibition about flirting when confronted by men with guns, breaking down in tears or bringing out photos of my children – whatever is required to get out of difficult and sometimes life-threatening situations. So far, it has worked every time.

But you cannot travel to Saudi Arabia as a tourist, unless you are one of the millions of pilgrims who travel to Mecca and Medina every year to perform the Haj. There is no tourist industry for non-Muslims. After all, who on earth would want willingly to travel to a country of shopping malls, traffic jams and desert and where – even on the white sand beaches of the Red Sea – women are segregated and entombed in their black abayas?

So I had to get official permission which entailed making frequent visits to the embassy of the Kingdom of Saudi Arabia in London's Mayfair where I was directed by the press officer to the embassy's representative for women's affairs, Dr Danish Elham. She was surprised and taken aback when I arrived in her office. She had never had a request from a journalist before who wanted to report on the condition of women in the Kingdom.

What was her job as representative for women's affairs? I asked. She confided that she had been summoned to London by King Abdullah himself to deal with the number of suicides among embassy wives, imprisoned in their luxury residences, unable to speak the language, not allowed to work and not permitted to join their husbands as they travel around the country or attend official events. Little wonder that to such women jumping from the top floor of a Knightsbridge apartment block came as a blessed relief. 'The king is very concerned,' she assured me.

I told her I wanted to make a film about the exciting new developments in the emancipation of women in the kingdom. A woman, Norah bint Abdullah al-Fayez, had just been appointed the Vice Minister of Education by King Abdullah and put in charge of a new department devoted to the education of girls. I told Dr Elham that I wanted to interview her and discovered that the vice minister has to conduct her meetings with male colleagues from behind a curtain. If Norah bint Abdullah al-Fayez agreed to an interview, I assumed that I and my cameraman would have to be on the other side of a curtain as well. I thought that this would make for an irresistible bit of television.

Despite the restrictions on her modus operandi, the move to appoint a woman as a minister in the twenty-first century was hailed as progressive on the part of King Abdullah by reformers. However, he was criticised by senior clerics who feared that by promoting the education of women, the king would encourage them to 'abandon their basic duties such as housekeeping and bringing up children' in favour of 'beautifying themselves and wantonness'.[11] The Saudi clerics' contempt for women apparently has no rationale and no limit.

I ferreted around for the names of other Saudi women who have achieved positions of public responsibility. Women who had been educated abroad and who were usually related to the royal family like Princess Loulwa Al-Faisal. The princess is a cousin of King Abdullah and is praised as a brave champion of women's rights. But, if I was looking for a woman with whom I might discuss the feminist movement in Saudi Arabia, I was disappointed to read that the princess says that Muslim women should be accorded 'equal though not necessarily the same rights as men'.[12]

I presented my wish list of women interviewees to Dr Elham. I was met with bewilderment and indifference and I doubt that any of my interview requests were delivered to the ladies in question. Dr Elham cancelled appointment after appointment. I have a string of emails from her assistant citing ill health and unexpected, emergency meetings (were there that many embassy suicides in London?). In the end, I simply wore them down. I visited the embassy every week for three months until my presence and persistence became a nuisance and an embarrassment. I believe that they gave me and my cameraman a visa just to get rid of me.

Which is how I found myself on a Saudi Air flight from Heathrow to Jeddah. There were a few Europeans on board, mainly oil men, and the kind of Saudis you see in London, businessmen accompanied by their abaya-clad wives with shopping bags, the type who clog up the aisles in the lingerie departments of Harrods and Marks & Spencer.

And then there were the young women, dressed in Armani jeans and Jimmy Choo stilettos. For them, the chance to live and study in London would have been the most liberating episode in their lives. Many of them would have acquired international driving licences but, on returning home, they would not be allowed to drive. They were returning to a life of arranged marriages and domestic incarceration in 'the world's largest women's prison'.

The author of the phrase, Wajeha al-Huwaider, had been educated in the United States. It surprises me that so many of the leading Saudi families allow their daughters this privilege. It is bound to lead to trouble and revolutionary thinking. Al-Huwaider says that, before she arrived in America, she knew she was a human being. 'However, in the United States I felt it, because I was treated as one. I learned life means nothing without freedom. Then I decided to become a real women's rights activist, in order to free women in my country and to make them feel alive.'[13]

I had read about these young women in the recently released book *Girls of Riyadh* by Rajaa Alsanea. The tease on the cover promises 'Love and lust, men and money. A taboo-breaking, bestselling tale of sex and the city'. It sounded like a rollicking account of drugs, sex and debauchery, in one of the most unlikely cities in the world. In actuality it was one of the most depressing books I have ever read.[14]

It traces the lives of four young women living in Riyadh – Gamrah, Lamees, Michelle and Sadeem – and is based on true stories. Most of them and their boyfriends had studied abroad and so they knew that there was another world out there, a world in which the equality of the sexes and the independent will of all young adults are normally respected. And yet they find themselves loving, marrying and having children in the most misogynistic and medieval country on earth.

I found the story of Sadeem the saddest. Sadeem and Waleed's engagement was arranged by their parents but, fortunately, they were immediately attracted to one another at their first meeting. They went to the register office to fill in the official engagement document. Sadeem was university-educated and she protested when she was not allowed to sign. 'My girl,' said her aunt, 'just stamp it with your fingerprint and call it a day. The sheikh says fingerprint not signature. The men are the only ones who sign their names.'

The couple were now in the 'milkah' period of their engagement which precedes the actual wedding. During this period, they were allowed to go out to restaurants together and watch films at home. Chaste kisses on the cheek moved on to passionate kisses on the mouth. Waleed gave the clear impression that he could not wait and so, one night, Sadeem allowed him to 'cross the line she had drawn for herself and for him'.

From calling her a dozen times a day, Waleed's calls stopped. Sadeem was wracked by worry. What could be wrong? Hadn't he initiated the crossing of the line? Was he not already her husband in all but the actual ceremony, 'the ballroom, the guests, the live singer and the dinner'? The message came from his family that Waleed was no longer comfortable with his bride. She had broken the strict Saudi moral code. Waleed went on to marry someone else. Sadeem's reputation was irreparably damaged.

The story was so cruel! All her life, Sadeem had been taught to obey the male members of her family. She was spending time with the man who was to be her husband and she obeyed him too. Waleed was the male in authority and Sadeem was programmed to follow his lead. But, after sex took place at his instigation, he no longer believed she could be trusted to be a faithful, obedient wife and to bring their children up to be good Saudis. He cast her aside like a common whore.

The story came back to me as the captain came on the tannoy and warned us that we would be landing in Jeddah in ten minutes. The Saudi young women on the flight all got up and, showing their tight jeans and cashmere sweaters to their best advantage, reached up to the luggage racks for the bags in which they had stowed their abayas. In a few minutes, they were transformed from young, fashion-conscious, contemporary women into a mass of black shadows whose beauty and individuality were obscured.

I pulled on my abaya and thought I had been so clever arriving in Saudi Arabia with no official interviews planned and, therefore, no government minder assigned to my case. On arrival, it looked as if I might have miscalculated. My cameraman, Tony Jolliffe, and I landed at the airport with the full panoply of TV filming gear. Immigration and customs officials did not know what to make of us or what to do with us.

They were mystified that we both had official journalist visas and yet there was no minder at the airport from the Ministry of Information to meet us, vouch for us and keep an eye on us. They put us in a holding area while they phoned Riyadh. The problem was that it was 2 a.m. in the morning by now and no one answered the phone. It looked as if we were in for a long, uncomfortable night.

To the embarrassment of Tony, I did what I always do when I travel to such countries alone: I sat on the floor of the airport and cried. Through my snuffles and tears, I spoke of my amazement that I could be treated thus after being welcomed so warmly at the Saudi Embassy in London where Prince Mohammed bin Nawwaf bin Abdulaziz Al Saud himself, a member of the royal family, was currently ambassador. 'The good prince gave me a visa and wished me luck on my journey to your country,' I lied to the astonished-looking officials, 'and this is how you treat me?' We were let go.

We were, as far as I know, the first TV camera crew ever to be let into Saudi Arabia without a minder and we made haste to take advantage of the situation. My first job was to buy an abaya to replace the one that a BBC journalist friend had lent me in order to arrive at Jeddah airport.

I explored the racks of garments in the shop, pausing at one in shocking pink. 'No!' the Bangladeshi male assistant warned me. 'For bedrooms only!' He steered me towards the rows of more acceptable black cloaks where I nonetheless found something a little more daring, in naughty navy and beguiling brown. I then had an experience that recalled the absurdities that Reem Asaad campaigns against. I put on the abaya and the male assistant then showed me how to arrange the scarf of the all-enveloping gar-ment around my head, carefully placing the ends under my chin, around my shoulders and tucking in stray strands of hair.

His proximity and touch were a paradox in a country that bans casual contact with the opposite sex. But then, of course, he was a Bangladeshi and, therefore, not considered by Saudi standards a real man. By the same token, women are routinely driven around by their Asian drivers with no apparent suspicion on the part of their male guardians. The mad mullahs clearly believe that it is only the Saudi man who must be protected from a woman's lustful intent and 'lack of capacity'. Later on in my trip, I was to discover that I was not a real woman either.

I contacted Fadwa Al Tayaf, a former TV presenter and now social worker and activist, and asked her to take me to the areas of the city where foreigners seldom go – where the poor and the destitute live in this country, which is one of the richest in the world. We walk through the narrow, dusty streets of the slums of

Jeddah. Men dressed in their long white *thobes* saunter down the alleyways. Women, encased in black abayas, drift anonymously like ghosts in the background.

We duck through an arch and into a maze of small mud-caked houses where Fadwa wants to introduce me to the women without an identity – the women without men. Women suffer at the hands of men in Saudi Arabia, she explains, but their lives can be even more perilous without them.

She introduces Fatima, a bedridden widow with diabetes. She lacks the medication for her condition because she can't get out to ask for help. She has no man in her life and is therefore unable to leave the house and get to the hospital or relevant government office. She is a prisoner in her house. Fadwa gives her food but, without the permission of the non-existent male, Fatima cannot be treated. She will die unnecessarily due to the lack of a man.

In the house next door we meet Warifa, a divorcee in her forties with four daughters. She is from the Yemen and her Saudi husband has left her for another woman. As an expatriate, she has no father, husband or son to ask for help. The family live on handouts from neighbours. Warifa summons the four daughters, aged between fourteen and twenty, from inside the house to meet me.

They emerge, shrouded in their abayas, shyly covering their faces with only their sad eyes visible. They are prisoners. Without permission from a man, they cannot leave the house, go to school or work. 'I pray every day,' says Warifa, 'that some nice man will come and marry one of them.' But how, I ask myself? What man is going to find them in this virtual jail in which they have been abandoned by the bad fortune to have been born in Saudi Arabia?

The predicament of women without men was a surprise to me. It has not been widely reported and it was not on my filming list when I arrived in the Kingdom. Another surprise was to find women who support the rules governing their lives as laid out by a misogynistic male clergy. I was mightily intrigued to learn of

Rawda al-Yousef, founder of the campaigning group ridiculously named 'My Guardian Knows What's Best for Me' and I eagerly asked for a meeting with her.

Yousef lives in an apartment in a gated community in a smart area of Riyadh where the Filipina maid shows us into a dark drawing room of heavy leather furniture and an excess of glass and gold decoration. I was expecting an over-made-up, over-coiffured, designer-dressed, simpering coquette, the kind of woman who, in my prejudiced imagination, would delight in being kept by an indulgent, controlling husband.

To my surprise, Yousef is a middle-aged, rather stout divorcee whose ordinary appearance is in sharp contrast to her extraordinary ideas. She has won favour with the royal family and senior clerics by arguing that Saudi Arabia is an 'ideal and pure Islamic nation' under threat from imported Western values and that women should stick to the role assigned to them by tradition.

She offers me tea and shows me a video that she produced and of which she is inordinately proud. It has women drifting around in modest, flowing silk robes looking adoringly and helplessly at their strong, muscular and heroic guardians set in some idealized, storybook past – a scene of marble palaces, flaming torches and men bristling with weaponry and puffed-out pectorals.

The ten-minute film has been shown regularly on Saudi TV, usually preceding a studio discussion promoting guardianship featuring Yousef sitting alongside severe-looking imams. To capture a wider audience, she has added English subtitles to the film. The translation is excruciating but nonetheless the message is clear: the condition of a woman is weak, ignorant, vulnerable and dependent. Her only hope of getting through life is to stick close to her guardian, whoever he may be. As for the divorced Yousef, her brother has to fulfil that role.

Digging my nails into my hands to stop myself from venting my wrath at this traitor to our sex, I do my best to conduct a civil interview. We start with the vexed question of driving. Yousef sees this as a straightforward practical problem. 'We are a tribal society and we are not ready to let women drive,' she explains. 'What happens if a woman has an accident while driving?' she asks. 'How can she go to a hospital or police station without her guardian? She might even be sent to prison. Her guardian is here to protect her from such a fate and for this reason he cannot allow her to drive.' But what about the women whom Reem Asaad wants to help? The women who can't work because they can't get to work? Yousef has a simple answer to this one. 'If she can't afford to get to work by employing a driver, how on earth is she going to be able to buy a car?'

And what about the women I was introduced to by Fadwa Al Tayaf, the women who could die because they cannot leave their houses to get to hospital? The young girls who will remain uneducated, unemployed and unmarried because they are prisoners in the ghetto of the Women Without Men? Yousef dismisses these women with a Lady Bracknell-type disdain as if it is due to their carelessness that they have found themselves in this situation. 'A woman simply cannot survive without a guardian and it is their fault if they have none,' she says, condemning them to their fate.

'I have the support of the majority in this country,' she boasts. 'My support comes from the conservatives and the moderates. As for the liberals, the only liberals I know have their women safely at home and it is only the freedom of other women that they support.'

Does she have the support of the majority? It is hard to know. In 2007, Gallup conducted a poll in Saudi Arabia which found that 66 per cent of Saudi women and 55 per cent of Saudi men said that women should be allowed to drive.[15] The same poll found that more than 80 per cent Saudi women and 75 per cent of Saudi men believed that women should be allowed to hold any job outside the home for which they are qualified.

I suppose it depends who you ask. A Saudi government poll in 2006 showed over 80 per cent of women disapproving of women being allowed to drive. A poll taken more recently, in 2013, by a woman lecturer at the elite Al-Lith College for Girls at Um al-Qura University in Mecca, allegedly found that about the same number of young students agreed. One of these privileged young women was quoted as saying that driving is not necessary for women in Saudi Arabia where 'every woman is like a queen. There is (someone) who cares about her; and a woman needs nothing as long as there is a man who loves her and meets her needs.'[16]

Which, sadly, was the view I found when I moved out of the realms inhabited by brave women activists and delved more into what could be described as ordinary life for the majority of Saudis. While in Jeddah and still without a government minder, I found it easy to contact brave, dissenting female voices like Reem Asaad, Wajeha al-Huwaider and Fadwa Al Tayaf. Jeddah is known to be more open and liberal. By the time I got to more conservative Riyadh, the authorities had caught up with me and I was assigned a minder.

Omar could not understand my attachment to the cause of women and alternative voices and made little attempt to help on this score, apart from introducing me to Rawda al-Yousef, the arch-conservative who could be trusted to deliver the party line. Like many Saudis, Omar had little enthusiasm for hard work. A third of Saudis under thirty are unemployed. The government tries to insist that foreign companies who operate in the kingdom take on more Saudis. Foreign bosses complain that it is difficult to find a committed native worker in a country where so many families are effortlessly rich on seemingly endless supplies of oil revenue.

Most employed men, like Omar, work for the state and he was no exception to the rule. He boasted about his family's wealth and clearly disliked his job at the Ministry of Information. He would meet me and my cameraman in the hotel lobby at 11 a.m.

97

and ask to leave by 5 p.m. This suited me because I could meet with dissidents and women activists before and after the formal working day with Omar.

However, one evening Omar made an exception. He offered to show us how decisions are made in his country and to illustrate just how irrelevant women are to the process. I thus found myself propped up against heavily embroidered cushions, sitting cross-legged on a thick woven carpet in a large room painted in white and gold, illuminated by enormous, crystal chandeliers and surrounded by fifty middle-aged men.

What passes for local government takes place on a tribal basis. Even in a city like Riyadh, the local tribal head will call a weekly meeting in his home of trusted males to discuss matters of local concern. I was invited to watch as the decision makers, dressed in traditional Saudi *thobes* and headdresses prayed and then deliberated on such topics as health, education and the appointment of a new imam for the local mosque.

I was, of course, the only woman in the room. After the formal part of the evening was over, the tribal head, Faiz Al Mahid, nodded in my direction to indicate that he was now ready for my questions. I started with the obvious. 'Why are there no Saudi women sitting here?' He raised his eyebrows in surprise and then, as if addressing a retarded child, replied, 'It is our custom and our tradition and, anyway, why should women be represented here. Why should they be among us?'

Because, I answered, women make up more than 50 per cent of the population and they should have a voice. 'They have a voice,' Al Mahid continued, 'in their house, in their home, with their children. They have responsibilities to their children, to raise them, to look after them. Here in Saudi Arabia, it is not like other countries. Here the man is supposed to support the family and the woman knows what she has to do. How can I do my work if there is not a woman at home to look after my children?'

With that, he gave me a look of irritated contempt and got up and left the room. Omar looked at me as if to say: 'You have your answer. Will you stop bothering me now?' He pointed out that, unused as he was to working late in the evening, we would have to start late the next day. I readily agreed to his request not to meet again until after lunch.

My trip was coming to an end. I never got to meet the handful of women who have been invited by the king to join his government. The few women who have made it into corporate boardrooms also turned down my request for interviews. The principals of the all-women colleges of further education, much boasted of by the king's propagandists as an indication of his progressive instincts, refused to allow me within their walls.

Women who have made it against the odds in Saudi Arabia clearly did not want to talk to a woman reporter who had come to their country for the purpose of telling their stories. Even the allegedly successful ones were apparently afraid to speak publicly. Maybe they hoped that by quietly going about their business without drawing attention to themselves, the resistant male population would not notice they were there?

More than 80 per cent of women in Saudi Arabia of working age cannot or do not work.[17] The poor remain prisoners in their homes. The rich can be observed in the shopping malls that are open to midnight. Leaving their drivers outside, the brightly lit shops filled with Armani, Gucci and Rolex brands are the only places where they can escape the house with the permission of their guardians. I saw no illicit contact with the opposite sex there, except with the 'non-man' South East Asian shop assistants. There are too many mothers and aunts accompanying young women for anything untoward to occur.

The men, of course, have more opportunities to amuse themselves. On my last evening in Jeddah, we came across the local chapter of the Saudi Harley-Davidson Bike Club as they pulled in to a service station to refuel. Motorcycling at speed along the near-deserted roads of the desert kingdom of Saudi Arabia is a favourite pastime in a country with no pubs or clubs. Tonight, it wasn't a desert ride that was planned but just a spin along the city's fabulous, palm-tree-lined corniche that borders the Red Sea. I ask the group of about ten bikers if they would take me along for the ride.

To my amazement, they agreed. I bundled my abaya into my bag and by wearing trousers and pulling a large helmet over my head, I looked suitably androgynous by the time I climbed onto the back of the Harley belonging to the group leader. Thus breaking all laws and customs governing contact between the sexes, we drove at speed through the traffic, past the mosques and the large billboards with pictures of a severe-looking King Abdullah to the northern end of the bay of Jeddah and to a bar they frequented for fresh lemon and lime drinks and to smoke the water pipes known as *shishas*.

I enjoyed the risk and so did they. I worried that if the morality police, the Mutaween, had found my companion with a woman riding pillion, he might have received an on-the-spot lashing and possible imprisonment. We laughed as we took off our helmets and walked towards the bar. Given the circumstances, I thought to myself, surely, I have found here enlightened representatives of the Saudi male, prepared to flout the law and custom. They must therefore possess what the rest of us might regard as normal attitudes towards women?

After ordering a round of non-alcoholic drinks, I interviewed the men. That was fun but why aren't your wives with you to enjoy it? My erstwhile biking companion answers without a hint of irony or shame: 'She is at home.' Why, I ask? Doesn't she have the right to some fun? 'Just because a woman stays at home,' he replies, 'it does not mean that we are not giving a woman her rights.'

He continues without embarrassment: 'She can sit at home, she can eat and she can drink, she is comfortable and everything is laid on for her. In our religion, men are responsible for women – my mother, my sister and my wife. They can stay at home and I shall look after them. If she wants to work, she can but only with my permission and I won't be forced.' I am reminded of what Rawda al-Yousef of 'My Guardian Knows What's Best for Me' said when she observed that the only liberals she knows are those who support other men's women while theirs are confined at home.

I turn to another member of the group with the same question. 'Women are equal to men in this country but there are some cultural differences,' he says. 'Women don't go on motorbikes or drive because they have a driver to take them everywhere. I bet you'd really like that for yourself in your country?' he asks me smiling. I get up and leave without returning his smile.

I realize, on reflection, that there had been no risk in inviting me to join them. I was no more a proper woman demanding protection than the Bangladeshi shop assistant is a man. The rules governing the behaviour of women pertain to Saudi women in Saudi Arabia. The young women who go abroad to study in Los Angeles and London experience a freedom while away from the kingdom that they will never experience again on their return.

It is for this reason that Wajeha al-Huwaider and her fellow activists despair at the deliberate infantalization of the female sex by the men of Saudi Arabia. '[I]t's the same kind of feeling they have for handicapped people or for animals. The kindness comes from pity, from lack of respect. The ownership of a woman is passed from one man to another.'[18] It is the ultimate misogyny – to treat a woman as a kind of subspecies, to feed and protect her while denying that she has the intelligence or ability that might allow her to be deemed an equal.

Al-Huwaider detects a cowardly rationale behind the system. 'Ultimately, I think women are greatly feared. When I compare the Saudi man with other Arab men, I can say that the Saudi is the only man who cannot compete with the woman.' She says now that more women go to university, men are even more afraid and determined to keep women from the workplace. 'If you do not face competition from the Saudi woman . . . you have the entire scene for yourself. All positions and jobs are reserved for you. Therefore, you are a spoiled and self-indulged man.'[19]

As I write this, King Abdullah has died. Hailed as a reformer, he allowed a woman to become deputy minister to a ministry devoted to the education of women and expanded the opportunity for girls to attend colleges of further education. In 2013, he allocated thirty seats to women in the Consultative Assembly of Saudi Arabia, the Shura.[20] The council, whose members are appointed by the king, can advise the monarch and question ministers but it has no power to make or veto legislation. The women members must enter by a separate door and sit in allocated seats, separated from the men. King Abdullah also passed a law to allow women to vote in municipal elections. But that was the limit of his reform for women.

The women's blogging community in Saudi Arabia has commended the political reforms. Writing in her blog, Sabria Jawhar observed that: 'To say that King Abdullah's decree to give women the right to vote and become Shoura Council members is a historic moment would be an understatement. The women's suffrage movement is only part of the story . . . The king took a giant leap forward, but it's only the first of many steps we must take. Now, if you don't mind, I'm going to hop into my car and drive up to Riyadh to apply for Shoura Council membership.'[21] There can be no real change in women's status until they can drive and until the guardianship rules are scrapped. But the women of Saudi Arabia fear that they have few allies in the outside world.

Disgracefully, the flags were flown at half-mast at Buckingham Palace, the Palace of Westminster and other public buildings in

London after the death of King Abdullah who had presided over thousands of public executions, funded terrorist organizations and reneged on his promise to let women drive. The prime minister, David Cameron, and the Prince of Wales attended his funeral and, only weeks later, Prince Charles was one of the first world leaders to fly again to Riyadh to pay homage to the new King Salman bin Abdulaziz Al Saud. So long as we buy Saudi oil and Saudi Arabia buys our arms, the House of Windsor is be expected to maintain a close relationship with the House of Saud.

The Queen, Diana, Princess of Wales, and Camilla, Duchess of Cornwall, have all pusillanimously kowtowed to this cruel regime, arriving with an array of 'Saudi-approved' gear on their frequent visits to the Kingdom. They step off the plane and into the desert heat wearing long dresses and long gloves, thus endorsing the stereotype of the modest and obedient Saudi woman. The forever fashion-conscious Diana even wore trousers under a dress lest a bare ankle offend her hosts. The arriviste Saudi royals apparently like to meet other royals and the older the pedigree the better, so long as they obey local rules. Ours fit the bill nicely and are always keen to oblige.

But I was delighted to see that the Queen did once stand up to the House of Saud, proudly telling a diplomat about an incident at Balmoral in 1998.

After lunch, the Queen had asked her royal guest whether he would like a tour of the estate. Prompted by his Foreign Minister, the urbane Prince Saud, an initially hesitant Abdullah agreed. The royal Land Rovers were drawn up in front of the castle. As instructed, the Crown Prince climbed into the front seat of the front Land Rover, with his interpreter in the seat behind. To his surprise, the Queen climbed into the driving seat, turned the ignition and drove off. Women are not – yet – allowed to drive in Saudi Arabia, and Abdullah was not used to being driven by a woman, let alone a queen. His nervousness only increased as the Queen, an Army driver in wartime, accelerated the Land Rover along the narrow Scottish estate roads, talking all the time. Through his interpreter, the Crown Prince implored the Queen to slow down and concentrate on the road ahead.[22]

Alas, the example set by the Queen had no effect on King Abdullah and would be unlikely to impress his successor, the 79-year-old King Salman. His reign has had an inauspicious start. There has been a considerable increase in the number of death sentences carried out in the kingdom and, despite international outrage, there has been no reprieve for the Saudi blogger Raif Badawi, who has been sentenced to 1,000 lashes for his blog that, according to the charges, 'propagates liberal thought'. He has also been punished for trying to champion the cause of women by posting a blog on Valentine's Day that pours scorn on Saudi Arabia's 'morality police', the Committee for the Promotion of Virtue and the Prevention of Vice.[23]

However, the king's most ominous move so far has surely been to sack the most senior woman in government, Norah bint Abdullah al-Fayez, from her post as deputy education minister for girls. Al-Fayez was the woman I asked to interview when I first turned up with my list of requests at the Saudi Embassy in London. I regret never getting the chance to meet her. Apparently she was trying to get physical education on the curriculum for girls in Saudi public schools, which provoked outrage from the ultra-conservative clerics who insisted that she be removed.

Fortunately, the geopolitics of the region is changing and Saudi Arabia may be forced to change. There has so far been no 'Arab Spring' in the kingdom because the rulers can buy its people's acquiescence. On 11 March 2011, I was in Riyadh when pro-democracy protesters called for a 'Day of Rage' to support the protests that were sweeping through the Arab world and to call for democratic rights in their own country. Some 30,000 people joined a Facebook campaign calling for action. I called a taxi the night before to take a tour of Riyadh and survey the preparations. The city was lined with tanks and soldiers. When I raised my mobile phone to take pictures, the car was stopped by soldiers and the driver ordered to take me straight back to the hotel.

The 'Day of Rage' never stood a chance. Days before, the leading cleric Sheikh Abdel Aziz Alasheikh reminded Saudis that 'Islam strictly prohibits protests in the kingdom because the ruler here rules by God's will.'[24] People who dared participate were warned of huge fines, lashings, imprisonment and loss of nationality. But it was probably the royal handouts that decided the day. Soon before the planned demonstration, King Abdullah announced an extraordinarily generous package worth about $37bn (£23bn) to pay for unemployment benefits, education and housing subsidies. What was there left to complain about? Democracy, freedom of speech and women's rights could be put on hold.

The day itself was a damp squib. There were more soldiers on the street than protesters. 'Report what you see,' a soldier told me as we looked for something for the camera to film. A lone protester, Halid, a forty-year-old teacher, approached the press party. 'I want freedom, I want democracy,' he said. 'This country needs a parliament and a constitution.' Our government minders and army officers were listening in. 'Aren't you afraid to speak out?' I asked. 'Why should I be? I shall go to prison but this entire country is already a prison.' I accompanied him to his car and asked for his phone number so that I could keep in touch. A police car pulled out after him and, sure enough, his family told us that night that he had been arrested and imprisoned.

But for how much longer can the House of Saud bribe and imprison its citizens? Saudi Arabia may still have one-fifth of the world's oil reserves but, thanks to the oil shale revolution, sales to the United States have plummeted. America, once the kingdom's most loyal backer, is no longer dependent on Saudi oil. To the fury of Saudi rulers, America has brought Iran back into the fold by way of the agreement on its nuclear energy programme and the State Department sees the Islamic Republic of Iran as a key player in the fight against ISIS forces in Iraq and Syria. In this realignment of allies, Saudi Arabia is at last being rightfully blamed for its support of Sunni terrorism.

The House of Saud is looking vulnerable. Some 8,000 princes are now on the royal payroll, paid to do nothing while around 40 per cent of the under twenty-fives in the country have no work. Eman al-Nafjan, a blogger on the 'Day of Rage' Facebook page, said she was disappointed that no one dared show their anger on the day but 'it will happen, give it ten years or so', she writes. 'The young unemployed are a ticking time bomb. The status quo, especially when it comes to women's rights, is impossible to maintain for long . . . The call for change and more rights is loud.'[25]

When I take leave of Reem Asaad, the academic who campaigns for a woman's right to work, she is playing with her daughters, aged two and five, in her home in Jeddah. She is despondent. Many of the women-only lingerie shops that she fought so hard for have closed because the owners could not find enough women employees. They found it too expensive to get to work. 'Will this ever end?' she asks. 'And, if so, will it end in my lifetime? I certainly hope that I shall see change or at least that change will come in time for my daughters.'

5

EGYPT

What Made Her Go There?

My memory of Egypt's Arab Spring is one of huge excitement and wonder at the prominent role played by women. Nearly every night, intelligent and articulate women journalists and commentators would appear on BBC News, beamed in from makeshift studios above Tahrir Square in Cairo, to explain in perfect English to the outside world what was going on. The cameras tilted down to the square below where, extraordinarily, women were standing alongside men shouting the slogans of the revolution. For eighteen days the crowds braved the bullets of the military and suffered many deaths until their end was achieved – to end the thirty-year tyrannical rule of President Hosni Mubarak.[1]

Ahdaf Soueif, writer and Pulitzer Prize-winning journalist, noted the phenomenon in the regular columns she writes for the *Guardian*. 'The revolution happened and with it came the Age of Chivalry. One of the most noted aspects of behaviour in the streets and squares of the eighteen days of the Egyptian Revolution was the total absence of harassment. Women were suddenly free; free to walk alone, to talk to strangers, to cover or uncover, to smoke to laugh to cry to sleep [sic]. And the job of every single male present was to facilitate, to protect, to help. The Ethics of the Square, we called it.'[2]

It was remarkable because harassment of women who dared to demonstrate in public places had been a well-known occurrence in Egypt. In 2005, when crowds came out onto the street to protest at Mubarak's crude attempts to rig the elections, the government used militias of ruthless thugs who were specially trained in demonstration deterrence to use different tactics for men and women. In the words of Ahdaf Soueif, 'They beat up men, but they grabbed women. They tore their clothes off and beat them, groping them at the same time. The idea was to insinuate that females who took part in street protests wanted to be groped.'[3]

But then, in 2011, something went wrong with the Age of Chivalry. On 11 February, day thirteen of the uprising, for 39-year-old Lara Logan, chief foreign correspondent for America's CBS News, and her TV crew, it was just another day covering the events of Tahrir Square. There was huge excitement. The day before, Mubarak had ceded all governing powers to his deputy. He was still refusing to renounce the presidency, but his position was looking increasingly untenable.[4]

Protesters in the square were elated; it looked as if they were winning. Millions more were travelling to Cairo to join the demonstrations that were paralysing the centre of the city. Unknown to the crowd and journalists, Mubarak would step down later that day. Meanwhile, the CBS crew were doing what TV crews do in such circumstances, filming the excited protesters and trying to find out what would happen next. Through her interpreter, Logan was asking: 'Who would replace the president? Did they fear a military coup?'

'. . . suddenly, before I even know what's happening, I feel hands grabbing my breasts, grabbing my crotch, grabbing me from behind. I mean – and it's not one person and then it stops – it's like one person and another person and another person. And I know Ray [my bodyguard] is right there, and he's grabbing at me and screaming, "Lara, hold onto me, hold onto me!"' But she was pulled away by the mob and separated from her crew for about half an hour.

. . . my shirt, my sweater was torn off completely. My shirt was around my neck. I felt the moment my bra tore. They tore the metal clips of my bra. They tore those open. And I felt that because the air, I felt the air on my chest, on my skin. And I felt them tear out, they literally just tore my pants to shreds. And then I felt my underwear go. And I remember looking up, when my clothes gave way, I remember looking up and seeing them taking pictures with their cell phones, the flashes of their cell phone cameras.[5]

Logan told this story in the CBS studio back in New York several weeks later. She said that 'What really struck me was how merciless they were. They really enjoyed my pain and suffering. It incited them to more violence.' And 'for an extended period of time', numerous attackers among a mob of 200 to 300 'raped me with their hands'.[6] The story became headline news all over the world and justifiably so. Most of us women reporters experience lewd come-ons and groping hands from crowds and occasionally drivers and other locals we employ to help us on foreign assignments. But most of us are so desperate to compete in what was until very recently a man's world and we are so afraid of missing out on the next assignment that we seldom complain.

Logan's attack deserves the publicity. It was a mob attack, horrific and a shocking example of the behaviour that was about to become the norm in Tahrir Square. Logan admitted that she did not know about the levels of harassment and abuse that women in Egypt and other countries regularly experienced. 'I would have paid more attention to it if I had had any sense of it,' she said. 'When women are harassed and subjected to this in society, they're denied an equal place in that society. Public spaces don't belong to them. Men control it. It reaffirms the oppressive role of men in the society.'[7]

But what changed to bring these attacks about? There were hundreds of deaths in the first few days of the demonstrations and Mubarak was later ordered to stand trial for the premeditated death of peaceful protesters. Women who took part in the early days of the revolution tell me that the profile of the protesters altered. The early, idealistic leaders welcomed the involvement of women; they were the ones who gave those early days the name of the 'Age of Chivalry'. But these young men were among those who were killed and arrested. Increasingly, the mob took over. And the military targeted the easier victims, women.

I arrive in Tahrir Square a year after Logan's attack. I want to investigate what happened to the women who dared protest. In February 2012, the square itself is a pale shadow of its former self. Where hundreds of thousands had occupied the square a year ago, there are only a few hundred people milling around here today. There are food kiosks, stalls promoting the candidates in the forthcoming presidential elections and rows and rows of photographs of the dead and missing. There are very few women. Those who stood shoulder to shoulder with the men in the first few days have disappeared, punished by the mob and the military alike.

I drive out to a dusty suburb of Cairo and wait for Samira Ibrahim outside a military court. She is the only one of sixteen young women who were assaulted in one incident in Tahrir Square who has dared bring the perpetrators, members of the Egyptian army, to account. I watch her as she makes her way through the gates and security checkpoints that lead to the main exit from the court buildings. She is looking dejected. 'They did not want to listen to my story,' she says. 'They called me a liar and a whore.'

We all squeeze into a small car – the driver, interpreter, cameraman Tony Jolliffe, all his equipment, me, Samira and her sister who accompanied her on the eight-hour drive to Cairo to attend the court session. Samira ends up sitting on my lap. I seldom get the chance to get so close to my interviewees and it was a good opportunity for her to pour out her fury and frustration. 'It is all political,' she says. 'There's to be a delay because they want to call more witnesses to support the soldiers. But it could be good for me,' she says, grinning broadly. 'It gives a chance for us to change the charge from just bodily harm to sexual abuse, which is what it was. And who knows,' she adds, 'maybe one of the other girls who were with me that day will join me when we go back into the court room?'

We fall out of the car and make our way up to my hotel room. While Tony sets about lighting the place to create a small studio in which I can interview Samira, we order club sandwiches and Coke and eat supper on my bed. Time is tight. We only have a couple of hours before Samira has to catch the bus back home. I plead with her to let us visit her village in the Upper Nile. I want to find out more about this extraordinary woman who, aged twenty-five, has the courage to take on the Egyptian army. But she won't let me. 'My parents are supportive but embarrassed at the same time. If journalists start coming to our house in the village, the neighbours could turn against us.'

The day that will be for ever stamped in Samira's mind is 9 March 2011, International Women's Day. Six weeks earlier, she and some friends from her village clambered onto uncomfortable buses to reach Cairo for the demonstrations. They had been there since the beginning, sleeping in school classrooms in the city at night and going to Tahrir Square by day. By 9 March, Mubarak had been allowed to escape to his seaside home in Sharm el-Sheikh and Samira and her friends still went to the square because 'we wanted to achieve all the goals of the revolution' which meant putting the former Egyptian tyrant and his cabinet ministers on trial.[8]

The attack on Lara Logan had already taken place and there had been many more, albeit unreported attacks on local Egyptian girls. Aware that going into the square could be dangerous, they stood outside the Kentucky Fried Chicken on one side of the square, leaning on the outside of the metal barriers which the soldiers used to cordon off the main demonstration taking place in the square. Samira goes on: 'There we were sitting outside KFC, and the army attacked us. One of the soldiers took my hair, and dragged me by my hair around the fence and to the museum on the other side of the square.' The army were using the Egyptian Museum of Antiquities as an operational base and torture centre.

'They dragged us to the gates of the museum and, putting our hands behind our back, handcuffed us to the railings. They started beating us and giving us electric shocks. They called us whores and prostitutes.' When the girls were taken inside the building, the beatings got even worse. 'They carried on with the electro-cuting and took off our headscarves, threw us to the floor and kicked us with their heavy army boots. At this stage, the beatings had been going on for seven hours and some of the girls started dying from their injuries. Others suffered permanent, disabling injuries. I think that is why these girls are so afraid today and won't testify with me.'

The girls who survived, about seven of them, were put in buses and driven to the headquarters of the military prosecutor. Samira thought the soldiers would question them and then allow them to go home. 'I could not believe it. They put homemade bombs, in bottles, and weapons on the table. They forced us to pick up the weapons and they filmed us. A few days later, the pictures were published in the Egyptian newspapers, with captions saying, "Egyptian thugs captured in Tahrir Square."' Now they were being called terrorists as well as prostitutes and whores.

The group was moved again, this time to a military prison where they were beaten again. A woman military doctor then arrived and told the girls she would be carrying out virginity tests on them. 'She told me to take off my clothes. I was so weak from the beatings and the electrocutions that I did what she said. She examined me in front of the soldiers who were watching, laughing and clapping as if it were a kind of public show. It was deliberate, public humiliation. I had gone to the square to call for freedom and they made me pay the price.' It was to get worse.

'The woman then said that the military officer in charge wants to test you himself. I was made to strip again. This was sexual abuse. If a man forces you to take your clothes off and puts his hand up into your private parts and leaves it there for five minutes – that is sexual aggression. I felt utterly degraded and defeated.'

Samira starts to cry and we take a break. I assure her we have nearly finished with the interview and I have only one more question. What message were the men who abused you trying to give with this kind of treatment? I ask. 'It is quite simple,' she says. 'They were quite open about it. They kept saying that we want to humiliate you in order to make you regret ever starting a revolution. We want to say that if you take to the streets to ask for freedom or social justice, we will violate your honour. This is the message they want to deliver to us and to society as a whole.'

But Samira refused to be cowed. She first took her case to a civilian court that promptly ruled that virginity testing should be prohibited. But her victory was short-lived. The military refused to accept a judgement from a civilian court and Samira took her case to the military court, which is where I met her as she came out of one of the hearings.

To no one's surprise, the military court eventually exonerated Ahmed Adel, the military doctor who performed the virginity test. The judge sympathized with the defence lawyer's argument that it is essential that a woman's virginity is tested when she is arrested and taken to prison. To go to Tahrir Square, he argued, and to mix with thousands of young men suggests that a woman is willingly putting herself at risk of rape and the soldiers who take her into custody want to avoid any blame.

When I spoke to Samira on the phone from London, she was angry and resigned. 'I wasn't really expecting anything from the military court,' she says. 'It is obvious, the military will never indict itself. I never stood a chance.' I ask her how she and her family are coping? 'Badly,' she says. Her parents have had a lot of trouble in the village and, far from supporting her, the majority of the Egyptian press keep asking: 'What made her go there?' Popular opinion seems to find it easier to blame a woman for going to a demonstration than apportioning blame elsewhere. 'Now the Egyptian woman is violated from two sides, one is the military and the other are the Islamists,' she says.[9]

Habiba Mohsen, a political researcher at the Arab Forum for Alternatives, tries to explain what she calls the 'twisted judgment' on women in Egypt. 'Women in Egypt face three times the pressures that men do: first, from the military regime as protesters; second from the society, just for being women, and third, from all sides for trying to claim their right to participate in public life. Different pretexts are offered, such as the supposed importance of traditions, culture, and even religion.' In short, she says, 'it's always the women's fault, as any "decent", well-behaving woman would not leave their home to protest or to take part in a sit-in. So, what made this woman take part in the protests in the first place? "What made her go there?"'[10]

I meet Hadir Farouk, one of the early women leaders of the protest in a cafe just off Tahrir Square and ask: 'What made her go there?' 'I went to Tahrir Square because I was fed up with Mubarak and the corruption he represented. I wanted real democracy and freedom of speech and, of course, I hoped that we women might gain something from the revolution, dignity and respect.' When she was approached by an army officer and asked to negotiate on behalf of the protesters with a major general waiting in a building nearby, she was flattered. At last, she thought, women are being recognized as leaders.

She now admits that she was hopelessly naive. She says:

> They pushed me into a room which turned out to be a torture room. There were girls inside already being beaten and raped and they threw me among them. The soldiers were using sticks to beat us brutally and they were clearly enjoying what they were doing. They asked us which hurt more, the beating or the violation? It was clear that they were targeting girls more than men because they wanted to make us afraid and because they wanted to make the men who were demonstrating feel humiliated and defeated for not protecting us.

No wonder, the women protesters began to disappear from the square.

The incident of the 'Blue Bra Woman' provides perhaps the most dramatic illustration of what a woman might risk if she takes to the streets. The image of an apparently unconscious young woman with blue jeans, trainers, slim, long arms and naked torso shocked all who saw it. Two soldiers are dragging her along the street, her black abaya has been rucked up around her head leaving her blue bra exposed. A third soldier has his boot poised inches from her breast, about to stamp on her. It was December 2011. Mubarak had gone, the army had taken over and protesters had staged a peaceful sit-in to protest at the army's choice of prime minister. The soldiers attacked the protesters brutally, women included.

Blue Bra Woman became an international celebrity but she has never revealed her identity. Like Samira, she may have feared potential repercussions against her family. Or, maybe she had not told her family that she had joined the demonstrations. Or, maybe she feared that her reputation would be ruined for ever as the horrific picture of a woman, naked above the waist apart from the blue bra, spread all over the world on social media and on the front pages of most international newspapers. She was, after all, wearing an abaya, which would suggest that she was a religious conservative. Or, she may have even been killed in the brutal torture rooms described to me by Samira Ibrahim and Hadir Farouk. We shall never know.[11]

With so much violence, I was astonished to discover that Egypt's most illustrious feminist, novelist, anti-FGM campaigner and militant Nawal El Saadawi made many visits to Tahrir Square in 2011 and even camped there for the night. She is tough and glamorous but, at eighty years old, might not be a match for teargas-throwing and baton-wielding soldiers. We sit down for tea in the elegant, book-lined living room in her apartment in Cairo. How did she cope with the thugs in the square? I ask. She gets up from her seat and, using Tony my cameraman as a target, she abruptly brings up her knee, stopping just inches from where it could inflict serious damage. 'I get them where it hurts,' she says laughing. Tony looks a bit pale.

I have come to Egypt to make two films, one about the women of the square and another about the prevalence of FGM. I have asked to see El Saadawi in relation to the FGM film. She tells me she was cut as a child. 'When I was six years old,' she says, 'the daya (the midwife) came into the room holding a razor, pulled out my clitoris from between my thighs and cut it off. She said it was the will of God, she was God's servant and that she must obey his command. I lay in a pool of blood, wondering what other parts of my body she might have been ordered to cut off.'

Born in a small village, she was an intelligent and rebellious child, one of nine children, who refused to conform to traditional expectations for a girl, which, in her village, would have entailed being married at twelve. In her autobiography she remembers her fury when her grandmother told her that a boy is worth fifteen girls. 'Girls are a blight,' she said to her granddaughter. El Saadawi determined to show her grandmother that she was wrong.

She was lucky. Her father was a progressive who believed in education for girls and so she achieved the near impossible for a woman in Egypt of the time and went to medical college and qualified as a doctor in 1955. She was appointed Egypt's director of Public Health, as a result of her campaigning against FGM. But she found it impossible to separate her anti-FGM campaign from her fight for women's social and intellectual rights. She was sacked, imprisoned under President Sadat and has never been given a government job again.

Just as she found it hard to stick to her brief when she worked for the government, our conversation about FGM is soon referred to in the context of the current political scene. Paradoxically, Suzanne Mubarak, the former president's wife, supported the campaign to eradicate FGM from Egypt. But now, El Saadawi fears, there will be a setback to the campaign. Anything that had been approved by the hated ancien régime, she explains, is likely to be opposed by its successors. All the work she did to get FGM banned in Egypt in 2008, at least in law if not in practice, is now in danger of being wasted. But she has no other regrets about the loss of the Mubaraks.

For this doughty, seasoned campaigner, the revolution of 25 January was what she had been dreaming of since she was a child.

I didn't expect twenty million people on the streets. It was when Mubarak started killing people that everyone, from all over Egypt, came to Cairo. This has been my dream, that one day the Egyptian people would wake up and revolt against slavery, colonization and tyranny. I have always been a rebel. When I was at medical college, I was fighting King Farouk, then British colonization. I fought against Nasser, against Sadat who pushed me into prison, Mubarak who pushed me into exile. I never stopped.

But after the initial euphoria, she confesses she was soon disillusioned. 'I am angry. Women, even old women like me, went to the square and participated, even with the dangers. Then, as soon as we achieved our first objective, the removal of Mubarak, Egypt returns to the old model and we find we are isolated. The constitutional committees which were formed to rewrite the constitution and prepare for elections were all made up of old men, so young people are also angry. We want at least 35 per cent female participation in all committees.'

She is depressed by the subsequent turn taken by the revolution. After Mubarak retired to his villa in Sharm el-Sheikh to await trial, the caretaker military government organized elections for early 2012. The Muslim Brotherhood's Freedom and Justice Party (FJP) won the largest number of seats while the Islamic hardliners, the Salafist Al-Nour Party, came second. They formed a coalition.[12] 'This will result in a backlash against women,' El Saadawi warns, 'worse than what we saw under Mubarak.' She hates religions as much as she hates dictators.

She was later to call the short-lived rule of President Mohamed Morsi and the Moslem Brotherhood, 'the age of jinn, spirits and nonsense'. She believes an individual's religion should be a personal thing and not forced by an outside authority. 'I am very critical of all religions,' she says. 'We, as women, are oppressed by all these religions. It is religious extremism that is the biggest threat to women's liberation today.'

I share the same birthday as El Saadawi so I feel an affinity for her and I agree with many of her ideas. And so it came as a surprise to me when, the following day, I find myself in the company of a woman Moslem Brotherhood MP whom I find warm, intelligent and very impressive. Hoda Ghaneya is a 43-year-old doctor and mother of four and newly elected MP for the constituency of Al-Qalyubiya, to the north of Cairo.

She invites me to join her on a walkabout in her constituency. It is a sprawl of concrete and breeze-block-built houses with a narrow, dusty shopping street where cars, motorbikes and donkeys compete for the narrow space available with the usual Middle Eastern cacophony of sound – car horns blaring, street vendors yelling their wares, panicked mothers screaming at children and everyone else shouting. Through the chaos, Ghaneya floats in her long blue abaya, looking serene and confident as her constituents rush up to greet her. 'I was born here,' she explains, 'and people know and like me.'

Even the men constituents approach her with almost deferential respect. The butcher, for example, leaves his counter and comes out onto the street to greet her. Why did you vote for a woman? I ask him. 'She has ability and skills and her party suffered a lot in the past and it's about time that they are given a chance and I hope she will work to make us happy and make this country better.'

The Brotherhood was a banned organization under President Mubarak although its political leaders were allowed to stand as independents in the elections of 2005 and 2010. Their slogan 'Islam is the Solution' left few in doubt about their intentions. When Mubarak attempted to boost his moderate credentials to the outside world and introduce a bill into parliament that would have allowed Christians and women to stand for the presidency, the Moslem Brotherhood supporters left the chamber, refusing to vote.

And yet while the Mubarak government sank into the mire of corruption, inaction and cronyism that would ultimately defeat it, millions of Egyptians were turning to the Moslem Brotherhood for practical help. The Brotherhood set up an alternative and very effective network offering social services in villages and neighbourhoods. No wonder people voted for them in their millions. It is these acts of good governance and charity that bring the people of Al-Qalyubiya out onto the streets to greet Ghaneya as she goes on her walkabout.

A woman grabs her sleeve and says, 'Thank you, thank you. My son would have died if you had not got him into hospital.' People stop to tell me and my translator how Ghaneya and the local Moslem Brotherhood team collected the money to buy a local hospital, how they give shelter to orphans and hand out food to the poor. One woman says, 'We voted for the doctor because she will fight for our rights. Our last MP made promises but did nothing for us.'

Ghaneya smiles at the woman and hugs her and then turns to me, 'You must be hot and tired? Let's go home.' Her house is a short walk away and we wind our way through a maze of unprepossessing two-storey buildings and litter-strewn paths. Broken children's bikes and deflated footballs lie scattered alongside piles of rotting food. 'I know,' she says looking embarrassed, 'we could do more on refuge collection but we have been concentrating on hospitals and orphans.' Ghaneya's house is bigger than most and the entire family appear to be waiting for her to come back for tea, even the male members.

I sit alongside the women, on long sofas. The men all sit on straight-backed chairs in a corner of the room. Ghaneya's mother and daughters prepare refreshments and I gratefully accept sweet black tea and Egyptian cakes. My cameraman, Tony, indicates that he is ready to start with the interview. We go through the history of the Moslem Brotherhood, how the state had tried to ban them but how they had become an increasing source of support for the poor. But what I want to know, I ask Ghaneya, is how a party with strict Islamic beliefs can be of benefit to the women of Egypt?

'From now on, I believe we will see change,' she says. 'We'll see the start of a real partisan life, solid democratic life in Egypt in a way that allows all citizens, including women, to join the political life knowing that the new politics is uncorrupted and based on rights for all. Therefore, I think that the participation of women and their impact in the parliament in the coming period will be completely different.'

Hoda Ghaneya is clearly a brilliant constituency MP but she is either being ridiculously optimistic about her party or she does not know the wider picture. Under Hosni Mubarak, women MPs had a quota of 64 seats in the 508-seat parliament.[13] After the fall of Mubarak, the constitution changed and there was no such quota. During the election campaign, the election posters and billboards for the religious parties might show, for example, six candidates. Four would be of men beaming out their confidence and their personalities to the passer-by. The two women candidates would be represented as anonymous black silhouettes. No wonder they did not do too well; only nine women MPs were elected.

I am in Cairo while the campaign is going on for the next election – for president. I meet presidential candidate Bouthaina Kamel as she is dashing from election meeting to 'must be seen at' social events. Not that she needs to raise her profile too much. A former TV presenter, Kamel is a well-known face in Cairo. Her life is hectic, she says, and I will just have to tag along and grab an interview on the hoof. In order to spend more time talking with her, I get into her car and Tony follows with the camera car. I need not have bothered. She was never off her mobile phone.

She screeches to a stop on a busy Cairo road, parks, gets out of the car and with a toss of her hair and with utter disregard for the oncoming traffic, she crosses the road in her high heels as cars screech to stop. 'Hey, Bouthaina!' drivers call out through car windows, 'good luck!' 'Yeah, I bet!' she mutters to me as we walk to the first appointment, 'men like that would never vote for me.' When her meeting with campaign workers gets going, she admits to us all that in the political climate in Egypt today, a non-headscarf-wearing, woman presidential candidate does not stand a chance of winning.

But winning is not the point of standing, she says. 'I want to show where women might go one day, if we keep up the momentum.' But, I point out, the fact that only nine women MPs got voted in at the elections might suggest that women in Egypt don't vote for women? 'Women make up 60 per cent of Egyptian society,' she points out, 'and the literacy rate among them is 70 per cent.[14] This does not help because many women simply don't know how to vote and it's their menfolk who fill in their voting papers for them.'

But it is the rise of the Islamic parties that really worry her. 'The political alliances have an Islamic bias which is detrimental to the status of women. For example, a committee for constitutional reform has been created without the participation of one single woman. I fear the worse for women's rights.'

Women like Bouthaina Kamel, with her flamboyant style, confidence and ambition, are right to be afraid of what the era of Islamic party rule for Egypt might mean for them. Secular, educated Egyptian women do not know what to expect. After a lot of phone calls and pleas to Egyptian journalist friends to intervene on my behalf, I manage to secure an interview with Nader Bakker, spokesman for Al-Noura, the hardline Salafi party, the ally of the Moslem Brotherhood in parliament. I asked him whether secular women, like Bouthaina Kamel, are right to be afraid?

He refuses to answer the question, instead he points out the injustices suffered by religious women in Egypt during the decades of the Mubarak era. 'What about the woman who wears the niqab who has been discriminated against in the past, prevented from entering university or being on the teaching staff? Also, they weren't allowed to work on television! They suffered systematic prosecution in the medical profession. The Islamic parties now have 75 per cent of the parliament. No one will be forced to do anything but we now have a greater chance to advise the rules of our religion, such as wearing the headscarf.'

We shall never know what the rule of the Moslem Brotherhood intended for the women of Egypt. Might there have been Saudi-type TV chat shows with niqab-wearing women, with only their eyes uncovered, arguing the virtues of submitting to the male members of their family? Would schoolchildren and hospital patients be confronted by fully veiled teachers and doctors? We shall never know because after only a year in office, President Mohamed Morsi and his Moslem Brotherhood government was deposed by a military coup, apparently supported by huge swathes of the Egyptian people.

Morsi claimed to be the candidate who would unite religious and secular interests in Egypt. After a few months in government, he showed few signs of embracing the latter. He was accused of bringing in a constitution biased towards Islam and of a heavy-handed, dictatorial approach towards opposition supporters and journalists. He had been brought to power by grassroots popular support and now those supporters wanted him to go, blaming the new president for the greatest crime in their eyes – raising prices and a collapsed economy.

And so the season of demonstrations started again in Egypt, in November 2012 to be precise, when the Morsi government tried to suspend the constitution temporarily and give the president unlimited powers. It was a move that brought thousands of genuine protesters – who saw democracy under threat – back to Tahrir Square and with them came the gangs of sexual predators.

But, by the end of the month, there was a new challenge waiting for them. The explicitly but not very elegantly named Operation Anti Sexual Harasment, OpAntiSH for short. On their website, they explain that their aim is 'to form a force that can fight against pre-planned forms of gang sexual assault on women during demonstrations and provide protection and support in those protest spaces'.

They are a group of young volunteers, men and women, including survivors of sexual attacks, who want to return the square to the short-lived Age of Chivalry, where men and women can protest or celebrate peacefully without fear of sexual assault. For security reasons, most of the volunteers refuse to give their names to avoid recognition when they are operating in the square. Only the names of the office-based staff are known, like Salma Said, one of the organizers, who says quite simply that, 'This is our revolution and our *midan* (square) and no one can take it from us.'

OpAntiSH study the tactics of the abusers. They learn that the abusers work in gangs, quickly isolate the victim, surround her, strip her and start abusing her. The abusers invite any man in near proximity to join in, thus giving the gang extra protection. OpAntiSH have six so-called confrontation groups, of fourteen men each, who infiltrate the circle of abusers and who are pre-pared to use physical force. Another team, the 'safety group', will be responsible for getting the victim back home or to hospital, whichever is appropriate. A third group work as coordinators to get the confrontation group to where it is needed. Emergency numbers are circulated to genuine demonstrators.

OpAntiSH set out to provide an essential service that the Moslem Brotherhood government refused to perform. The Human Rights Committee of Egypt's Shura Council, the upper house in Egypt's bicameral parliament, showed little sympathy to women who wanted to join demonstrations. In February 2013, committee member Major General Adel Afify said they 'know they are among thugs. They should protect themselves before requesting that the Interior Ministry does so. By getting herself involved in such circumstances, the woman has 100 percent responsibility.'[15] Once again, the 'What made her go there?' mentality.

The committee went on to confirm that the government was not prepared to risk deploying its own security personnel to help demonstrators. It was, they said, just too risky. Which left Fatima, who attended an anti-Morsi demonstration on 25 January 2013, dangerously exposed when attacked by a gang.

> They were pulling the kefayya around my neck and chok-ing me and dragging me by it . . . I couldn't breathe . . . The more I screamed the more savagely they attacked me. Right in front of me, I saw someone (I remember the way he looked: less than twenty years old and short and with the utmost savagery) cutting my sweater and cutting my bra and stripping it off of me. He kept grabbing my breasts and at the same time people were violating my body everywhere. I was so disgusted and felt sick. I felt like I was going to pass out. I was really scared I was going to fall to the ground. The shoving and the hands multiplied, and suddenly I stopped screaming, I couldn't breathe and I got really dizzy, and I was afraid I was going to fall down and die, I really felt that death wasn't far at all.[16]

There were twenty-five violent sexual assaults that day, too many for the OpAntiSH to handle them all. The volunteers who assem-bled on that day complained that it was difficult to identify who in the crowd was trying to help them and who wanted to get in on the abuse. 'It was chaos,' says one volunteer. 'I was being hit trying to get to the girl, not knowing whether the people I hit back were harassers or trying to help.' Some men claimed to be rescuing the woman or to be a family member or friend, only to start assaulting her once they got close enough.[17]

The demonstrations accelerated, as did the sexual assaults. On 30 June 2013, forty-six violent sexual assaults were recorded. According to Injy Ghozman of OpAntiSH, most of the victims required immediate medical attention. On the organization's Facebook page, they wrote: 'Our team intervened in a case where a survivor of a horrific mob sexual attack was about to undergo a virginity test by a female doctor in a police booth inside Tahrir metro station.' They were able to intervene before the test actually took place. The security forces refused to help protesters but they had the personnel ready to carry out virginity tests.

On 3 July, President Mohamed Morsi stepped down after just a year in office. In a post on his Facebook page that day, he commented, 'the message will resonate throughout the Moslem world loud and clear: democracy is not for Moslems.'[18] Egypt's first democratically elected president was put on trial to face charges including the murder of protesters. In March 2014, 529 of his supporters were sentenced to death.

Since then, Egypt has reverted to type, a military dictatorship. So what did Egypt's Arab Spring accomplish? Writing in the *Guardian*, Ahdaf Soueif observed that: 'Like a sci-fi monster, the blocks of the old regime break and dissolve only to rise again in a new configuration.' She adds, 'Are we in a worse place than we were before 25 January 2011? Our loss, the grief of which is immeasurable, is the thousands of people murdered and maimed, and the years tens of thousands have lost, and are still losing, in unjust imprisonment. Every tally has to start with these.'[19]

It is believed that 846 protesters were killed during the 2011 uprising. Only three low-ranking security force personnel were ever convicted and sentenced to prison. The security forces turned their guns on Moslem Brotherhood demonstrators in July and August 2013, killing approximately 1,150. No charges have been brought against a single member of the security forces.

And the sacrifice and bravery of all those women, what did it achieve? All the women demonstrators in the square who went there because they passionately wanted to change Egypt, Samira Ibrahim and others who suffered 'virginity testing', Hadir Farouk who was beaten and raped to punish her for being one of the demonstration leaders, feminist and author Nawal El Saadawi, who at eighty years old was prepared to camp in the square and to encourage the young, and Blue Bra Woman. What did they manage to do?

I asked a lot of Egyptian friends and commentators this question and I found that Shaimaa Khalil, a BBC correspondent who was born in Alexandria, got closest to what might be the cruel truth. I have worked with Shaimaa in Saudi Arabia, Lebanon, Syria and in Egypt and, as an Egyptian who covered much of the revolutionary period, she has no delusions about her country. She suggests that women might have been disingenuous to ever think they could bring about change.

> The problem is that during this time, women's rights issues were not a priority. Things like gang rape, sexual harassment and FGM were just allowed to fester. There is this notion that women's rights are a separate and, more annoyingly, not an important part of human rights in Egypt as a whole. It is a luxury that you can deal with after you've sorted other important issues like the economy and security, without considering that women's rights are part of sorting out security and the economy.
>
> Right now, it's all about security. It's about saving Egypt from impending dangers on every border. It's about conspiracy theories and nationalism that verges on fascism. So, to conclude, women's rights never were and are not now on a priority list.

The targeting of women protesters by the security forces continues. As I write this, another video from Egypt is scoring thousands of hits on YouTube, like Blue Bra Woman. This time the victim has a name. Shaima al-Sabbagh, a mother, a poet and political activist, joined a small demonstration to mark the anniversary of the 25 January 2011 revolution. She had left her five-year-old son at home near Alexandria and travelled by train to Cairo because she wanted to lay flowers in Tahrir Square for the victims.[20]

The video shows a petite, attractive woman with curly brown hair wearing a blue denim jacket over slacks. She is with a small group of twenty or so demonstrators, carrying flowers and banners. She stands next to a man in his sixties. None of them look threatening. She walks down Talaat Harb Street toward Tahrir Square.

Four shots are heard on the video. A uniformed officer is directing a masked gunman who crouches down when he fires the third shot at the backs of the small group of protesters as they walk away. It was this shot that killed al-Sabbagh. The subsequent medical report said that she had been shot in the back and the neck with birdshot, from a distance of eight metres.

One of her friends picks her up and takes her across the road, away from the group of protesters and police fire. Sayyid Abou al-Ela carries the small, rag doll-like body in his left arm while holding what appears to be her handbag in his right and lays her carefully on the pavement. Al-Ela later told Human Rights Watch that he was arrested by a police officer and a police brigadier general who arrived on the scene as he was holding al-Ela's hand while she lay dying. Others who came to her assistance and eyewitnesses who gave evidence to the state prosecutor were also arrested.

If the case ever comes to court, no doubt the state prosecutor will ask those who knew Shaima al-Sabbagh: "What made her go there?"

6

FROM RUSSIA WITH LOVE

Sex Trafficking

Aija is an attractive, twenty-five-year-old Latvian with blonde hair, the body of a ballet dancer and a fierce desire to escape the drudgery that has blighted the lives of Latvian women for most of the twentieth century. The collapse of the former USSR in 1991 has done little to help. The main industry in her home city of Riga is sex tourism but a girl of her age is in danger of being excluded from even this unwholesome and dangerous business.

The trouble is that the daughters of their former colonizers, the Russians, are muscling in on their patch. They are often younger and are prepared to get paid less for the work offered by the organized street prostitution, massage parlours and striptease clubs that now fill the streets of the attractive old city of Riga with its cobbled streets and colourfully painted houses. Aija's only chance is to seek work abroad.

She walks past the sex clubs, ignores the cat calls from a group of men from Cardiff on a stag weekend and ducks into a basement internet cafe squeezed in between a club offering lap dancing and the Pussy Café. She finds a website appealing for waitresses, dancers and chambermaids to work in the countries of Western Europe. She types in: 'I want a job. I am 22, nice looking and have dance experience. What do I need to do to get work?'

The reply is immediate. It is from Denmark. 'Hey Aija!' the respondent writes in an email. He identifies himself as Albert and assures her, 'you need no experience. If you like, you can start this week.' She is told to buy a ticket to Copenhagen and, if questioned by immigration, to say that she is a tourist. She must take a taxi to 'Club 8' where she can start straightaway as a dancer. Albert says he is the club owner and promises to reimburse all her travel expenses.

Aija turns to me and asks, 'Shall I do it?' I am sitting beside her in the cafe because I have asked Aija, a journalist, to help me in an investigation I am carrying out into the sex trafficking business. Aija is glad to help because, she says, 'I see it as a mission. I find it sad that so many girls from the Baltic States get caught like this, tempted by the prospect of earning a living wage for the first time in their lives and then end up destroying their lives.'

I ask her if she is happy to take the risk and she agrees. I phone the appropriate departments at the BBC to arrange full protection for Aija and we fly to Copenhagen. From the airport, as instructed, Aija takes a taxi to Club 8 and we follow in a car, park outside the club and watch her as she goes in. We discuss long and hard whether she should wear a hidden radio microphone but decide against it. If it is discovered, she could risk being beaten and punished before we can get into the club to help her.

Later Aija tells us what happened: 'A woman called Luna greeted me and took my passport, saying she would put it in safe-keeping. She showed me around, first to the dormitory which, she explained, I would be sharing with four other girls and then we went down to the public areas. "This is the bar," Luna said, "here is the sauna and the room next door is where we hold the sex parties and everything after that takes place in the rooms upstairs." I said to her, "Forgive me, I came here to dance. Do you mean I have to have sex with the clients?" "You are here to dance, have sex and you start tonight," she replied.'

About an hour after Aija goes into the house and before we see any clients arrive, we contact the Danish police and report an incident of kidnapping and the threat of rape. They arrive and arrest the owner, Albert, and Aija's co-workers, four Hungarian girls. They retrieve Aija's passport from Albert's safe and let her go. The police see the case as essentially an immigration problem. The Hungarian girls are deported the next day. There are no statements taken about how they got to Denmark, their treatment at the club or whether they had been forced to have sex against their will. No charges are brought against the club's management.

Dorit Otzen, a Danish lawyer who has spent most of her life trying to help the victims of sex slavery, is in despair. She has lost count of the number of times she has begged the police to give these girls witness protection so that they can testify in order to bring about a successful prosecution. 'The police do not want to know anything about sex trafficking. You can get up to ten years for selling or importing drugs into Denmark but the longest sentence anyone has ever received for importing a woman is a year. And even then the judge apologized to the man in court, saying it was a long sentence. You could cry!'

And what about the girls? 'The police give the girls twenty-four hours (after a raid) and then they're out,' says Otzen. The pimps just go and collect another batch, week after week, month after month.' Sure enough, I phone the club a few weeks later to find that Albert is still in business. On a recorded message, he advertises the girls they currently have on offer: a Lithuanian, a Pole and two Russians. He gives their bust dimensions and describes their sexual attractions.

The sex business is condoned, covert and dangerous. Latvian girls have died in Denmark. We shall never know how many because the murders are likely to take place in subterranean clubs and bars from where bodies can be easily disposed of. Natasha Pavlova had such high hopes when she arrived in Copenhagen in

1996. I meet with Natasha's mother, Eugenia Pavlova, in her tiny flat in Riga where she offers me tea and we talk while her six-year-old grandson watches cartoons on TV. 'After a few weeks, Natasha phoned to say that she was getting married.' It was the fulfilment of every Latvian mother's dreams. 'She said that they were just getting settled and that she would be bringing over her son, little Andrei, to live with them and that she wanted me to come too.'

We don't know whether the boyfriend ever existed, whether he was in fact a pimp and how her plans ended in what the Danish red tops at the time called the Massage Parlour Massacre. Magnus, a young IT technician who lives and works in the same street as the massage parlour remembers 'an Asian woman emerging from the basement, naked, covered in blood and staggering around from her wounds'. Neighbours called the police.

As one officer looked after the woman, another went down to the massage parlour and called back up, 'You can forget her. Look what we've got down here. It's much worse!' It was Natasha Pavlova, brutally knifed to death and lying in her own blood. 'Whenever the phone rang,' says Eugenia Pavlova, 'little Andrei thought it was his mother to tell him that she was coming for us. It took me six months to find the courage to tell him the truth.' No one was ever charged.

This all took place more than ten years ago but little has changed. It was not until 2012 that the Danish government, in compliance with an EU directive, raised the maximum penalty for trafficking to ten years. Since 2010, the police have prosecuted about a dozen men a year for sex-trafficking offences. Penalties for these convicted have ranged from nine to thirty months imprisonment.

Denmark is not alone in its relaxed attitude to the problem. Traffickers operate in Nigeria, Thailand and Eastern Europe to provide sex slaves to meet an increasing demand in the richer countries of the world. They find it worth their while; it is a low risk, high reward business.

I go back to Riga to find out more about how it works and meet twenty-one-year-old Sveta and nineteen-year-old Ljuba. They are typical young Latvians: well-educated, ambitious and attractive. They cannot find work and they dream about jobs abroad. The streets of their city are beginning to boast fashion boutiques and shops selling the latest smartphones. Girls their age, in designer shades and heels, can be seen stepping out of new BMW cars to shop at them. These are the 1 per cent. Go to the seedy areas around the bus station and you see how badly these countries suffered after the collapse of the Soviet system and before they became members of the European Union. Old people sleep on the benches of the bus shelters, a bowl of thick gruel from the soup kitchen in the evening is the only meal for many, people look downtrodden, destitute and in despair. No wonder the young take crazy risks to escape.

Tatiana Kurova paints a bleak picture over a coffee in her threadbare office in a centre for women in Riga: 'Women will go, no matter what because there is simply nothing to eat here. There are people living in unimaginable poverty. It is difficult to stop these young people and make them think. They see their parents live on crumbs of bread and they don't want to do the same. They want to change their situation and they don't want to wait.'

Sveta and Ljuba know that the wealthy and young in Latvia, if not involved in the world of crime, will have contacts and joint business ventures in the West. When I meet them, they are in a cappuccino bar sifting through jobs pages. They find an employment agency offering jobs as domestics in the Republic of Ireland. Such a job – they admit it might not get them access to the best boutiques just yet, but it's a start. 'I am so excited,' says Ljuba, with a toss of her long black hair. 'It will change everything. We pore over maps and our old geography books and talk non-stop about the trip. We have even started packing!' Sveta, a pretty blonde, is the more serious of the two. 'I am desperate to go abroad to earn enough money to complete my higher education.' Her dream is to become a vet.

The next day, they tell me they are confused and apprehensive. Edgar, the owner of the employment agency has asked them to have an Aids test. Another girl they met in the waiting room and who was coming back for a second appointment had been asked by Edgar to bring a photo with her and her bust measurements. Is this normal? they ask. I assure them that it is not. Edgar tells them that he can send them to work for a Mr Con Foley, the owner of Foley's Hotel and Restaurant on the High Street in Portumna, County Galway in Ireland. He says he has already sent several Latvian and Lithuanian girls there who have phoned to tell him that they are all enjoying the work. I advise Sveta and Ljuba to stay put while I go to Ireland.

If the subject of my investigation were not so serious, the fact that I find myself in Portumna looking for an essential link in an international sex-trafficking operation would be comical. The expression 'one horse town' could have been devised to describe Portumna, a small, sleepy town on the west coast of Ireland. The tourist office boasts horse riding and a visit of local ecclesiastical sites as its chief attractions. 'Where's Latvia?' said one old man walking his dog when I ask him if he has seen any Latvians in town, 'somewhere in Yugoslavia?' At Portumna post office they confirm that no Latvians have been seen, 'but we had a Spaniard here last year' the postmistress adds, helpfully. Nor, she tells me, is there a Foley's Hotel and Restaurant on the High Street.

I find a Mr Con Foley, though, flipping hamburgers in the local Burger Express. His sole outlet is in an internet cafe; it's a booth squeezed in beside the plastic tables and the jukebox, leaving no room for a team of Latvian waitresses. I struggle to understand how he came to be known in Riga as an importer of girls from the

Baltic States into the Irish Republic. Foley is an amiable character who is embarrassed and very cross about his unwitting connection. He shows me how he had posted a job vacancy on the web, looking at the possibility of employing a waitress from abroad. There is nothing unusual in this. During boom years, the service industry in Ireland was desperately short of workers. In one year, the Irish government issued 10,000 work permits, 1,000 of them for Latvians. In the end, Foley filled the vacancy locally. And if you get a girl from Riga, would you ask her to have an Aids test? 'Good God, no,' he replies, blushing.

I move on to Dublin where a local journalist arranges a meeting for me with a player in the vice trade. He works until late and our rendezvous is after midnight in the red-light district of Smithfield village. As he gets into the back of the car, he says he will talk but only if I guarantee his anonymity. He has a theory about the Portumna connection. 'It makes sense for the traffickers to use a bone fide employer as a front to bring Latvian girls here on work permits for the service industry in the high season. The government is handling thousands of work permits a month, it's a new game for them and it would never occur to them that someone could be abusing the system.' That someone, he explains, would be an insider who can get his or her hands on the official work permit application forms 'and they're making a lot of money out of this'.

The traffickers would arrange for the girls to fly to Dublin with legitimate work permits where they would be met, but they would never see Portumna. From Dublin, he continues, the sex trafficker uses the free movement between the Republic of Ireland and Britain 'to fulfil the vice requirements of London, Birmingham and Manchester. I know one of the big names in vice here in Dublin who is transporting the girls to Belfast and, from there, they are taken to Britain.' The fact that the girl might have obtained a work permit for the Republic of Ireland, he explains, will make her even more vulnerable. 'She will find herself in the UK illegally and the pimp will use this to his advantage. He will seize her passport and tell her that it cost £10,000 to £20,000 to get her to the UK. He forces her into prostitution, arguing that this is the only way he can pay back her travel expenses. Payback time often involves servicing up to twenty clients a day. The girls are effectively prisoners for as long as the pimps can make use of them.'

I go back to Riga and meet up again with Ljuba and Sveta. I tell them that Mr Con Foley is innocent in all this but that the risks are too high for them to travel with an agency that clearly does not know where they are sending them to. They are devastated. 'I had so many hopes, about paying for my education and getting a good job,' Ljuba says. 'I had a life plan but now my future is in tatters.' Sveta looks utterly dejected. 'I feel terrible. It has been an eye-opener. I now realize that there are people out there who just see us as prey.' But have Ljuba and Sveta really learned anything from their interaction with Edgar? I get the impression that they are quite cross that I have shattered their dreams. A few days later, I come across them in the same cafe. They are poring over the job adverts again.

I went back to see Tatiana Kurova, of the women's centre in Riga and ask why the authorities are not doing more to stamp on the sex-trafficking business and, in particular, agencies like Edgar's. 'We are overwhelmed,' she says. 'Look at me. I would love to get into the schools and warn the girls who are about to leave school about the dangers out there but my life is spent caring for those who manage to escape and who get back to the city in a terrible, terrible state.'

She reaches for one of the many files piled on the shelf behind her. 'Where do I begin to explain? Yes, look, this girl came here and told me that she was in a concentration camp in Poland where there were some three hundred women. The camp had fences with barbed wire and was guarded by dogs. The women were sex slaves and they were starved. Three of them managed to escape, travelling at night to avoid busy roads and immigration controls. The girl who I am helping was one of them. She literally crawled here into my office.'

She asks me to return that evening so that I can hear first-hand the story of one of the girls under her care, Irina. The chain-smoking twenty-six-year-old was already a sex worker in Riga when she was told she would get better pay in Israel. 'We were told that we would be paid $1,000 a month. They took us all over Israel, selling us to different pimps. The first time I got sold, it was for $15,000, the second time was for $10,000 and the price kept dropping until no one wanted me any more. We were expected to service fifteen clients a day. I serviced thirty-three in one day. I think I must have made $20,000 to $35,000 a month for the pimps. But I didn't get a penny.' The pimps love it, she says, when the traffickers can find them young, naive girls like Sveta and Ljuba. 'They are easier to terrorize, you see. There was this one young girl who answered an ad to work as an au pair in Israel for $600 a month. The traffickers said they had found a family and sorted all the travel arrangements for her. When she arrived in Tel Aviv, they took her straight to a brothel and sold her, just like they did with us. They boasted to us about her.'

And it is not just Latvia and the Baltic States. I have made more film reports on sex slavery than I care to remember. I have followed the trade of fair-skinned young Nepali women who have been sold to the brothels of Bombay and have traced the sad procession of Aleksandras, Ludmillas and Nataliyas from the Ukraine to the lap-dancing clubs of America. It is utter despair that makes people take such risks. Just as Syrians and Somalians today risk drowning in the Mediterranean while travelling in overcrowded dinghies from Libya to Lampedusa, the former citizens of the Soviet Union were taking similar risks fifteen years ago. The Soviet Union was untenable and deserved to collapse but the security, the cradle to grave certainty of state care, however inadequate, went with it. The cost in terms of human misery has been enormous.

Some of my worst recurring nightmares come from this era. I remember the smell of faeces and sweat in the cell of the juvenile prison I visited in the newly renamed St Petersburg where there were twenty boys under the age of eighteen in a subterranean cell designed for four with no window. Some of the children were as young as twelve, imprisoned indefinitely for stealing bread to help their starving families. The state could not afford the procedures to send them to trial, it could not pay for enough prison officers to allow them the luxury of recreation or the medicine to cope with the TB raging through the prison.

There was a pattern of misery repeated throughout the former Russian empire. And if there is a literal 'hell on earth', it could be in Magadan, in the Russian Far East where people live in the area once notorious for Stalin's gulags. To get to Magadan, you drive down the 'Road of Bones', built by gulag prisoners who collapsed as they worked and whose bones, the locals tell you, are ground into the road's foundations. In a spartan and freezing-cold old people's home I met Natasha Lvov who, although released from a gulag on Stalin's death in 1953, cannot afford the journey home to Leningrad and remains in the land of prisons. During the 'Great Patriotic War', as Russians call the Second World War, she had been building railway tracks in 1943 near the city of Rostov as part of the programme to move all essential production lines eastwards, away from the German advance.

'The manager handed us all boots for the work. My feet are small and all he had left were men's boots. I put them on and I laughed. I was only eighteen and so I started clowning around, dancing on the tracks and all my fellow workers laughed too.' She was accused of sabotaging the war effort and was sent to a gulag, 4,000 miles away from home. She has been there ever since. Although Stalin's network of punishment camps have almost disappeared from sight in the harsh climate where the land is covered with snow for six months, the people there are still prisoners. During the Soviet era, engineers, doctors and teachers were persuaded to work in this harsh environment with generous hardship pay bonuses for the duration of their contracts and with guarantees that they would get their houses and jobs back on their return home.

But when the Soviet Union collapsed in 1991 and the rouble went into freefall in 1998, all such guarantees became worthless. I met Vladimir Leteninkov in the main hospital in Magadan in 1999. He is a brain surgeon from the Ukraine. His country is no longer even part of the Russian empire but, like Natasha, he lost everything. He cannot even afford to get a train back to Kiev. His patients pay him in slices of reindeer meat.

But I think the saddest stories of all come from a country that seldom appears in the headlines except for its current distinction for being the poorest country in Europe, Moldova. Like Latvia, Moldova was a former member of the Soviet Union but when the empire collapsed in 1991 the country was wide open to the brutality of the free market. The country barely survives on agriculture and remittances from Moldovans working abroad. For the past twenty-five years, Moldova has been haemorrhaging people.

I go to the village of Scoreni in Moldova, to the west of the capital, Chişinău. It is a typical Moldovan village with one-storey wooden houses, a well in every backyard and an Orthodox church with onion domes that glitter in the sunlight. It is Sunday and I stand at the back of the church and watch as the service draws to an end. The air is thick with incense. The priest is circulating with an icon of the Virgin Mary encased in a heavy gold frame. Old women and young children genuflect and make a sign of the cross as he passes them. It is not unusual for women to be responsible for the spiritual welfare of their community. What is unusual here is that there are no women between the age of sixteen and forty. I talk to the women as they leave the church. Where have they all gone? I ask. 'They go to Italy, Portugal, Turkey and even Moscow,' says one woman. 'I can't tell you how many but for sure they've all gone.' 'There's no work or money here,' explains another. 'All those state enterprises, collective farms and factories that we got in the old days have closed. We now have nothing.' 'She promised to send us money,' says another, crossly, 'and we have heard nothing from her.'

I meet with Yeva, a sixty-year-old woman wearing the long full skirt and flower-patterned headscarves favoured in the region. Sitting at the kitchen table in her cottage, she offers me black tea in a glass and spoonfuls of home-made cherry jam. The tea glasses and the little ceramic dishes with the jam are placed carefully on hand-embroidered doilies. Yeva offers me matching napkins. Old-fashioned, intricate embroidery is what the women of the village do. Unfortunately, it is of little interest to local entrepreneurs. She doesn't have many photos of her daughters, Tanya and Daniela. They don't have cameras or the kind of phones that take pictures and so she can only show me formal school and family group photos which reveal two lively, happy-looking girls in pigtails. 'They were eighteen and twenty-one when they left,' she says.

An agent from the local town came to the village, promising work as waitresses in a smart hotel in Italy for any woman under the age of thirty. 'The language is similar to ours,' the agent, Svetlana, said, 'the girls will soon fit in.' Tanya and Daniela did not hesitate. Like all the school leavers in the area, there was nothing for them at home. The area was rife with rumours of generous remittances being sent back to families in other parts of the country. Yeva, a widow confronting an impoverished old age, encouraged them.

The girls were told to meet at the central bus station in the town. The friendly agent was there to reassure Yeva and other anxious parents and offer comfort as mothers and daughters sobbed into one another's arms as they said goodbye. The bus left and she hasn't seen her daughters since. 'But rumours are circulating the village she says,' choking back her sobs, 'something about kidnapping and bars and much worse besides.' Yeva is now crying so much that she can barely talk. I comfort her as best I can and get up to leave. 'Go and see Ana,' she says, indicating a house on the other side of the church. 'At least she knows which city her daughter is in.'

I walk down the muddy paths that separate the brightly painted wooden houses of Scoreni. The scene looks almost medieval with women filling buckets of water from the wells, geese pecking at their heels and the occasional horse-drawn cart clip-clopping through the village. There may be more men than women in the village; but they don't look well. This could be because few of them have two kidneys intact. Scoreni has two main exports – young women, and the sale of kidneys to rich patients in Istanbul and Israel, for often risible sums.

Ana and her family pull out plastic chairs for us all to sit on under a plum tree in their garden. 'At first we all welcomed the agent when she came to the village,' she explains. 'She seemed a nice enough woman called Tanya. There was no work here for my daughter, Elena, and the agent seemed like a godsend. Tanya said that she had friends in Istanbul who ran hotels and needed smart, hardworking chambermaids and that she knew other families who wanted au pairs.' Tanya drove off with Elena in her car, with her family's blessing.

But Tanya got caught a few weeks after she had left with Elena. In a rare display of curiosity by border police, she was questioned as she left Moldova with her latest batch as to why she had three young girls in the car with brand-new passports. She is now awaiting trial on charges of procuring girls for the bars and broth-els of Istanbul. The case was widely reported, even in Scoreni. But the arrest was too late to save Elena; she is presumed to be in Istanbul.

'How could this happen to us?' asks Ana. 'I trusted that woman with my daughter. That woman took our little girl and sold her. My husband died because of it.' Ana takes out a photo of Elena from her handbag and grabs my hand. 'Take it!' she says. 'Go to Istanbul, I beg you and find my daughter.' She is so insistent, I cannot refuse. I take the photo and try to impress upon her the difficulty of the task. I have been told that there are some fifty to sixty girls leaving Moldova for Istanbul every week. I promise to try but plead with her not to raise her hopes.

I fly to Istanbul with my cameraman Ian O'Reilly. We meet up with Liviu, our Romanian fixer (Moldovan and Romanian are the same language), and start trawling through the bars of the sleazier parts of Istanbul, around Taksim Square, Aksaray and Istiklal Avenue.

The three of us have often worked together before; we once made a film in Romania exposing the illegal sale of babies. We wanted to show how easy it is to buy babies in Romania and we managed to 'buy' seven babies in seven days, always withdrawing before the final handover of money.

As we go from bar to bar, Liviu tries to negotiate his way through the zombie-like pole dancers, and attempts to take the girls aside as they come off stage for a break. He then shows them the photo. The pimps get angry: 'If you want to spend time with a girl,' one yells across the dance floor to Liviu, 'it costs $100 an hour!' No one recognizes the photo. As I look at the girls in their tank tops, their tiny, naked waists and their fishnet stockings, I begin to have misgivings about bothering with the club scene at all. The photo of Elena is of a shy, plump eighteen-year-old, with a mop of brown curly hair and rosy cheeks, a typical country girl.

She is wearing the Moldovan equivalent of a Shetland sweater. I just don't see her fulfilling the role of pole dancer, whatever the coercion. Her homely looks are not for seductive display but her body could always be sold to serve the more basic requirements of the sex trade. I shudder as I imagine her in one of the basement brothels and massage parlours like the one where Natasha Pavlova was found dead.

The next morning, we go to the city's main bus station. There are so many buses coming from the Moldovan capital, Chișinău, every day that there are always huddles of Moldovan drivers standing around talking and chain-smoking. We get our first break. At least one man and a woman recognize the photo of Elena. 'Yes, she was here a month ago, looking for a job,' says the man. 'I saw her running down the street towards the bus station,' says a woman. 'I suppose she had escaped from the bar or brothel or wherever she was being held and wanted to go home. But, of course, she would have had no passport and no money so she couldn't.'

And there the trail runs cold. I go to the Missing Persons Bureau in Istanbul located on the edge of a park behind the Blue Mosque. A neat row of male typists sit hunched on small stools with their typewriters on small tables at the ready in front of them. Everyone has to fill in an official form before entering the building. I complete the form with the typist shouting out the questions in quick succession. 'Name? Date of Birth? Address? Nationality? When was she last seen? And with whom?' 'A known trafficker called Tanya,' I said. When he asked my relationship to the girl, I simply asked him to type 'friend of the family'. He ripped the document from his machine and handed it to me, and sighed wearily: 'I do dozens of these every month for you Moldovans.'

I go into the building and to an office marked 'Duty Officer, Bureau for Missing Persons', and find myself standing alongside anxious families who seemingly represent all fifteen former Soviet republics. The traffickers clearly throw their net wide. When I am called in, I am rewarded with another sigh when I utter the world Moldova. The duty officer reaches for the Moldovan file on the shelf behind him. It is the biggest of them all. 'I am sorry,' he says as he punches holes in my document, slots it in and slams shut the file. 'We have thousands of Moldovans on our records. Your search is hopeless.'

The budget does not, alas, stretch to a return visit to Scoreni for me to be able to give Ana the news personally. Liviu calls her. She is disappointed although, she admits, that she was not holding out much hope. She is strangely reassured that at least there is now a document with her daughter's name and photo in a government office in Istanbul. Liviu is careful not to tell her of all the weary sighs with which the officials meet news of yet another missing Moldovan.

So what happened to the other girls from the village like Yeva's daughters, Tanya and Daniela, who clambered onto the bus, thinking they were headed for jobs as waitresses in Italy?

Once the bus crosses the border into Romania and heads west, the atmosphere abruptly changes. The friendly agent, Svetlana, the one who comforted the weeping mothers, disappears and is replaced by a male trafficker. The bus takes them to the notorious staging house in Belgrade, in Serbia, where the traffickers get the 'first go' on the girls, for their personal sexual gratification and to more easily terrorize the girls into submission. After the girls – many of them virgins – have been raped, the human auction begins. They are told to strip naked and parade in front of the 'buyers' who have journeyed to the house from the brothels of Europe. The buyers are then invited to sample the goods and the girls are raped again. The next day, the buyer will leave with his selected purchases and drive across several borders to the brothels of Sarajevo, Kosovo, Istanbul, Amsterdam, Copenhagen and London. The pimps take their passports and the girls are drugged or threatened into silence as they pass through international frontiers.

I learn all this from the few who manage to escape. These lucky ones are usually sent home by staff working for the UN's International Organization for Migration (IOM), which has a presence in the main centres for sex slavery. The staff at the IOM's shelter in Chişinău allow me to meet some of the girls, shortly after they get off from the plane bringing them home from the Bosnian capital, Sarajevo. They arrive at the shelter clutching plastic bags, with the UN logo stamped on them, in which they carry pathetically few possessions. They seldom have passports but have to be issued with emergency travel documents by the UN. The pimps and bar owners from whom they have fled keep their passports and all the money they ever earned for them.

They sit on the edges of the metal beds in the austere dormitories of the shelters, heads bowed and twisting their fingers nervously. They tell me how they blame themselves for their stupidity, of their eagerness to see something of the world outside their impoverished villages, for their sincere hope that hard work might enable them to send money back home and earn prestige in the eyes of their families and friends and their inclination to trust the agents sent into the villages to find them.

In tears, the girls describe the effort of survival, month after month, year after year, in sordid cubicles in seedy bars and hotels, rarely seeing the light of day. They tell me of the beatings inflicted on them by traffickers, pimps and bar owners and of being locked in their rooms when they are not working. With no contact with home, with their passports seized and no wages paid, there is seldom a chance of escape. Now that they are back in Moldova, will they go back to their villages? Monica, who spent six months in a bar in Sarajevo, is sure her parents will reject her. 'I just couldn't tell them anything. This is the problem. My parents are strict people and I am scared. They simply would not understand how it happened. The agent was so friendly. He took three of us girls and promised us jobs as teachers' assistants in Italy, but we found ourselves in that house in Belgrade . . .' at which point she breaks down and cannot speak any more.

Through no fault of their own, they feel that have failed. In these deeply conservative, rural areas of Romania and Moldova, which the agents target precisely because of their unworldliness, the idea of illicit sex and prostitution, even forced prostitution, is incomprehensible. It just doesn't fit into the world of incense-filled churches, wooden cottages, home-made doilies and a life so isolated that when a smart stranger called Svetlana comes to the village and offers the answer to your problems, you are flattered and you believe her. The girls are too ashamed to go home.

A woman called Marianna works alongside the UN's IOM in Moldova and welcomes many of the returned girls into the huge shelter in Chişinău that she runs for street children and the victims of sex traffickers. She tries to recreate a family atmosphere at the home. The children and young adults are all expected to eat together and the older ones read to the younger ones before they go to sleep. It is therapy for them all and, from the constant sound of chatter and laughter, it appears to work.

She arranges for lessons in dressmaking skills and cooking for the girls returned from Sarajevo, mainly just to give them a purpose and to keep them busy. Moldova is being flooded with cheap fabrics from China decorated with American logos and there is unlikely to be much demand for the kind of dresses that the girls painstakingly produce on ancient sewing machines. They live a prison-like existence. They are warned not to go out alone. Men are seen loitering on the streets around the safe refuge. They are waiting for the girls to get so bored and desperate that they will escape their secure accommodation. And then the traffickers and pimps are waiting to pick them up again.

Before I leave, I ask Marianna to give me an estimate of the numbers for Moldova. Flicking open huge files, she says they have seen 500 repatriations over the last three years. They believe that about 7,500 girls and women left their villages during that same period so she assumes that 7,000 are irretrievably lost.

'The girls we lose are between twelve and forty years old. They take young girls as young as twelve and destroy them. So you see, they are also destroying our womanhood and even the future of our country.' Marianna's phone rings. Another flight has landed from Sarajevo and there will be more broken lives to attempt to put together again.

But why were so many flights from Sarajevo?

7

BOYS WILL BE BOYS

Where There Are UN Peacekeepers There Are Traffickers

The new arrivals are sitting in the communal room in the shelter in Chişinău, Moldova. They look dazed, tired and very frightened. The woman from the International Organization for Migration explains who I am and how publicity about their abusers could help protect girls in the future. Most shrug their shoulders and leave the room and I can hardly blame them. They have learned to trust no one and are too consumed by their own agony to be able to think ahead about someone else's future. Only Monica stays to talk to me.

Monica comes from Chişinău, and is better educated and more sophisticated than the girls the traffickers recruit from remote villages. She now realizes that when her boyfriend said that he had found them both jobs in Italy, he had in fact sold her to a pimp. After travelling for three days, she found herself in the Vila Bar in Sarajevo in Bosnia. She was appalled by the seediness of the bar, the lap dancers and that a woman had the cheek to tell her that she had to get undressed and join them.

'At first I thought it was a joke,' Monica says. 'I told her, I'm not staying here. Then she said I had to stay or the owner of the bar would beat me. She told me that he had my passport and that I couldn't leave. She said I had to have sex with any man who asked for me. The next day, I met the owner of the bar who told me that the journey to Sarajevo had cost a lot of money and that I had to pay back the men who had brought me there. I had to go with up to eight men a night.'

But what Monica said next was the most startling: 'A lot of the men were United Nations' peacekeepers – soldiers and policemen who had come there to help people. I pleaded with them, especially the young ones, to help me. None did.' After the Bosnian War, thousands of peacekeepers arrived, allegedly to help rebuild the country, support civic and democratic institutions and restore law and order. Ask any local and they will tell you that, as soon as the peacekeepers arrived with their fat, monthly pay cheques, the sex traffickers and their victims soon followed.

After six months of hell, Monica seized an opportunity. 'It had been a busy night and the pimp was drunk and left the door unlocked. I crawled down the corridor and through a window onto a fire escape. I ran, and ran down the road until I found a woman in the street. I screamed and cried but she could not understand me. She took me to the police and they took me to a safe place.'

Monica was taken in by the remarkable Célhia de Lavarène, five foot tall and elegantly dressed with beautifully coiffured blonde hair. She speaks English with a beguiling Parisian accent and isn't afraid of anyone. With her team of mainly British and Irish policemen, Célhia is the founder of the charity STOP. She has been given a mandate by the head of the UN Mission in Sarajevo to tackle the sex-trafficking trade in Bosnia and has personally been responsible for shutting down dozens of bars and rescuing hundreds of girls in Sarajevo.

We meet during one of the weekly briefings with her hand-picked team of police officers. They exchange notes on recent

December 2011: Sue in London.

Late 1970s: Prince Charles with Sue on a royal visit to the former ITN newsroom on Wells Street, London

July 1995: Sue with His Holiness the Dalai Lama at Alexandra Palace in London. Sue was a big supporter of the Tibetan cause and did a lot to raise money and awareness. The Dalai Lama called her 'London Sue'.

December 2011: Sue with the Emmy Award she won in 2011 for her film for BBC World, *Inside the North Korean Bubble*.

August 2013: Imam and President of the Supreme Islamic Council in Gambia, Muhammed Alhaijie Lamin Touray laughing as he discussed with Sue the many benefits of female genital mutilation for women.

March 2009: The Grandmothers of the Plaza de Mayo march to Argentina's presidential residence in Buenos Aires, in memory of their children and grandchildren, who disappeared during the country's dictatorship era of the 1970s and '80s.

February 2013: Some of the Grandmothers of the Plaza de Mayo look through photographs of their children and grandchildren with Sue, Buenos Aires.

September 2014: Sue with Mary Merritt, a former laundry worker at Magdalene High Park Laundry in Dublin, visiting the mass grave where her co-workers were buried.

February 2013: A Magdalene laundry ledger. The four religious orders are refusing to contribute to the Irish government's compensation scheme for former laundry workers.

March 2012: Sue in a shop in Jeddah trying on the abaya she wore in order to work in Saudi Arabia.

September 2013: Saudi Arabia is the only country in the world where women are not allowed to drive. In 2013, fourteen women were detained by authorities as activists published videos on YouTube showing women driving in defiance of the ban.

May 2012: Egyptian activist Samira Ibrahim stands next to a mural depicting her in Cairo. Samira was forced to undergo a 'virginity test' while in detention by the military after protests in Cairo. She later filed an unsuccessful lawsuit against a military doctor.

January 2015: Shaima al-Sabbagh is carried away after being shot during clashes with police during a left-wing protest in central Cairo, Egypt, on the eve of the anniversary of the 2011 uprising against Hosni Mubarak. Al-Sabbagh later died of her injuries.

August 2001: Scoreni, Moldova: a mother asking me to find her daughter in Istanbul. She was taken away by an agent promising her work in a bar or hotel but it's likely she was tricked into becoming a victim of sex trafficking.

December 2011: An Egyptian woman holds up a picture of 'Blue Bra Woman' at a protest in downtown Cairo to denounce the military's attacks on women and call for an end to violence against protestors. The woman in the image, who had been stripped and beaten by riot police a week earlier, quickly became a visual symbol of abuse of power by the Egyptian military.

September 2010: Kathy Bolkovac, an American with over a decade's experience with the US police force, was hounded out of her job as a UN International Police Force monitor after her attempts to expose sex trafficking in post-war Bosnia. A film, *The Whistleblower*, starring Rachel Weisz, was based on her story and premiered in 2010.

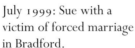

July 1999: Sue with a victim of forced marriage in Bradford.

December 2009: From left to right, Banaz Mahmod, Samaira Nazir, Surjit Athwal and Heshu Yones, all victims of so-called 'honour killings'.

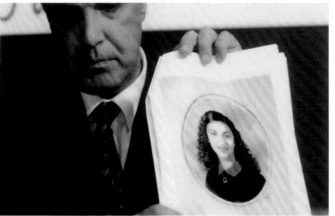

September 2003: Commander Andy Baker holds a picture of Heshu Yones, at a police press conference. Heshu's father, Abdullah Yones, was jailed for life after murdering his 16-year-old daughter because she had become too westernized.

December 2015: Protestors are joined by the mother of Jyoti Singh in a march to mark the third anniversary of the brutal gang rape and subsequent death of the young woman, who would later become known as 'Nirbhaya' ('India's Daughter'). Jyoti's attackers were convicted and sentenced to death, but are still awaiting execution.

December 2012: Demonstrators hold placards demanding stricter laws against rape in Hyderabad, India.

April 2009: 'Mamma Masika' Katsuva survived a brutal gang rape in 1999, but refused to be bowed by her experience and now helps other women in the Democratic Republic of Congo who have been abused. Here, she tends to a woman in labour who was abducted by soldiers and held as a sex slave for five months, before escaping while pregnant as a result of her rape.

March 2009: With her baby on her back, a rape survivor plants corn on Masika's land, a combination half-way house and vegetable farm just outside Goma. It is a sanctuary for violated women, providing support to them while they get back on their feet and build new lives for themselves and their children.

April 1991: Sue with her two children, Sarah and George Morris, on holiday in Cyprus.

October 2005: Sue with her husband Nick in Palma, Mallorca. They lived in Fornalutx, Mallorca, from 2003.

events. John, a British policeman in his early thirties, shares a story he's heard from one of his contacts in the club underworld. It's of a girl who, for two days, refused to go with any of the clients. 'And so the club owner decided to make an example of her,' John relates. 'She was put in a room and stripped and people actually paid to watch her being raped by the bar owner and his favourite clients.' Terry, a young Irish policeman who has just joined the team, looks shocked. 'They are not people,' he says. 'They have no feelings, nothing. They treat the girls as if they are just merchandise.'

The team agree to take me 'brothel busting' with them. Célhia instructs me and my team to arrive at her office the next day at 4.00 a.m. We leave in a convoy and, about an hour before dawn, draw up in a fleet of police cars and vans at the brothel, a nondescript, suburban house on the road leading west out of Sarajevo. The STOP team beat on the door. We can hear shouting and chairs scraping on the wooden floor from inside. 'The men inside are yelling at the girls to run out the back,' says the police translator. 'Get round the back!' Célhia screams at one of the policemen and to the others, 'Break down the fucking door!'

We burst in. The pimps have already fled out of the back door, leaving cigarettes butts, half-drunk cups of coffee and piles of money on a table in the front room. Célhia races up the stairs and we follow to find eight girls in their sordid cubicles, dazed and too exhausted by the previous night's work to obey the pimps' instructions to run. Pale and shaking with fear, they are bundled into minibuses and driven to the local police station where Célhia attempts to assure them that they are among friends and they are now safe. It is a difficult job – the girls have long since learned not to trust anyone, especially men in uniform. Célhia is angry over the behaviour and hypocrisy of United Nations employees. 'Wherever there are UN peacekeeping forces, the human traffickers follow,' she says. 'It is the greatest scandal in the United

Nations today and yet those in charge of the men just shrug their shoulders turn a blind eye.'

Célhia and I hit it off straightaway and have remained friends ever since. After hearing the stories from the girls in Moldova, I have persuaded the editor of the *Correspondent* documentary series at the BBC to let me investigate the involvement of United Nations peacekeepers and soldiers in the business of sex trafficking. We call the film *Boys Will Be Boys*, which is how their behaviour is all too often justified. The girls Célhia has rescued in the raid come from Moldova, Romania and the Ukraine. They will stay in the safe house in Sarajevo until the UN's IOM team can arrange transport for them back to their countries. Occasionally, a girl will ask to testify against her abusers. Monica was brave enough to refuse transport home in order to stay in Sarajevo and expose the men who pimped her and to identify her abusers.

'I had to have sex with any man who asked for me. I had to have sex at least three times a night, sometimes seven or eight times in one night. The majority were Americans. They like to have fun and you can't imagine how they act. They drink a lot, they speak loudly they make fun of the girls and treat us like rubbish. I wanted to stop them behaving this way. They shouldn't do this. It is not fair, not only for me but for all the girls in this situation.'

Her clients, she explains, were members of the UN peacekeeping forces, the SFOR or Stabilisation Force, and the UN-appointed IPTF, the International Police Task Force, policemen who had been recruited from all over the world to help the process of nation-building in Bosnia in the late 1990s. It was these men, tasked with rebuilding a broken country, who refused to help Monica when she pleaded for help. 'They said that they didn't want to get into trouble because they weren't allowed to go to these types of bars. They said that if they helped me, they might lose their jobs. I had to get out of the situation by myself.'

At the police station, Monica identified four members of the International Police Task Force and four members of the peace-keeping forces as her abusers. She said that she was prepared to go to court and testify but she never got the chance. 'That's because I was sent home. I don't know the reason. I don't know why. I wasn't in a hurry. I told them that once I had started, I wanted to do whatever I could to stop this happening to other girls. I am very angry. I had always believed in justice but there was none. Someone should do something but I don't think anyone cares. They are covering up.'

It turned out that the cover-up had been going on for years and anyone who tried to expose it was made to suffer. I met Kathy Bolkovac after she had been hounded out of her job in Bosnia. Bolkovac is a blonde, statuesque police officer who had had ten years' experience in the police force in America when she applied for a job in Bosnia in 1999.

'I was ready for a change. I felt that I was at a time of my life when I was ready for something more. I was approaching forty and felt that I didn't want to remain an officer on patrol, doing simple investigations. Furthermore I had always wanted to see the area of the world where my grandfather, my father's family was from, which was Croatia, and it seemed a good way to do all these things at once.'

She sent off her application to the American company DynCorp, a private military contractor that had recently won the contract for Bosnia to run pretty much everything from managing warehouses and cafeterias to recruiting American policemen. Within a week, she learned that she was hired for the $85,000-a-year job. There was no interview, she simply had to turn up for a week's training in Fort Worth, Texas. 'The recruits were either very young, I could hardly believe that they had the eight years' experience stipulated on the application form. Or they were retir-ees. Most had never seen a pay cheque for more than $20,000 a year in their lives.' But her excitement at the prospect of going to Bosnia persuaded her to ignore any misgivings and she flew with the forty-two new recruits to Sarajevo.

To begin with, she did well. She reaches for a photo album and shows me pictures of herself, as part of a line-up in which she received a medal from the UN Head of Mission, a French Canadian called Jacques Klein. Her six-month contract was extended three times and she was decorated and promoted. 'My particular job description when I was made manager of the gender office was to oversee all investigations involving gender issues, anything from trafficking to sexual assaults to domestic violence cases throughout the country.' Increasingly, her job was dominated by the thriving sex industry. She was appalled to learn about the sex-trafficking operations and assumed that her colleagues would share her outrage. On reflection, she realized that she was hopelessly naive. 'I would drive by on patrol and see many UN vehicles parked outside the bars. At first I thought, OK, they're having a drink and checking up on things.'

It was one woman in particular, Viktorija from Moldova, who opened Kathy's eyes as to who were the true users and abusers. Kathy was in her office one morning when one of the local police cars, a white Yugo squad car, pulled up at her office. A young girl 'barely older than a teenager' stumbled out of the car wearing a short skirt and tank top with her hair matted with leaves and mud. The accompanying policeman explained that she had been found wandering, alone and incoherent, along the banks of the River Bosna.

Bolkovac ushered her into her office along with her language assistant. The girl did not speak Bosnian. Bolkovac was surprised. There were few enough jobs available in the war-torn country and, as far as she knew, no immigrants came to Bosnia looking for work. While they struggled to understand her, Bolkovac noted that she had red marks and bruising on her neck. Eventually, they established that her name was Viktorija and that she was from Moldova.

Apart from 'Viktorija' and 'Moldova' the only other word she kept repeating was 'Florida'. At first, Bolkovac could not make sense of it and then she remembered a desolate-looking nightclub called Florida next to one of the best restaurants, renowned for the favourite local dish of stuffed cabbage, perched on a riverbank on the outskirts of Sarajevo. 'I would always see UN trucks in the Florida lot,' Bolkovac recalled, 'I assumed it was just overflow parking from the restaurant.' As soon as Bolkovac showed that she understood about the Florida, Viktorija grabbed her hand and stared at her, pleadingly.

Bolkovac organized for Viktorija to be given a hotel room with a policeman assigned to stand outside the door. This was before Célhia de Lavarène had arrived on the scene and there were no shelters for trafficking victims. She drove to the Florida with a local police officer and translator. As they walked in, they found the bar completely empty – 'no servers, no bartenders, no patrons. A few half glasses of beer lingered at the bar, a smoky, sweaty odour hung in the air. Nightclubs with nothing to hide do not clear out this hastily, and it was apparent that someone had alerted them to our arrival.'

Bolkovac then found what looked like a metal gun box filled with US dollars. 'Why would American dollars be exchanging hands here, in this depleted place fortressed by forest and mountains and on the way to nowhere?' she asked herself. And then, as if in answer to her question, she found a bundle of passports belonging to girls as young as fifteen, from Ukraine, Romania and Moldova – including Viktorija's passport. Bolkovac needed air and she walked out of the building, trying to assess the significance of her findings. She noted a fire escape going up the side of the building to a wooden door. She called Goran, the local Bosnian policeman, to accompany her up the steps. He tried the door. It was locked. 'No one there,' Goran concluded. Using her military-style boots, Bolkovac kicked the door in. 'There, on the other side, in a stuffy, attic-like room, huddled seven wide-eyed young women, their terrified faces all too familiar.'

There were two stained mattresses on the floor, which the girls now sat on, shaking with fear. Their clothes were stuffed in plastic bags and there were condoms hanging over the waste bin. 'We are going to take you to someplace safe,' Bolkovac told them through the translator. 'Are there any other girls hidden here? Please tell me, so that we can help them too.' A blonde, blue-eyed girl pointed out of the window, to the gurgling stream below, and in a shaky voice she said, 'We can't say. We don't want to end up floating.'

Bolkovac's interviews with these young girls in Sarajevo mirrors the stories I had learned from survivors in Chişinău in Moldova. 'They were so young, so vulnerable, girls who had willingly left home to find jobs in the West,' Bolkovac recalls. 'They had been intimidated by their traffickers and pimps who forced them into a life of prostitution. You don't just take the girl off the street and put her in a brothel and tell her to start working. You basically rape, abuse and mortify these girls through horrible, traumatic acts in order to get them to do that.'

The problem was that the girls from the Florida were so traumatized that, although they vaguely described men in uniform among their clients, they refused to testify against their abusers and pimps for fear of reprisals. Within days they were repatriated back to their home countries by the IOM. Bolkovac could not forget the metal gun box with the stash of US dollars. The only place to receive US dollars in Bosnia was on American military bases. There was something very wrong here.

Bolkovac had better luck on a raid a few months later, on the La Vila bar in the town of Doboj, where Monica had worked. The women who were found there were prepared to talk. 'These women were implying that international police were involved in visiting the bar for sexual services. The women were describing American men in uniform. They were describing tattoos. They were describing many things that would allow for identification. As a police officer, we would be able to identify these people and these women were prepared to testify.'

Kathy came up with what she thought was a clever way of helping the investigation process. She sent her boss, the commander of the American contingent, an email in which she suggested that the girls identify the men from the photographic IDs which every police officer in Bosnia had to wear. The next day, every member of the American contingent got an email warning of Bolkovac's plan. 'I really felt that he had blown the whole investigation. If indeed there were Americans involved, then this gave them the opportunity to make up a story about their whereabouts and to cover for one another.'

But, on further reflection, she was prepared to believe that perhaps there was some genuine confusion. She thought it might be helpful to spell out the details of sex trafficking to men who might not understand. She wrote an email to everyone in the American contingent explaining:

Prostitute – someone who willingly sells their bodies for sexual services with actual material or financial gain who is free to say 'no' whenever they want. **Trafficker** – someone who buys, sells, transports, enslaves, entices, promises, kidnaps, receives, assaults or coerces a person for material gain. **Trafficking victim** – most of the women, children, some who you are referring to as prostitutes.

Clientele – some local people, SFOR, IPTF, local police and international humanitarian employees in Bosnia Herzegovinia.

Bolkovac concluded her email by explaining what motivated her to come to Bosnia. She admitted that the money was an incentive but that she never forgot her main mission of serving and protecting people. 'We will leave the mission with money in our pockets,' she wrote, 'medals on our chests and bars on our collars that we would never have earned in our home countries, departments or military. Some of us may have had the opportunity of assisting one or two "prostitutes" with getting out of a very dangerous and desperate situation. We may get accused of THINKING WITH OUR HEARTS INSTEAD OF OUR HEADS, but at least we were able to THINK.'

The next day, Bolkovac was accused of being 'psychologically burned out' and she was moved from her job. She was later fired for allegedly falsifying a time sheet, which she denied entirely. She felt threatened even as she packed up her things. 'There were cars parked outside my house, night and day,' she remembers. 'Some fellow officers even told me that they feared for my life.' Kathy Bolkovac had left Sarajevo by the time I arrived with a film crew. But I found the officials left behind, especially the women who were unnerved and angry about the incident. I ask Madeleine Rees, the head of the UN Human Rights Commission whether it was accurate to describe Bolkovac as psychologically burned out? 'Based on what?' she replies. 'There was never any sort of evaluation. It was decided without any consultation with her or with anybody who was in an appropriate position to make that sort of estimate.'

So, I ask, why was she prevented from doing her job? 'I think clearly because she was the front-line person interviewing trafficked women. She therefore interviewed about every single woman who was trafficked and who went through the IOM programme and she was very, very good at her job. And she was finding out from these trafficked women the extent of IPTF involvement.' Bolkovac filed a claim against DynCorp Aerospace, the British subsidiary of the company that had hired her in the United States, for unfair dismissal. In 2002, the tribunal sitting in Southampton on the south coast of England, found unanimously in her favour. Some of the police officers she named were dismissed but, because of the immunity from prosecution they enjoyed while serving in Bosnia, none of them were prosecuted or punished.[1]

I caught up with Bolkovac ten years after I first met her when she was in London promoting the book that she wrote on her experiences in Bosnia, called *The Whistleblower*. Her story was also made into a film of the same name with Rachel Weisz playing the lead role. I was asked by Amnesty International to interview Kathy in the theatre of their smart new offices in Clerkenwell, after which she took questions. She was asked whether she is still angry about what happened? 'The anger comes and goes,' she said. 'Sure, I won my lawsuit, but I never got any real answers.'

Another questioner asked her about the attitude of the men she found herself working with. Bolkovac answers that there existed a 'Come on, this is war' attitude among senior officers. She described the sexual harassment that the women police officers suffered from their male colleagues and sums this up as all part of the 'boys will be boys' atmosphere that prevailed. She despaired at the utter contempt the men showed for the women they abused: 'That these women are whores of war, they're just prostitutes, they want it.'

I go back to my notes of that early interview with Bolkovac, before she won her court case, where she tells me, ruefully, 'There are times when I feel it really wasn't worth anything. That I ruined my career. I ruined my credibility. I gave up a very good life in America to go to Bosnia and work internationally. But then there are times when I realize that sometimes it does take just one person to make a difference, to get the ball rolling, to keep pushing.'

No one can doubt that Bolkovac is bold and brave and deserves acclaim for what she did. But did she make a difference? Sadly, evidence suggests a sex industry involving vulnerable young women is always likely to follow hard on the heels of a large, male-dominated, international peacekeeping force. But given the now-proven inevitability of the phenomenon, how do we account for the cover-up at the very top of the command structure?

I travelled to Romania to meet with another of the girls who were rescued from the La Vila bar. We meet in a small village close to the town of Braşov in western Romania. Unusually, her parents welcomed her back home after her ordeal and I am able to interview Alina in the shady orchard beside her home, under the apple and pear trees. 'We had to make 200 DM [Deutsche Marks] a night. If we refused, the boss used to threaten us, saying he had to get his money's worth out of us and that he couldn't afford to house and feed us unless we worked. If we continued to refuse, we were beaten up. If we didn't talk nicely to the clients, we were beaten up.'

Alina was lucky. After only two weeks working in the bar, one of her clients took pity on her, an Argentinian working for the IPTF. He paid 3,000 DMs to the bar owners to let her go; like a slave, he bought her freedom and helped her get back to Romania. She planned to forget about Bosnia and rebuild her life. To her astonishment, a few months later, the head of the UN Mission in Sarajevo, Jacques Paul Klein himself, came to Bucharest on business and sent a car to bring her to the city to meet him.

She told me that Klein showed her a photograph album with pictures of twenty IPTF officers. I asked her how many she could identify as former clients at the bar? 'It was only three that I could not identify out of the twenty he showed me. I identified them but nothing happened to them from what I know. He was only interested in one person, the man who helped me. They wanted to get the evidence against him for frequenting such bars so that they could repatriate him. They were after the one person who offered to help me.'

I went back to the UN Mission headquarters in Sarajevo and asked Jacques Paul Klein about this extraordinary encounter. Why did he, the Head of Mission, the UN Secretary General's Special Representative in Bosnia, take time out to interview a victim of trafficking in Romania? 'I am a former criminal investigator,' he explains. 'I was a special agent, I had credentials and a badge. I've done more criminal homicide, fraud and other investigations than most of my IPTF people. So the fact that I did this in Romania in the context of doing something else, (there is) nothing illogical or illegal about that.'

So, what did he get out of the interview? 'She identified, one person, I believe. That individual was disciplined and sent home.' I told Klein that I had spoken to Alina two days earlier and she said she identified seventeen policemen. 'That's a direct and outright lie. I have a document. She did not identify seventeen people to me. That is an absolute falsehood.' Are you protecting these people? I ask. 'Come on now, be serious,' he replies with indignation, 'I thought you were a serious journalist.' I asked Klein's office for the document which he implied confirmed his recollection of the interview. Serious journalist or not, they did not give it to me.

It is the word of a victim of sex-trafficking from a small village in Romania against one of the most senior officials in the United Nations. We shall, no doubt, never know the truth. I asked the head of the Human Rights office at the UN Mission whether she was surprised at Jacques Paul Klein's intervention at that level of investigation. 'I think if you asked, he would say that it was because he wanted to find out for himself the truth of the involvement of IPTF in trafficking,' said Madeleine Rees. 'Nonetheless,' she added, 'if you have that seniority and that position, you don't go and interview someone who has been trafficked because someone who has been trafficked needs support, she needs counselling and she is not exactly in the shape to give evidence in that sort of manner. It was an extraordinary and entirely inappropriate thing to do.'

In Klein's defence he did send dozens of IPTF police officers home because of their involvement in the sex-trafficking business in Bosnia. But that is all he could do. He explained the limits of his powers to me during our interview in Sarajevo: 'My policy here is zero tolerance, they're sent home. Any time you or anyone else can walk into my office and give me the name of any officer anywhere using the service of a prostitute and he will be fired immediately and sent home. The problem is that your country and no other country will waive diplomatic immunity. It's just that simple so nothing is going to happen. No matter how much you and I conjure about what should be done, it will not happen.'

As if emphasizing the relevance of the infamous email that Bolkovac sent and that got her sacked, Klein uses the word prostitute here. Was Bolkovac right? Did he, along with most of the men serving under him, simply not understand the distinction between a woman who can say 'no' and a victim of trafficking?

Bolkovac left Bosnia and Klein appointed Célhia de Lavarène and her STOP team to tackle the problem and go brothel-busting. They were instrumental in closing over a hundred brothels and the team repatriated 300 girls.[2] Nonetheless, Madeleine Rees dismisses much of this activity as mere show, for public consumption, dramatic, headline-making activity to try to suggest something is being done by the UN to tackle the problem. But, she says, the situation is more complex and, more importantly, market driven.

The traffickers aren't stupid. They don't sit around waiting for brothel raids. No, of course not. There is too much money at stake. They are still going to continue forcing these women into prostitution but in different circumstances where they are not going to be so easily prosecuted. Instead of having women in bars, now you've got mobile phone numbers and women being delivered to apartments, to a hotel or to restaurants. They are not seen as night clubs or bars but there are now restaurants where you find there are rooms upstairs where you can buy a woman and take her upstairs.

STOP may have raided hundreds of bars and clubs but there were few prosecutions of bar owners as a result. Proper disciplinary procedures against international peacekeepers did not take place in Bosnia,[3] nor in the next destination where they were called upon to help.

From Sarajevo, I go to Kosovo where the war broke out six years after the Bosnian War. In the capital, Pristina, every second car belongs to an international agency. The locals call the red and white cars belonging to the international police force 'Coca-Cola cars'. At its height, there were 50,000 international peacekeepers in the country.[4] The Americans inhabit a formidable base, called Bondsteel, complete with cinemas, pizza and hamburger outlets to help comfort the men who are allegedly confined to barracks during their leisure time. Nonetheless, there is an onsite clinic that offers treatment for STDs (sexually transmitted diseases). I ask the doctor on duty whether the incidence rate of STDs in Bondsteel is high? 'We do have cases,' he replies. 'Which have been contracted here, while the men have been based here?' 'Yes, ma'am,' he says.

I leave Bondsteel and drive around the city. There are many more bars here in 2002 than I remember when I first came here ten years earlier during the war. It is not very original for a journalist to seek information from a taxi driver but they are, nonetheless, often a good source. As I sit in the back of his cab, I ask Bashkim which came first, the soldiers or the bars? 'The bars started up after the troops came.' And do you take soldiers to them? 'About every second night,' he replies. 'Sometimes they are in uniform and sometimes they change their clothes in my car – from military to civilian. People around here don't like it and think it is a bad example for our young people but soldiers will be soldiers and they won't stay put if there's a night club outside the barracks.'

Boys will be boys, again. When the peacekeepers first arrived in Kosovo, they were welcomed for providing much-needed protection for the local Albanian community against attacks by the ruling Serbs. But now locals are wondering whether they don't need protecting from their protectors. Already, the city of Pristina has all the trappings of a well-worn sex-trafficking industry with the clubs, massage parlours and secret houses with girls imprisoned in attic rooms.

Concerned NGOs help the girls who flee from such places and set up shelters where they can find refuge. In one of these shelters, I meet a fourteen-year-old girl. At first glance Luljeta looks like any other teenager, dressed in jeans, trainers and a Minnie Mouse sweatshirt. She is sitting at a table in the kitchen beside a middle-aged woman who is encouraging her to draw. Luljeta is frowning in concentration as she chooses from an array of coloured pencils. I look at her pictures. The first shows a little girl beside a car, then a naked little girl and the third shows the same girl, scarcely visible, with men beside her and on top of her. 'They raped me, all the time,' she says.

Her carer and therapist Svedie believes in drawing as part of the healing process and asks Luljeta to tell me her story. It was a year ago, when she was thirteen, she says: 'I was walking down the street with a friend on my way to school. A woman stopped me and asked if I want to come and work in a bar and make some money. I said no but she forced me to go with her. She took me by car through checkpoints with soldiers and then into a house where the soldiers were – she threw me inside. I told them I didn't want to but they forced me. They beat me. I told the woman that I didn't want to and she beat me as well.'

Luljeta tells me that she knew that they were foreigners by the way they spoke and because she saw them arrive in foreign cars. What kind of cars, I ask her? 'Red and white cars,' she says. Svedie gently encourages Luljeta to get on with her drawing and leads me into another room, out of the child's hearing. She tells me that several of the members of the international peacekeeping and police forces who have raped young girls in Kosovo have been sent home. But are any of them punished? I ask. 'No, they have their immunity. You cannot arrest any international soldier or policeman here because they have their immunity, an immunity for the internationals. Whatever happens, even if they rape a minor, even if they kill!'

No wonder the women who dare fight back despair. Kathy Bolkovac loved being a policeman but she never got another chance after her court case and the notoriety produced by her book and the film. 'It is a small community,' she says 'and I am infamous.' These days she has a desk job for an international auction company. 'What can I say? I did the best I could. I worked hard and can only pray that one day things will change.' But she is not hopeful.

Célhia de Lavarène and her STOP team continued working in the Balkans, first in Bosnia and then Kosovo for two years. They raided and closed down hundreds of bars and clubs and helped many young women with counselling, repatriation and rehabilitation. From the Balkans, she was employed to do the same when the UN employees moved to Liberia and women were being trafficked from Asia, North Africa and, as in the Balkans, from the poorest countries of eastern Europe to meet the appetites of the peacekeepers.

One of her first jobs in Liberia was to rescue thirty girls from eastern Europe who had been brought to Liberia for foreigners who wanted prostitutes but refused to sleep with African women. They asked for white flesh. Even in Liberia, she was horrified to discover the international ramifications of the trade. While UN peacekeepers were demanding the import of white girls from Romania and Moldova, '[w]e have noticed trafficking from Liberia to London because I had someone in London calling me and explaining to me that Liberian girls were trafficked,' says Célhia.[5]

I stay in touch with Célhia and we meet up again some twelve years after we went 'brothel-busting' together in Sarajevo. Over lunch in a restaurant in Spain, she tells me that the situation in Liberia is almost identical to what we both saw in the Balkans. 'The girls have their passports confiscated, they are locked in rooms, raped, drugged, beaten and forced into prostitution and it is the same old client base – the so-called international peacekeepers.'

Her eyes well up with tears as she describes a fourteen-year-old girl from Sierra Leone who was kidnapped while walking back from school one day and sold as a sex slave to a club in Freetown, Liberia. She was able to rescue the girl and send her home. She got to know the girl well during her stay in STOP's shelter. It was, she says, one of the most heartbreaking cases she has ever come across. But her mission in Liberia is coming to an end. 'I am not going to claim that we have been successful,' she says. 'The trafficking business may be on hold but, as soon as I leave, I fear that the traffickers will know I have gone.' Célhia de Lavarène has gone on to work with UN missions in Cambodia and East Timor. 'There will always be work for us,' she says sadly.

8

FORCED MARRIAGE

From Kashmir to Bradford

I was excited because whenever we went back to Pakistan for the summer holidays, Mum would buy a new salwar kameez and sandals for me, my younger sister and two brothers. All my uncles would be at Islamabad airport to meet us. We would spend time in the town of Mirpur and then at a farm owned by an uncle and aunt. They had a son of about twenty years old; he was skinny, tall, had a hunchback and was very ugly. His face was packed with pimples, his eyes were green and he looked wicked and scary. He always used to talk to me when there was no one else around. I used to feel very scared, but I tried to be pleasant because I was a guest and he was a cousin. I was fifteen and planned to finish school and go on to university. He used to say that we'd be getting married soon, but I didn't take it seriously because everyone said he was a bit soft in the head. He is now my husband.

Nazish is in hiding in Islamabad. Sitting on a sofa with the curtains drawn against inquisitive neighbours, she is beautiful, painfully thin and calms her nerves by chain-smoking. In her memory, her childhood years are filled with the irreconcilable culture clashes

THE WAR ON WOMEN

that must dominate the lives of so many young Pakistanis in the UK. 'At home, it was all discipline and respect for the elders and very male dominated. I was even told I must respect the word of my brothers. I couldn't understand why my friends were allowed to go shopping on Saturdays. I wasn't. I had to go with my mum and brother. It was so embarrassing bumping into a friend or a boy from school.'

She was expected to wear a headscarf and a voluminous scarf. 'Every morning, I would dump my scarf in the bin at the back of the house and take out my make-up and my file which I covered with pictures of my favourite pop stars and actors. I just wanted to be like the other kids.' She did her GCSEs and was working on her A levels. 'Everything was OK until one day there was a telephone call and a guy was asking for me. My parents would always listen in to all my phone calls with friends and they were convinced I was seeing the boy.' To discipline her, her parents took her to Pakistan supposedly to attend a cousin's wedding. It was a trap; Nazish was being forced to marry.

'During the ceremony, my mother was gripping one arm and my grandmother the other. They were hurting me and telling me that unless I went through with it my grandfather, who has a weak heart, would die. He would die of the shame, they told me.' The groom was the cousin who had looked 'wicked and scary' to her as a child. He spoke no English and was illiterate. 'He would skip work and watch pornographic films with friends all day. He would come back and force me down and tell me he wanted me to do the things he had been watching. It wasn't love; it was rape. I would be clutching the sides of the mattress, waiting for it to end. Every time he went with me, it was rape.'

Her mother-in-law was as bad. 'She was determined that her smart daughter-in-law from the UK would do all the work. It was a small farm with buffaloes. I had to look after the buffaloes. I had never even seen a buffalo before! I had to clean the house, do the washing-up, wash the clothes, sweep the yard, clean the animals' shit and then cook lunch. I had to cook in pots on open fires. I had never done anything like that. I didn't even know how to light a fire and I was burning myself all the time and my mother-in-law would yell at me.'

Nazish starts crying as she remembers the day her father visited.

It was about a year after the wedding and I was five months pregnant. He had flown in from Bradford. He came into the backyard and saw me there with burns all over my hands and arms and tending to the buffaloes. I was in a terrible state, I hadn't had a bath and my clothes were dirty rags. I would go for days without washing. I wouldn't comb my hair or brush my teeth in the hope that my husband wouldn't come close to me. My father looked so shocked and I gave him a look as if to say, 'Remember me? I am the one who dreamed of becoming a doctor?' But his shock did not last long. After all, this is all about family and honour and fulfilling his side of the bargain.

A year after her son was born, Nazish managed to flee rural Mirpur and escape to Islamabad, where fortunately she found a job as a nanny and English tutor to a wealthy family. She and her son lived quietly in the staff quarters of the family's guarded compound.

After interviewing Nazish in Islamabad, I drive two hours south-east to Mirpur, part of Pakistan-governed Kashmir, with cameraman Ian O'Reilly, and Razia Sodagar from Bradford. We are making a film for *Newsnight* on forced marriage and Razia, an activist and campaigner against forced marriage is helping us. We have been in town for a couple of days and are conspicuous by our whiteness, our camera gear and the questions we are asking local police and journalists about the hundreds of British girls who are brought to Mirpur every year, held against their will and forced to marry men they have often never met and have little in common with.[1] The word is getting around, hence the note written on pink paper waiting at reception at the Jabeer Hotel in Mirpur. It is addressed 'to the BBC staying in Mirpur' and reads quite simply: 'I want help. Please come tomorrow and I shall try and be alone, Koheema' followed by a local address.

From our hotel balcony, we have a good view of the high street while we stand and discuss our reaction to the note. Mirpur is a man's world in every sense of the word. There is not a woman in sight on the street below; they are kept behind closed doors. Camels, goats and gleaming, new SUVs are driven down the street past smart-looking banks promising 'swift foreign money transfers' and there are numerous travel agents. Such are the links between the Pakistanis of Mirpur and Bradford that there is even a branch of British Airways here. I notice the accents of those queuing up at the post office to make international calls are from West Yorkshire.

The connection between Mirpur and the UK goes back to the 1950s, after the construction of the Mangla Dam on the Kashmir–Punjab border flooded a huge swathe of agricultural land in the Mirpur region. The government paid compensation to those who had lost their homes. There were job opportunities in the textile industry in West Yorkshire and much of the compensation money was used to pay for airline seats for the men leaving Mirpur and heading to new lives in the UK. Now, however, it is pay-back time for those extended families back in Mirpur. In return, they want the daughters of those who have settled in Britain to marry their sons so that they too can get to the UK.

We agree that we must try to meet with Koheema and Razia volunteers to go to the house with me. Razia runs a self-help and advocacy group in Bradford called 'Our Voice'. I have known her for some time and watched her square up to local MPs and even an immigration minister to give her opinion on how the British government is colluding in forced marriage. Her courage and confidence are not in doubt but, just in case of trouble, we tell our driver to wait outside so that we could leave in a hurry if necessary. We're acutely aware that things could quickly turn violent.

We enter the house. To our consternation, there are a number of women milling around. Razia asks for Koheema, explaining that she is a school friend from Bradford and I am a family friend. To begin with, a one-to-one conversation is impossible. Koheema's mother sits resolutely by her daughter's side, holding her arm in a vice-like grip. Razia does well regaling the group with stories from her and Koheema's pretend past and then says: 'Hey, Koheema, have you forgotten your English manners? What about a cup of tea?' The mother relaxes her grip and the two young women and I go into the kitchen.

The story spills out in breathless snatches interrupted by nervous looks at the door. Koheema tells us that she was studying for a science degree at Bradford University and had been tricked into coming to Pakistan to attend a cousin's wedding. She wants to be a pharmacist but her parents do not want her to continue at university. They fear losing control over her and believe that she is being influenced by the promiscuous behaviour of her fellow English students.

As soon as they reached Mirpur, however, she realized that the wedding being prepared by the extended family is her own. She had a boyfriend back in the UK and she vehemently refused to cooperate but she was beaten into submission and the ceremony took place. She is now expected to apply for the right to settle in the UK for the husband she loathes. 'Do you want us to try to help you?' I ask. 'Yes, please,' she replies with desperation in her voice. 'What would your parents do if they knew you were talking to us like this?' 'They would kill me,' she says. We notice guns in the front room as we leave the house.

Koheema's story has the ring of truth about it because we have been meeting these women wherever we go in Pakistan, at clandestine meetings set up by Razia and our Pakistani fixer, Homaira. A Foreign Office official tells us that there are probably hundreds of girls in situations like Koheema's, in transit between the UK and Pakistan at any one time. These girls are being held against their will and are often being threatened, beaten and finally dragged to take their place beside a hated groom at an unwanted wedding ceremony.

The problem now is how to help Koheema extricate herself from this situation. We call on the local police station, walking past rows of prisoners crouching on their haunches in cells where there is no room to stand. We are ushered into the office of Superintendent Karishi. He tells us about a visit they had from the West Yorkshire police the previous year and what a good time everyone had. Did they discuss forced marriage? I ask. 'It was not on the agenda,' he replies. I tell him about Koheema, without using her name, and how she fears for her life. He tells us that he can only help a woman if a male member of their family asks for her to be taken into protective custody.

The atmosphere in the police station is hostile and unfriendly to women. No wonder none of them ask for help; custodial rape is routine. I am reminded of a previous filming expedition in Pakistan when I invited my fixer, Homaira, to have a drink with me after a particularly gruelling day. As I poured whisky into tumblers from a duty-free plastic bottle I asked, 'What would happen if we were discovered sitting in this hotel room, drinking?' 'Oh, quite simple,' she said. 'We would be taken to the local police station and raped. We would then be moved to the district jail and raped. Then you would be released and I would wait in jail for months for a trial, all the while being raped.'

Despairing of help from the police, we call on a human rights activist who shares an office with the local Mirpur newspaper.

He says he tries to help the young women from West Yorkshire who find themselves in Mirpur defenceless against the demands of their families. He shows us the files on hundreds of them who have appealed to him for help. 'But what can I do? If the police won't help, who else is there? Why doesn't the British government do something?' he asks. 'After all, they gave these girls British passports and so they should help them. There should be some place here in Mirpur where they can turn for help.'

I did not pin much hope on the British High Commission in Pakistan after what Nazish had told me.

When I was truly desperate and needed support, the first thing that came into my mind was to call the British High Commission. I was pregnant and was afraid that all the beatings and sexual abuse would make me lose the baby. I knew that they would help and I was so relieved and comforted to hear a British voice on the phone saying 'How can I help you?' I said, 'Look, I am upset, frightened and need some support.' He asked for my name which I gave him. 'But you're a Pakistani,' he said, 'you have a Pakistani name.' I said, 'Yes, but I have a British passport.' He said, 'Sorry, we can't help,' and put the phone down. I really went to pieces after that. It was like someone had hit me.

Mark Kettle, deputy head of the consular section, looks embarrassed when I tell him this story. He explains that it is a problem for those with dual nationality. According to Pakistani law, a British girl of Pakistani origin is regarded as Pakistani when in Pakistan. 'We cannot go out and get her,' he says. She has to get to the High Commission, a patch of British soil behind a barbed-wire fence in the diplomatic enclave in Islamabad before the British government can do anything to help. I look at the mass of people outside the High Commission being shepherded into an orderly

173

queue. Just standing in the queue can be dangerous as two girls from Bradford discovered the year before. Fleeing the prospect of forced marriage, they made the difficult, three-hour journey by bus from Mirpur to Islamabad only to see the uncle who had threatened to kill them join the queue shortly after they arrived. He had bribed a guard at the High Commission to tip him off if the girls turned up and he was armed with a knife. Eventually, after several narrow escapes, the girls were safely repatriated to the UK and the guard was fired.

So you do repatriate girls, if they can get here? I asked Mark Kettle. 'Yes,' he says, 'we will do that.' The problem is getting Koheema to Islamabad. The ever-resourceful Razia Sodagar arranges a third party to liaise between us and Koheema. We tell her to tell her family that she has been told by the High Commission that they must come to Islamabad to make a set-tlement application for her husband. The staff at the commission have done their best and a flight has been booked, a 'safe house' made ready and everyone has been briefed to be careful not to arouse suspicion.

The family arrive with their settlement application forms in their hands and we identify them to Kettle. He approaches them and asks for a private word with Koheema. The parents look con-fused and angry but, intimidated by the busy office environment and by what is at stake, they let her go with him. Once they are alone in an interview room, Kettle explains that they can get her out of the country immediately and that there are a network of shelters for women in the UK for Asian women in her situation to take refuge in. She refuses the offer. Kettle calls me in so that Koheema can explain herself. 'I am really grateful for all that you have tried to do but I have decided not to accept your help. I have run away before and they have always found me and beaten me. If only I had had somewhere to go before they married me. I would have run away but now it is too late. Now that I have been forcibly married, they'll never let go. It may take two, three years but they will find me even in the UK and they will kill me.'

Maybe she is right. Some years later Nazish returned to the UK after we had met her in Islamabad and she still fears for her life. I went to meet her in the village where she has settled with her then six-year-old son. She seems happy and healthy. She has put on a bit of weight and she has a new partner but Nazish misses Bradford and her friends. 'I could never go back there,' she explains, 'my family would know in minutes that I was back. They would come looking for me to kill me.' To further conceal her whereabouts, she has taken her partner's surname but, without a divorce, she can't marry him. The benefits office was refusing to pay her the child benefit she's due because she is using a false name. 'Don't they realize,' Nazish says, 'that these people are clever, they have spies everywhere. If I used my real name, they would soon find me out.' I wrote to the Home Office on her behalf, explaining my knowledge of her case and, as best I could, why she feared for her life and needed to use a pseudonym. It helped. She now receives her benefits.

Families from South Asia will use all the resources at their disposal to find missing female family members, including employing bounty hunters.[2] It is a brisk business in London, West Yorkshire and the West Midlands. I meet one of them in Bradford who agrees to talk to us, on condition of anonymity. I start our meeting in a poorly lit basement restaurant in Bradford but Tahir keeps looking around himself nervously. 'I can't afford to be seen talking to you,' he explains. He suggests we get into his car and record the interview as he drives.

We drive around the streets of Bradford in the dark as he talks. 'I have lots of ways of finding girls. I talk to shopkeepers and taxi drivers a lot. They normally know where they are and what they are doing. When I find them, they are scared at first. I tell them, "Don't run away from the problem. Face it!" When I find them,

I never tell the parents where they are. It just causes problems. If they want to meet their parents, I arrange it in a neutral place like a cafe in the city centre.' How much do you get paid? I ask. 'I won't tell you because I like to see myself as a community mediator. For example, I once found a girl and her father said he would kill her and when I took her home, I made sure he didn't.'

He goes on:

Another case involved a seventeen-year-old girl whose parents wanted to take her to Pakistan to marry a thirty-five-year-old cousin. She went missing and the parents called on me. I found the girl and told her, 'If they try and take you to Pakistan just tell Security at the airport.' We all sat down for a meeting and I told her father that she didn't want to get married. He said, 'I've hired you and paid you. I'll take it from here.' I said to him, 'She's your daughter not your enemy. Why are you forcing her to marry one of your wife's relatives who is old enough to be her father?' I told the girl to contact me if she had any problems. After a couple of months, the father arranged the trip to Pakistan and she phoned me. I told her to hand her passport to the police, which she did. After a while, the father just gave up. She later went to college and married a guy of her choice.

Is most of his business due to failed forced marriages? 'Yes, I would say so. Mind you, I don't approve of forced marriages and I know parents are prepared to kill girls who won't obey and I've been involved in many cases that have ended tragically. On the other hand, I don't agree with the police operation and use of these shelters. They're too keen to move the girls into those places and they don't consider mediation. The police don't understand. The Asian community works totally differently to the white community. We go into a room and talk out our problems.' It is getting late. The pubs are emptying and we have driven around the block so often that the ladies of the night begin to think that we are kerb-crawling and approach the car with their offers. Tahir pulls in to the parking area of our hotel. His mobile phone has filled with messages during the time he has spent with us and he has to get on. As we make our farewells, I ask him whether he enjoys the work? 'It's getting too much for me – in the north one day and in the south the next. There is too much work and there are not enough of us able to do it. The only answer is for the government to set up some Asian-run agency to do it.'

The next day is Friday, the day of prayer. I am keen to know whether many men are as moderate and conciliatory in their views as Tahir or whether most of them believe in absolute control over the women in their lives, and in forced marriage. With a view to asking them as they leave the mosque after prayers, Ian O'Reilly sets up the camera and I arm myself with a microphone and we wait on the pavement outside. I have hardly begun asking when an aggressive, bearded man in salwar kameez and topi comes up to Ian and says, 'Take that thing away or I'll smash it to smithereens.' We do not argue.

It seemed safer to book an appointment with Dr Ghayasuddin Siddiqui, president of the UK Muslim Parliament. Are forced marriages endorsed by Islamic law? I ask. 'No, not at all,' he replies. 'In Islam, marriage is a social contract where the consent of both parties is essential. Without consent, the marriage is null and void. In fact, the situation is that any sexual relationship within a forced marriage is rape. What is happening here is that we have brought over extra cultural baggage from the subcontinent. It's a subcontinental culture that exists mainly in the rural areas. It is not a religious practice.'

What about the absolute control that men in the family wield over their women? Time and time again, I have heard young men from West Yorkshire say it is the Koran that gives them this authority? 'The Koran does not give anyone this authority but what happens is that these young men have learned these practices off their parents and from their imams and they mistakenly believe it comes from the Koran. What is actually happening is that the majority of our imams are from rural Pakistan and they are brought here more for their piety than their learning. They teach and repeat what they themselves have learned from their parents and forefathers and so this tradition continues.'

It is a familiar story that we hear in the UK. Those who claim to represent British Muslims, like Dr Siddiqui, shake their heads in horror at the way local imams preach about forced marriage and jihadism in Britain's mosques. 'They are not mainstream', 'they do not represent correct Muslim thinking', 'they misrepresent the Koran' they say, wringing their hands in despair. And yet there appears to be no system for policing and restraining the vile and violent messages that are delivered during Friday prayers. Certainly, the message does not appear to be reaching the Mirpuris of Bradford.

The West Yorkshire police admit that they are overwhelmed by the problem. They receive hundreds of calls from girls asking for help every year and the special shelters run by social services to hide and protect them are filled to bursting. I go along for a ride one day with Philip Balmforth, community liaison officer for West Yorkshire police, forced marriage troubleshooter and knight in shining armour for many of the Asian women in the community. 'I dealt with 300 cases last year. I have dealt with 300 cases already this year and it's only July. Next year, it will be over one thousand,' he tells me as he drives his smart police Range Rover through the streets of Bradford.

He receives a call from a woman called Samira. He has been to her house before, called out after a case of domestic abuse. She sounds hysterical as she says that the man she was forced to marry has been beating her. She says: 'He has just left. Please come and get me.' Balmforth executes a neat U-turn and makes for the terraced house in north Bradford. Samira opens the door as soon as he knocks; she looks frightened. Putting her finger to her lips, she tells Balmforth to leave immediately. Her husband has returned and he'll beat her again if he gets to know that she has been communicating with the police.

'We can only intervene when the women ask us to,' he explains. 'There's a lot of nastiness going on behind closed doors but it's only when they call on us that we get to know. There's no doubt that there are more and more out there who are in trouble.' When he can get a woman out of her house, he takes her to one of a network of shelters in Britain. Even in a shelter, the woman can still be at risk from an angry, vengeful family and so they will always put a woman from Bradford in, for example, a shelter in Leicester. A woman from Birmingham might be sent to Bradford and so on.

The shelter in Bradford looks a bit like a girls' boarding school or convent. Set in a leafy suburb, it is surrounded by high brick walls with a security man at the door. Each woman has her own room and there are common areas. In a small sitting room, Ian sets up the camera for me to interview Fozia. Her story is beginning to sound familiar. 'I was in love with someone here in Bradford when they took me to Pakistan. I cried throughout the wedding. He didn't love me. He only married me to get into the UK. He was a rotten husband and father and he would beat me for the slightest thing. For example, if there wasn't enough salt in the chapattis.'

A woman opens the door and comes into the room, looking agitated at the sight of the camera. 'Take it away!' she yells and starts to get hysterical. A member of staff comes in and we take her into the adjacent room. 'You can't take pictures of us,' she says frantically. 'My family might recognize me or someone here might mention my name and then my husband will come and get me,' and she breaks down, sobbing. I explain as gently as I can that the camera lens was pointing directly at Fozia and there was no way that there could have been a glimpse or a reference to her. She is shaking with fear and takes some persuading. The atmosphere in the shelter is quiet, subdued and hopeless. Such is the fear that the women have for the families they have fled from that they will be living here for decades. Even though the cities they now live in are hundreds of miles away from their homes, they are too scared to even go shopping or out to a cafe together. They are comfortable but they have as much freedom as prisoners.

Razia Sodagar blames the British government for allowing the situation to get out of control. We meet up again in Bradford where she holds the weekly meeting for her campaigning group 'Our Voice'. She invites us to film but half the women insist that their faces remain hidden. One tells me that her brother would beat her up if he knew she attends such meetings. For such a subversive and apparently provocative gathering, the tone is most restrained. 'We are not against arranged marriage,' Razia says, 'and we are not against Islam. We simply want to campaign against forced marriage and the immigration laws that got us in the mess we are today.'

In 1997, the new Labour government abolished the Primary Purpose rule, claiming it was racist and anti-family.[3] Up until then, the rule had been one of the cornerstones of UK immigration law. The rule stated that if, when considering a claim for permanent residence for a spouse in the UK, the presiding immigration officer felt that the primary purpose of the marriage was for the non-British partner to gain residence in the UK, the application could be denied and usually was. Labour candidates campaigned on the issue in the run-up to the elections in East London, the West Midlands and West Yorkshire and the scrapping of the bill was greeted enthusiastically by the exclusively male members of Britain's Asian community organizations. As a result, the number of girls and women who were forced into marriage increased substantially.[4]

'Nonsense!' says Razia when I remind her of the Labour Party's claim that the rule was racist and anti-family.

> We have to work really hard to get these men over here from India, Pakistan and Bangladesh. We have to work, we have to have a house, we have to be paying taxes and, even when these guys get here, we normally have to carry on working because they can't speak English and can't get jobs. So once they get their permissions for permanent stay, they shouldn't be allowed to go back out to the subcontinent or wherever they have come from and just marry again, perhaps to the girl they wanted to marry before the parents arranged things. They dump us, divorce us and then they apply for settlement rights for their new wife, sometimes two or three times!

We are sitting on a bench in Bowling Park in Bradford and Razia is raising her voice as she gets more indignant. People passing look at her in surprise: 'You see, they are not used to hearing an Asian woman's voice,' she says. 'It is only British Asian men who are listened to in our community. We British Asian women are being used and abused but the women have no say. A lot of women haven't got the guts to say "Listen to us"; they just stay quiet and suffer. They let the men deal with their problems. But when the problems do arise, it is the women who suffer and not the men.'

We drive to a meeting where the then immigration minister, Mike O'Brien, will be addressing one hundred or so Asian community leaders on the subject of forced marriage in a school hall in Keighley. We take our seats among rows of men. Razia, myself and one other girl who attends the Our Voice meetings are the only women there apart from the then-local MP, Ann Cryer, who sits alongside O'Brien on the platform. O'Brien assures the audience that there is no question of bringing back the Primary Purpose rule but appeals to the community to put their own house in order 'so that the small minority of arranged marriages which are forced can be stopped by the community working with us to ensure that women are not forced into an unacceptable situation'.

There is no applause, no dissent, nothing. O'Brien looked quizzically at the unflinching, stony-faced Asian men sitting in rows in front of him but he gets no reaction. The meeting is over. Pushing his aides out of the way, Razia confronts the minister. 'The government has to do something because they won't,' she says, indicating the men who were making their way out of the hall in silence. And, in words that would make Nigel Farage applaud, she adds, 'Why don't you in government realize that you have to stop the riff-raff who come to this country as our supposed loving husbands. Can't you see what is happening? It's just an immigration scam!' O'Brien looks startled, makes his excuses and leaves.

So what gives Razia her balls? Her confidence must come from her strong family and, in the context of West Yorkshire, her incredibly enlightened father. After the meeting, we go to her home, a large, handsome end-of-terrace house in central Bradford. Her parents came from Mirpur in the 1960s, they have five children and have done well. Her father speaks English; her mother does not. Razia's marriage was arranged and not forced but, when it broke down, they welcomed her back into the home without recrimination. They allow Razia to hold her Our Voice meetings in the front room and, whenever I cross the threshold, I get a warm welcome along with platefuls of curry and chapattis.

Razia's husband wants her to agree to a divorce now that, thanks to his wife, he is a British citizen. He wants to bring the new wife he has married in Pakistan to live with him in Bradford.

Like many unskilled Asian men in West Yorkshire, Mohammed Sodagar is a taxi driver. Razia tells us where he works, we wait for him to pull up at the rank and I approach him with a microphone. 'Good morning. Your wife, Razia, tells us that you have married again in Pakistan, even though you are still married to her?' 'So what?' he says, 'I am a Muslim. I can get married two, three, four times. No problem. I treated Razia very nicely but the problem with Razia is that she didn't understand what I want.'

Given that I am interviewing him on the pavement at a public taxi rank, it strikes me that he is being very obliging. Many people cornered like that would just get in the car and drive away. But then, I wonder as he continues, is he enjoying showing off while vilifying Razia in front of his fellow Pakistani taxi drivers? 'She doesn't know how to live with a husband,' he continues, 'she always tries to fight with me. She abuses me very badly. She goes out every day and sometimes at night. She doesn't listen to me. Why should I keep her? I shall divorce her.' And, of course, according to the law in the UK, he only has to wait for two years' separation for the divorce to go ahead.

I take the interview recordings back to London and, in the edit suite with my mainly female colleagues at *Newsnight*, we have a good laugh. It is a good bit of television and we ridicule the arrogance of a man talking of his wife in such an outdated way as if she is a servant who has to ask permission to go out. Sadly, it turns out to be a timely lesson for me in the culture clash between traditional East and liberal West. When the programme is transmitted, Razia is mortified. The idea that she goes out at night, however innocently, suggests that she has loose morals. To the non-Asian viewer she is a heroine; to the conservative, Asian community she is a harlot. Her family are not pleased.

With the amount of criticism that Keighley MP Ann Cryer has levelled at the local Asian community, it is a surprise that she managed to keep her seat throughout the Labour government from 1997 to 2010. She has confronted the community about forced marriage, honour killings and called for essential English language skills for immigrants entering the country.[5] More recently, she was one of the first to draw attention to the grooming scandal, the young Asian men who groomed mainly white girls in care for their sexual use.[6] In her constituency office, Ann Cryer tells me she is not prepared to exercise restraint on the subject of forced marriage. She fears that the practice produces 'seething resentment' in the men brought over as husbands from Mirpur which all too often they take out on their wives and she believes it is dangerous for society as a whole.

> They find themselves in a situation where they feel like a second-rate person because they don't speak English, they can't get a job and they're often stuck at home while the wife goes to work. In effect, he becomes an emasculated male. This can lead to resentment and worse against his wife. After all, he has come from the subcontinent where the tradition is one of a very patriarchal society, where men are regarded as superior to women and he is brought over to an alien society where he is, in many ways, subservient to his wife.

She meets with the Asian women in her West Yorkshire constituency and tries to persuade them to look elsewhere for sons-in-law. She says that most of their daughters are not averse to arranged marriages, 'but they are averse to marrying a man from a totally alien lifestyle. If these girls had been allowed to make their own choices, they wouldn't have married them. They would have married a young, capable, English-speaking Asian Muslim from West Yorkshire and most of these problems would not exist.'

But Cryer is forgetting the Mirpur factor. The traffic between the two countries is so busy that the flights from Manchester to Islamabad are called the 'Mirpur Shuttle'. Mirpur is today by far the richest region in a depressed area of Kashmir. There are more marble mansions here than anywhere else in rural Pakistan and building contractors do a brisk trade in classical columns and grand porticos. They are built from the money sent back to the region by successful immigrants in the UK, either for the benefit of parents and extended families left behind or as future retirement homes.

Close family ties and obligations to those extended families mean that Koheema, Nazish and Fozia were all forced to marry men from Mirpur, with tragic consequences for them all. The men have it all, says Razia bitterly, 'Look, once a man from Mirpur gets a British passport, it doesn't matter who he is, what he's like or whether he's good-looking or not. He can have his pick. For all women on the subcontinent, it is their dream to marry someone like that and to have a life of wealth in the UK.'

The consequences for young Asian women who rebel against forced marriage has a much more sinister aspect than we have touched upon in this chapter. In far too many instances the men who want to kill them get away with it because it is called 'honour killing'.

The year after I made films on forced marriage in Pakistan and in Bradford for the BBC, the Labour government set up the Forced Marriage Unit, run jointly by the Home and Foreign Offices, to help girls who were being coerced into marriage, mainly from South Asia. It was not until 2014 that the Conservative government was brave enough to outlaw forced marriage. In her weekly column in the *Independent*, in which she celebrates the first prosecution under the new law, Muslim columnist Yasmin Alibhai-Brown congratulates David Cameron for delivering these 'long-overdue legislative measures (in contrast to all those Labour MPs who, fearful of losing "ethnic" votes, had shied away from opposing forced marriages).'[7]

Alibhai-Brown has long campaigned against the practice and

she quotes a chilling letter she received from a father who made his daughter, a singer, marry her cousin in Pakistan. 'You write all this [sic] things about strict parents. You know nothing. She wanted to sing. How can I show my face to people if she is doing that? So Rahman was a good boy, my brother's son. He made her into a good, obedient wife. Then in Pakistan, she took poison and killed herself and the baby inside her. She cannot go to paradise. I wish this daughter was not born.'

'These are the attitudes we have to overcome,' opines Alibhai-Brown.[8]

9

HONOUR KILLINGS

Murder to Preserve Honour

There is desert scrub for as far as the eye can see and, in the distance, treeless, craggy mountains. A bearded vulture swoops down from a precipice to explore the possibility of a meal on the plain below. Rivers wind their way through gorges which over the ages have provided the way for armies to invade neighbouring Afghanistan. Balochistan accounts for 44 per cent of the land mass of Pakistan and yet, because of the lack of water, only 5 per cent of the population live here.

I drive from the parched plain to a village which nestles in the foothills of the Sulaiman Mountains. There are dusty roads lined with date palms, houses of mud, camels and turbaned men wearing salwar kameez in what feels like one of the remotest spots on earth. It is easy to believe that the unthinkable can happen here. The population is so thinly scattered and so autonomous. Law is decided at a tribal level; the man is master in his own house.

But what is harder to fathom is how what happens here finds its way to Acton, Mitcham and Warrington. British police chiefs and Home Secretaries may go on TV fulminating against so-called 'honour killings' which, they say, are not honourable and have no place in British society today. But people do not abandon entrenched customs as they fly over the white cliffs of Dover. Their beliefs come with them. So what provokes an 'honour killing'?

'He killed her because he saw her talking to a boy when she was betrothed to another,' a woman tells me when I enquire about a recent case in the village in the mountains in which a father killed his daughter. 'He started by attacking her arms and legs with a knife. "Please don't kill me," she called out to her father. She fell on to the ground and tried to crawl away but he cut her throat and then chopped off her hands. "Please don't do it like that," her mother called out to her husband, "please, just shoot her."'

They call it *karo kari* which, translated literally, means 'black male, black female' or adulterer and adulteress. But it is invariably only the woman who is at fault. The killing in the village was a common enough occurrence. Fourteen-year-old Nawara wanted to marry a boy from a family who lived in a large compound on the other side of the village. Her father wanted her to marry a forty-five-year-old man, a recently widowed cousin. A handsome dowry was expected and the family prefer to keep the money in the family. For this reason, she had to be killed, as an example to her sisters.

Nawara's father would not be punished. In Pakistan, the right to waive *qisas*, or punishment, is given to the family of the victim. Given that the murderer and victim are father and daughter, the family will automatically pardon the murderer and will call the event an 'honour killing', dictated by necessity. It is a convenient way of controlling women, safeguarding family wealth, sorting out inheritance problems and settling local feuds. It is thought that 'honour killings' take place at the rate of two or three a day in the country as a whole. Recent figures from Pakistan's Human Rights Commission say that 'more than 3,000 women have died in so-called honour killings in Pakistan since 2008. The Aurat Foundation, a rights group in the country puts estimates even higher and maintains that these incidents claim the lives of 1,000 women every year.'[1] It is probable that many more take place in situations where the body is quietly disposed of without intervention by or the knowledge of the authorities.

Sophisticated Pakistanis like to think that it is something that happens 'out there' in the wilds of Balochistan or Sindh province. Until April 1999, when 28-year-old Samia Sarwar was shot dead in her lawyer's office in Lahore by a gunman hired by her family. And, more recently, in May 2014 when a pregnant woman was bludgeoned to death by her father, brother, cousin and former fiancé on the steps of Lahore's High Court. Thirty-year-old Farzana Parveen had gone to the court to defend her husband against her family's accusations that she had been abducted by him. She wanted to tell the judge that she loved her husband and had married him of her own free will. She never got the chance. The family mob, twenty members of Parveen's family and fifteen of the jilted fiancé Mohammed Iqbal's family, was waiting for her with bricks and stones which they used to beat her to death as the police stood by.

The murder was so public and caused such horror worldwide that, unusually for Pakistan, the men were charged with murder and sentenced to death. During the trial Parveen's father was quoted as telling the arresting police officer that, 'I killed my daughter as she had insulted all of our family by marrying a man without our consent, and I have no regret over it.'[2] During the trial, it also emerged that Mohammed Iqbal had killed his first wife some years earlier in order to marry Parveen. The son from that first marriage told journalists that the family had persuaded him to forgive his father for murdering his mother, so that he could get out of jail. The men are appealing against their sentences.

Back in the village in the foothills of the Sulaiman Mountains, they have not finished telling me about the recent murders there.

As I walk to an appointment with Bibi Fatima, I pass stalls piled high with melons, onions and eggs which are sold individually, then carefully weighed and wrapped in newspaper. There are no women. Stallholders and customers alike are all men; women are not allowed out, even to shop. You catch rare glimpses of them – shrouded in heavy wraps as they balance on the back of passing bullock carts or hastily closing the door of their houses against the inquisitive stranger.

Apart from the young girls chattering in excited groups on their way back from school, I am the only woman walking freely along the muddy streets. I stop to talk to the girls who tell me they must be careful not to catch the eye of a boy as they make their way home. 'If our brothers see us talking to boys, they say we are kari,' ten-year-old Hanni explains, 'and they threaten to kill us. If we go to school and talk to a boy, they threaten to kill us.' They tell me that a ten-year-old girl and a fourteen-year-old boy were recently murdered for such a crime.

I meet with Bibi Fatima in a room behind a curtain inside the family compound. She is surrounded by sisters, daughters and female cousins. They are still clearly traumatized by the murder of a cousin two months earlier; none of the women have dared leave the house since. Bibi Fatima tells the story in a high-pitched wail with other family members chipping in with missing detail. She says her cousin had gone down to the riverbank to wash clothes when her husband saw a man watching her. When she got back to the house, he told her he was going to kill her. 'She was innocent,' says Bibi Fatima, tears rolling down her wrinkled cheeks. 'She said, "Why are you killing me? What have I done?" She swore on the Koran that she was innocent and she said, "Let's go to my father's house and talk?" But he shot her.' 'He beat her first,' interrupts a woman sitting beside the main raconteur. 'Yes, that is true,' says Bibi Fatima, 'he beat her first and then he shot her. He did it for money. He got 10,000 rupees from the man he accused.' It was, she said, a settlement of an ongoing dispute between two neighbours. The murderer got the money and, after burying his victim, he also got a new wife.

The murders took place in the small village of some five hundred souls within the same year. The police are unapologetic about the murder rate of women and even children on their patch. 'They see it as a business,' says Inspector Akbar Marri. 'The men see it as a way of making money. Afterwards, they come with their weapons and say that they have murdered a woman but that "we're allowed to", they say.' And why don't you tell them they are not? I ask. The inspector shrugs his shoulders: 'They think of it as their right.'

The problem for Pakistani women is that the law is ambiguous. After Samia Sarwar was murdered in her office in 1999, leading human rights lawyer Hina Jalani was encouraged when a Member of Parliament moved a resolution condemning 'honour killings'. She had set up Pakistan's first ever all-female legal practice in Lahore in 1980 and this appeared to be the breakthrough she had been campaigning for during the intervening decades. But the resolution was thrown out, she says, 'by those Members of Parliament who say that it is part of our culture. This is totally unacceptable.' There was further cause for optimism when an amendment to Pakistani law in 2004 ruled that 'honour killings should be treated as regular murders'. But Jalani points out that there are still two anomalies in the law that protect the killers. Under Pakistan's Hudood Ordinances, introduced in 1979, the status of women remains inferior to that of men and puts women at a crucial disadvantage within the justice system. The new amendment also fails to address the fact that the offender can negotiate with the victim's family and can be forgiven in the name of God, in which case the charges are dropped. 'And that's why the person who actually pulls the trigger walks free,' according to Jalani. 'We are calling for this law to be changed but, to be honest, I don't think that the government wants to address the issue.'

Pakistan has long struggled between the Islamists and the secularists in government but the problem is more fundamental than the make-up of its legislation. It begins with the lamentable status of women in Pakistan society: the birth of a boy is the cause of celebration and the birth of a girl can lead to a day of mourning. In some tribal areas, only 10 per cent of girls are allowed by their fathers to go to school. Girls are expected to obey and wait on their fathers and brothers, older and younger. The men in their family rule their lives, decide who they can marry and will kill them with impunity if and when they think fit. The woman has no control over her life and no voice. As Hina Jalani puts it, 'The right to life of a woman in Pakistan is conditional on her obeying social norms and traditions.' And, even in the twenty-first century, there is little sign of radical change in those entrenched traditions.

When the Mangla Dam was constructed in Mirpur in southern Kashmir in the 1950s, mainly male Pakistani migrants arrived in the UK to be given jobs by the steel and textile industries and, later, by the NHS. Most of them settled in Bradford, Oldham and Birmingham. The numbers increased with the arrival of wives and families in the 1990s and so 'honour killings' came to the UK.

It would be a gross calumny to suggest that every Pakistani family who arrives in Britain carries the vengeful and violent tradition with them. As we have seen, the family of Razia Sodagar was tolerant and understanding of their daughter. However, according to the Home Office in 2000, more than half the cases of forced marriage investigated in the UK involved families of Pakistani origin. Ninety per cent involved Muslim families.[3] When I first reported on the phenomenon in the UK back in 2004, the police believed that there had been a hundred murders or disappearances of young women in the previous few years which deserved investigation as 'honour killings'.

Shafilea was born in Bradford and in 2003 her family were living in Warrington. She did well at school and wanted to be a solicitor. She was frightened when her parents took her to Pakistan for an arranged marriage to a cousin who was ten years older than her, spoke no English and who would expect her to give up all her dreams. In despair, she drank a bottle of bleach. The marriage did not take place and, on her return to the UK, she required constant medical treatment. Her father explained that in the middle of the night, in the darkness, she had mistaken the bottle for mouthwash.

There was a history of violence in the family and the attacks on Shafilea increased after she refused the marriage. Teachers voiced concern when they saw bruises on Shafilea's neck and head. Social workers investigated but invariably interviewed the family as a whole and Shafilea was intimidated by the presence of her father. It was when she failed to turn up for medical appointments and missed school that the official search and police appeals for information began. The police remember her father, Iftikhar Ahmed, a taxi driver, being obstructive and angry rather than concerned by his daughter's disappearance. He insisted that she had just run away and that she was over sixteen and could do what she liked.

The police suspected the parents and put listening devices in their house where they overheard Iftikhar and Farzana Ahmed warn their children to 'say nothing at school'. They picked up on Ahmed saying that the system in the UK works on proof. 'Without proof, even if you sisterfuckers kill forty people, until it is found, they can't do anything to you.' Six months after she disappeared, her badly decomposed remains were found in the River Kent, near Kendal in the Lake District. The murderer had obviously covered his tracks well. Two post-mortems failed to prove how she had died but an inquest in 2008 ruled 'unlawful killing'.

It took almost ten years for the murderers to be brought to justice. Seven years after her disappearance, Shafilea's sister, Alesha Ahmed, told police that the fatal attack on her sister was provoked by the clothes Shafilea had chosen to wear to her part-time call centre job that fateful day in 2003 – a T-shirt and tight-fitting trousers. Her parents had killed Shafilea in front of their four other children. She said they pushed Shafilea onto the sofa, stuffed a plastic bag in her mouth and suffocated her. She said that she remembers her mother saying, 'Just finish it here!'

The Cumbria coroner Ian Smith concluded that Shafilea had been the subject of 'a very vile murder'. She wanted to live her life the way her school friends did and not according to the rules of the small village in Pakistan from where her parents came. Shafilea was ambitious, hard-working and wanted to follow a career in law. These are just basic human rights and they were denied to her.

Two years after Alesha confessed to the police, in 2012 Shafilea's case came to Chester Crown Court. Iftikhar and Farzana Ahmed listened impassively as they were each sentenced to twenty-five years' imprisonment. While sentencing them, Mr Justice Evans told the couple: 'A desire that she understood and appreciated the cultural heritage from which she came is perfectly understandable, but an expectation that she live in a sealed cultural environment separate from the culture of the country in which she lived was unrealistic, destructive and cruel.' Judges, policemen and politicians expressed horror. Meanwhile, the murders continued. At about the same time as the police in Warrington were investigating Shafilea's death, two hundred miles to the south, police in West London were struggling to understand the brutal murder of sixteen-year-old Heshu Yones by her father, Abdullah.

Abdullah was an Iraqi Kurd who had come to Britain ten years earlier with his wife and two children, fleeing Saddam Hussein's Iraq as a political refugee. He was confronted with a clash of cultures that he could not comprehend. He was appalled by what he deemed as the promiscuous behaviour of the young women he saw as he walked down Acton High Street. The short skirts, the high heels, their confidence and uninhibited swagger made him fear for Heshu's future. He admitted in court that he was worried that his popular and fun-loving daughter would become too westernized and would dishonour her family.

When he discovered that she had a Christian boyfriend, an eighteen-year-old Lebanese teacher, his suspicions were confirmed and he started beating her. She planned to run away and wrote a letter to her father in which she said: 'me and you will probably never understand each other. I'm sorry I wasn't what you wanted, but there's some things you can't change. Hey, for an older man you have a good strong punch and kick. I hope you enjoyed testing your strength on me, it was fun being on the receiving end. Well done.'

Before she had a chance to leave the house, he stabbed her and slit her throat. When the case came to court the following year, Judge Neil Denison said, 'This is, on any view, a tragic story arising out of irreconcilable cultural differences between traditional Kurdish values and the values of Western society,' and sentenced Abdullah Yones to life imprisonment. It was found that the extended family had conspired in a cover-up and the police investigated other members of the Kurdish community for perverting the course of justice, although no charges were ever brought.

It was time for me to go to the Middle East, to examine in greater detail the prevalence of 'honour killings' there. I started my enquiries in Jordan, a country that stands out as an oasis of stability and calm in an otherwise turbulent region. The West feels reassured by the succession of Sandhurst graduate kings with their American-educated, non-headscarf-wearing wives. The US is happy to subsidize King Abdullah II to the tune of $1 billion a year and the United Nations Development Programme extolls the country's 'high human development'.

To my surprise, I find that in a country that boasts a 97 per cent literacy rate and progressive and liberal thinking, the tradition of 'honour killing' is very much alive and well. The official figure is twenty to twenty-five killings a year,[4] about a third of that in Pakistan if you take into consideration that the population of the Islamic Republic is thirty times that of the Hashemite Kingdom. But there is no sign that the figure is falling or that enthusiasm for the tradition is waning. A recent Cambridge University survey of more than 850 teenagers – average age fifteen – in the capital, Amman, found that 46 per cent of boys and 22 per cent of girls agreed with at least two honour-killing situations. The report's author, Professor Manuel Eisner, points out that the basis for the belief was not necessarily a religious one. 'While we found the main demographic in support of honour killings to be boys in traditional families with low levels of education, we noted substantial minorities of girls, well-educated and even irreligious teenagers who consider honour killing morally right, suggesting a persisting society-wide support for the tradition.'[5]

I found a most articulate exponent of this credo in a high security jail, built on a bleak plain of sandy soil an hour's drive from Amman. The prison is modern and impressive: the staff are courteous and betray no surprise that I am here to interview Ahmed Hamid, a sister-killer. I am shown into an inner courtyard pleasantly planted with acacia trees, shrubs and black irises to await the prisoner. He arrives flanked by two officers who do nothing to restrain him and they leave him alone with me. Hamid is smartly dressed in a well-ironed shirt and trousers; he's in his thirties. He is an engineer who was working with a respected company in Amman. His sister was a secondary school teacher.

There is only one question you can ask when you find yourself sitting on a bench with someone who has committed sororicide and the camera is rolling: why did you kill your sister? 'I had to, I had no choice,' Hamid says with complete equanimity. 'It was agreed that one of us four brothers had to kill her and I said I would gladly do it. She left the husband we had arranged for her to marry for a man she said she loved. And then, what might have happened? She might have run away with another one hundred men and where would that have left the family honour? The entire family would have been dishonoured and none of us would have been able to get married, not even a distant cousin.'

What went through your mind as your hands tightened around her throat? 'I prayed,' he replies. 'I prayed to Allah for the strength to do what I had to do and, while she still had some breath in her body, I told her to pray too but she didn't and so I prayed to Allah to forgive her.' Before Hamid is led back to his cell, I ask him how many women killers there are in the prison with him? 'There are dozens of us here and we are all treated with respect by the other prisoners and by the guards. Anyway, we are only here for a few months.'

The interview is over and he begins to walk away and then suddenly wheels around and takes a step towards me. The guards do nothing to rein him in. He looks directly, threateningly into my eyes. 'You must realize,' he says, 'this is no passing thing that will end in a couple of years. We are in charge of the chastity of our women. If she loses her chastity, the honour of the family is lost. This thing will continue, and rightly so. It is our way.' When Hamid is released in a few weeks' time after serving a six-month sentence, he is assured of a hero's welcome back home.

My prison visit is not over. While the murderers inhabit cells with a view over the courtyard garden, the women in the building next door are in rooms from which they can freely access a courtyard which would be ugly and bare were it not for the lines of colourful washing that criss-cross the space. These are not murderers or even thieves; in the eyes of the male members of their families, they are worse. These women and girls fled from men they did not want to marry or from abusive husbands and are in prison for their own safety. The authorities call it protective custody. Their brothers and fathers may have already tried and will certainly still want to kill them and so they choose prison rather than freedom and certain death.

Fatima is hanging out her washing on the communal line when I ask to speak with her. She agrees, so long as we don't show her face. 'Even though I am in prison, the men of my family are clever and desperate,' she explains. 'They would even come here to get me.' She tells me that after she fled an abusive marriage her uncle shot her twelve times. She was in hospital for six months before the police brought her here, for her own safety. 'I know I did wrong,' she says with sincerity. 'I made a mistake but I have been here for four years now and my uncle was in prison for only two weeks. It doesn't seem fair.'

Premeditated murder in Jordan carries the death penalty, except for men who kill female members of their family who have committed adultery or behaved in a way the male members of her family deem morally unacceptable. There have been numerous attempts by civil rights organizations to change the law. 'We have to change the whole mentality of the nation. To spill someone's blood that easily has become a socially acceptable practice,' says Reem Abu Hassan, a leading activist. However in 2011 when the government tried to introduce a bill to make the punishment more appropriate to the gravity of the crime, it was rejected by Members of Parliament who, just as in Pakistan, argued that it would encourage waywardness among the country's women and promote adultery. The majority of the bill's opponents came from tribal backgrounds and feared upsetting their supporters. The campaigners were confronted with another defeat. 'The tribal mentality is the main driving force that makes this phenomenon spin out of control,' said Reem Abu Hassan, adding sadly, 'there is no political will in this country to fight so-called honour crimes.'

A few of the campaigning groups who fight for change in the law in Jordan also offer shelter to those fleeing the guns and murderous hands of the male members of their families. This is how I met Rana, mother of two, whose father has already tried and still wants to kill her. We sit in the back of a near-empty cafe in Amman for the interview. Once again, the cameraman is asked to film only the back of her head. She is on the run. 'I was seventeen when I was forced into marriage. I had never even thought of marriage. I loved school and wanted to finish my education,' she says. 'It was like being forced into prison, the prison of marriage.' Her husband beat her; she bore him two children. The dislike was mutual and so he divorced her and insisted on keeping the children. Rana went back home and planned to start her life over again, but her family told her that she had effectively ended theirs. The family had lost its honour, her father said, and he had to kill her. Rana, happy to be back home, thought he was joking. After the evening meal on her first night back, he took a gun from his desk drawer, entered her bedroom and shot the weapon twenty-three times.

Fortunately for Rana, he was not a good marksman. When she took me with her on a routine medical check-up the day after our interview, the doctor showed me where four bullets had entered her body, three in the leg and one in the shoulder. 'It was God who saved me,' Rana says. 'My father kept shooting at my head, my hair was flying everywhere, sparks were flying as the bullets singed my hair. I think he must have thought he got me in the head because he dropped the gun and left the house.' Rana's mother got her to a doctor. The doctor, an enlightened man, urges Rana to go through with the court case she is pursuing, with the help of a women campaign group. 'Don't drop the charges,' he says to her as she leaves, 'I can show the court all the photos of the gun[shot] wounds.'

Rana and I walk down the streets of Amman to our next meeting, with her lawyer. Smartphone shops stand side by side with fashion boutiques and luxury car salesrooms. Pictures of the apparently thoroughly modern monarchs, King Abdullah and Queen Rania, adorn every shop wall. The Jordanians have been rightly praised for the super efficiency and extraordinary generosity with which they have hosted over a million refugees in their country since the uprising began in Syria in April 2011. The outside perception is one of a sophisticated and humane leadership and yet there is this medieval, incomprehensible exception – those twenty-five or so extrajudicial executions of women and girls in Jordan every year.

Rana's lawyer is waiting for us outside the imposing metal gates of the Courts of Justice. She has news. The case will be heard the following week. 'If your father can persuade the judge that it was an attempted honour killing, he will get just three to six months in jail. But it is important that we go ahead,' she says. 'We need the publicity to draw attention to the scandal of the short prison sentences handed out to the so-called "honour killers".' Rana tells her lawyer that her father has contacted her to ask her to drop the charges. If she does so, he promises to leave her alone and to let her get on with her life. 'Don't do it,' says the lawyer. 'You can't trust these men. It is too much of a risk.'

As Rana and I walk away from the court building, she begins to cry. 'What is the point of any of this?' she asks. 'He may go to jail for a bit but he will always be out there, stalking me, wanting to finish the job. I can't get work without the permission of a male member of my family. I shall be living in hiding for the rest of my life. I am twenty-five and my life is over.' The situation in Pakistan and Jordan appear similar. These violent killings are prompted by deep-rooted tribal beliefs which are adhered to even by sophisticated and educated men like Hamid, the engineer and sister-killer. Right-minded doctors, lawyers and some politicians do their best to change a tradition that has no place in the twenty-first century. In each country, the law makes a token recognition of the crime and yet the punishment falls far short of what might be expected for brutal, irrational and premeditated murder.

Next I go north-east to Kurdistan. Some of the most harrowing cases to come to court in the UK recently are from this land that exists only in the minds of Kurds who live in a vast area that straddles Syria, Iraq, Iran and Turkey. Diyarbakir, the ancient Roman town on the edge of the River Tigris whose giant black basalt walls can, I am told by a local, be seen from the moon is the capital of Turkish Kurdistan. It is a wild, semi-autonomous area which the Turkish authorities have difficulty in controlling. Locals also tell me that some two hundred women were killed in the name of honour in the area last year, 1997.

Here too the women who manage to escape their trigger-happy men live in shelters provided by brave activists who are determined to defy tradition and provide a place of humanity and safety in this murderous, misogynistic part of the world. Fatima also keeps her back to the camera as she tells how, after the death of her husband, his family told her she must marry her brother-in-law. She refused. 'My mother-in-law started beating me and said, "You are our property and you must obey us. My son will kill you."' Fortunately, she managed to escape before he had the chance.

'It's the Kurdish way,' a man explains to me in a cafe in Diyarbakir that night although surprisingly he is prepared to admit different degrees of honour and reprisals. 'If a daughter runs off with a boy, you can do a deal. You can negotiate. But, if your wife runs away or disobeys, there is no negotiation. This is a point of honour. You have to kill her.'

'I disagree,' interrupts the man sitting next to him who introduces himself to me as Serhat. 'My sister would be as guilty as
my mother if she disobeys me. In fact, she told me that she did
not want to marry her forty-year-old cousin. I am a kind brother
and so I gave her a chance. I warned her that I would have to kill
her if she did not obey. She married him.' Fortunately, some
twenty years' experience of interviewing such people has refined
my ability to look indifferent. I thanked the young men for their
time and got up and left.

It is the Kurdish way and the Jordanian and Pakistani way.
I hear this phrase in every country I visit. The more I hear
about women being ordered to marry men they do not love and
fourteen-year-old girls being given to middle-aged men in their
forties like parcels of land to seal business deals and cement relationships, the more I am convinced that this is to do with the
status of women. Women are seen as unthinking, unfeeling items
of property to be denied any chance of a mature, mutually loving
adult relationship. Their virginity and unquestioning obedience
are associated with family honour and honour is so important that
it is worth killing for.

I was among several journalists who at the time were taking a
close look at Turkey's human rights record. Turkey had applied to
join the EU and the mandarins in Strasbourg were asking difficult
questions about Turkey's treatment of its Kurdish population. The
1980s and 1990s had seen near civil war in large Kurdish region
of Turkey. In the 2000s, the Turkish army and police still exer-
cised martial law there, Kurdish language radio and TV stations
were forbidden and many hundreds of Kurdish political prisoners
remained in jail.

Turkey was also told to put right its dire record on women's
rights and warned that lack of progress on this could impede
the country's entry into the European Union. Legislators were
persuaded to modernize the law regarding 'honour killings'.

As in Pakistan and Jordan these killings were still considered crimes of passion and a family affair, and they were dealt with leniently, if at all, by the courts. In response to pressure from the EU, Turkey imposed life sentences on the so-called 'honour killers'. Unfortunately, the result has had unforeseen and tragic consequences.

The guidebook recommends that you give the town of Batman a miss. After you have paused to take a photo of yourself beside the eponymous road sign, drive on. It advises you to carry on exploring the more beautiful parts of Kurdish south-east Turkey. Batman, 50 miles to the east of Diyarbakir, was a village of a few hundred souls until oil was discovered in the 1950s. Now around a quarter of a million people live in the ugly town of concrete and breeze-block buildings thrown up in a hurry between the railway station and the refineries.

The guidebook does not mention Batman's more recent claim to fame – as the female suicide capital of Turkey. According to the women's support organization KA-MER, over a hundred women, mainly young girls, have killed themselves since the introduction of the new penalties.[6] The only logical explanation is that parents who want to avoid seeing their sons incarcerated for life are persuading their disgraced daughters to kill themselves instead.

Ayten Tekay, a caseworker for KA-MER explains, 'Rather than losing two children, they opt to lose a daughter.' From the hundreds of girls and women who appeal to the organization for help, they hear of girls being locked in rooms and left with a rope, some poison or a pistol. 'We have to bring these killings out from the shadows and teach women about their rights,' she says. 'The laws have been changed, but the culture here will not change overnight.'

A year after the law was changed and 'honour killers' faced lifelong prison sentences, thirty-six women killed themselves in the first six months of 2006, according to an investigation by the United Nations envoy Yakin Ertuk, who concluded that the majority of the deaths were 'honour killings disguised as a suicide or accident'. Most of them had taken place in the town of Batman or nearby villages. An added riddle to the story of Batman comes from the bizarre fact that the Turkish author Orhan Pamuk, winner of the Nobel Prize for Literature, had based his recent novel *Snow* on a suicide epidemic that had taken place in Batman at the turn of the century. Amateur psychologists speculated about copycat deaths; others warned of the curse of Batman.

There is a more prosaic explanation. The majority of women who seek help come originally from the remote, rural areas of south-eastern Turkey whose families have followed the oil rush to Batman. Most of them are uneducated and illiterate: few if any of them will have read Pamuk. Nonetheless, they will have access to the shopping channels and to MTV and will be aware that there is a more open, fun-loving world out there. And yet these women are expected to ignore the modern world around them and obey the male members of their family.

The modern, technical paradox for seventeen-year-old Derya is that she was receiving love messages by text from a boy at school. When the family learned of her immoral behaviour, they used the same technology to send her orders to kill herself. Her uncle texted her saying, 'You have blackened our name. Kill yourself and clean our shame or we will kill you.' She received fifteen such messages in one day. She threw herself into the Tigris but did not drown and then made a botched attempt at slashing her wrists before a policeman brought her to the safety of the KA-MER refuge.

'My family attacked my personality and I felt I had committed the biggest sin in the world,' she says. 'I felt I had no right to dishonour my family, that I have no right to be alive. So I decided to respect my family's desire and to die.' After counselling, Derya says she will no longer try to kill herself but she is still depressingly pessimistic about her future and that of other girls in the area: 'This region is religious and it is impossible to be yourself if you are a woman. You can either escape by leaving your family and moving to a town, or you can kill yourself.'

And the other option – emigrate to another country – can hold as many dangers. I eventually get back to the UK in North London where I live; Kurdish shops sell *dolma* and *kofta* and the music of the nationalist Kurdish singer Şivan Perwer blares out from the shopfronts. The majority of Turkish Kurds came to Britain during the fighting in the 1980s and 1990s. They brought with them welcome additions to the fabric of London life, such as their spicy, exotic food and heart-rending music. They also brought their traditions.

By now, Scotland Yard has set up a special taskforce devoted to investigating 'honour killings' led by Commander Andy Baker, head of the Metropolitan Police's Serious Crime Directorate. 'I want to get one thing straight,' he told me in an interview, 'there is nothing honourable about honour killings.' He hoped that the sentence meted out to Yones would act as a deterrent to those who stayed silent about the maltreatment of women in their community. 'Violence in the name of culture will not be tolerated. Murder in the name of honour will be punished by the severest penalties available in law.'

And yet, a scandalous lack of understanding and sensitivity was demonstrated by the police handling of the case of Banaz Mahmod from Mitcham who disappeared in 2006. She contacted the police five times to say that she feared for her life from an abusive husband and a threatening family. The CCTV video at the police station as she tells a woman police officer how her husband wants to kill her shows a beautiful young woman of nineteen years, her dark hair neatly tied back in a ponytail, hazel eyes and a heart-shaped face, wracked with fear.

'He slapped me, he beat me, he raped me, he kicked me in the head and he dragged me by my hair. I was only seventeen when I got married. I didn't know whether this was normal,' she tells the policewoman referring to the Iraqi Kurd whom she was made to marry in 2005. It was an arranged marriage. He came straight from northern Iraq and, according to Banaz, 'he has the thinking of fifty years ago. He always has to have his own way. In our culture, we are not allowed to call husbands by their names in front of other people. We had guests around and I called him by his name. He told me he would kill me if I ever did that again. I told him, but this is Britain!'

Banaz walked out of the unhappy marriage and fell in love with a Kurd from Iran, Rahmat Suleimani. There was no way she could keep the relationship a secret. She soon felt that her husband had sent men to follow her. She told the police: 'When I go out, one guy is always following me in a car. This is the reason I came to the police station. If anything happens to me, it's one of them.' She said to the WPC, 'Now that I have told you, what can you do for me?' The police did nothing. There was no follow-up and no security given to the young woman who feared for her life.

On New Year's Eve 2006, her father persuaded Banaz to meet him at her grandmother's house in Morden. Banaz's older sister, Bekhal, saw him leave 'with a bottle of alcohol in one pocket of his jacket and a big blade in the other'. He plied Banaz with brandy. 'I drank something I had never drunk before,' she said later. 'He told me to drink it very slowly. The curtains were closed and it was very dark. He went out of the room and came back wearing Reebok trainers and gloves. He told me to sit down and that I would feel sleepy and he left the room again.' Realizing he was going to kill her, she fled out of the back door and smashed a neighbour's window to attract attention before finally collapsing in a cafe.

Bleeding from the wounds to her hands and wrists from breaking the window, she was taken to the local hospital where staff said that they had never seen anyone so afraid. Rahmat met her there and had the presence of mind to record her account of events on his mobile phone. But the WPC who came to interview Banaz about what had happened refused to believe her story, accused her of being drunk and considered charging her with criminal damage for breaking the window. There was no connection made with the young woman who had come to the police station pleading for help.

Banaz disappeared a few weeks later and the case was handed to the Metropolitan Police, to Detective Chief Inspector Caroline Goode. The details of Banaz's murder that came out in court in 2007 were harrowing. Her father and uncle organized a gang of local Iraqi Kurdish thugs to kill Banaz. In secret recordings in prison while awaiting trial they boasted of sexually abusing her; strangling her; 'stamping on her neck to get her soul out'; cramming her body into a suitcase; and driving it to a house in Birmingham where it lay in a shallow grave under an abandoned fridge-freezer for three months before it was discovered. The uncle, Ari Mahmod, who was the mastermind behind the killing, got a twenty-three-year prison sentence. Banaz's father, Mahmod, got twenty years and their accomplice, Mohamed Hama, seventeen years. Two other accomplices, Mohammed Ali and Omar Hussain, who were cousins of Banaz, fled to Iraq. In an unprecedented extradition operation between the two countries they were brought back to the UK by DCI Caroline Goode in 2010. They were tried and sentenced to eighteen years in prison.

DCI Caroline Goode went on to receive a Queen's Police Medal for her handling of the case. As a result of her experience, she called for more education, training and communication on 'honour killings': 'We must talk about this issue and not sweep it under the table in the name of political correctness.' A subsequent Independent Police Complaints Commission report into the initial handling of the case by Surrey police found that Banaz Mahmod had been badly let down. It concluded that, although on some occasions the standard of service had been satisfactory, at other times it fell far below what should reasonably have been expected.[7] Meanwhile, the murders continued.

In 2009, the Metropolitan Police reported that there had been a huge rise in recorded incidents in the name of 'honour'. In the six months between April and October, there had been 211 incidents of which 129 were criminal offences. An independent NGO, the Iranian & Kurdish Women's Rights Organization (IKWRO) did not believe the figures saying they were too low. By using free-dom of information requests, they contacted all fifty-two police forces in the country and revealed that the police had recorded 2,823 honour attacks in the UK in 2009/10. London recorded the most with 495 attacks, followed by West Yorkshire and the West Midlands.[8]

The CPS chief prosecutor for the north-west specializing in forced marriage and 'honour killings', Nazir Afzal, also believes that the number of murders of young British women is under-estimated. 'We also have the export of murder,' he says. 'The victims are taken abroad and killed overseas and so don't feature on police records. He believes alarm bells should ring whenever a child is withdrawn from a school early. 'It's important not just to concentrate on the victims but also on potential victims,' he says. 'Often, if a girl or boy is taken out of school early, it's a trigger that a forced marriage may be on the cards.'

A recent Home Office paper revealed that in Bradford alone, 250 girls aged thirteen to sixteen were taken off their school reg-isters because they did not return from a visit abroad.[9] Former MP Ann Cryer is prepared to stick her neck out again. 'The problem is that it is just not in anyone's interest to pursue what is happening to these children. Parents, schools and the community simply do not want to look into it but that is just not satisfactory. I don't care who does it, but someone has to ask questions as to why these children are not in school.'[10]

And so it goes on. Like female genital mutilation, these obscene customs degrade British society. Education, integration of ethnic communities and a better awareness by the police, schools and social services would help. There must be a stubborn refusal to use euphemisms and to obfuscate about 'honour killings'. More must be done to challenge centuries'-held beliefs.

I walk down to the Kurdish Workers' Association clubhouse in Finsbury. I know the building well. I used to come here for advice from Kurds living in London before leaving for Turkey and Iraq to report on human rights abuses against the Kurds in these countries. They were always friendly and would put me in touch with community leaders and their families back home. I came here during the first case that dramatically brought to attention the involvement of Kurds in 'honour killings', the murder of sixteen-year-old Heshu Yones by her father. Today, young men mill around in designer jeans and hoodies and are plugged in to their iPods. It is a typical twenty-first-century scene.

I order a strong, bitter coffee and sit down with a group who are relaxing between turns on the billiards table. I ask them if they believe in 'honour killings'? 'If a woman, a wife or daughter disobeys or runs away, she takes away a man's honour,' Samir tells me. 'To restore it, he has to punish or kill her. It is our tradition. We have to do it.' Ahmed, an older man, adds, 'When someone kills a woman, it is invariably because family and community pressure has got to him and he believes he has to kill to get back his respect again.' I could have been back in Diyarbakir ten years ago, in the ongoing Dark Ages.

1 0

INDIA

The Worst Place on Earth to
Be Born a Woman

Manemma says:

> I liked the dress. It was pink and red with bits of gold on it
> and Mummy put jewels around my head and down my face.
> She told me it was a special day and I was so excited. There
> were a lot of people and lots of noise. I was six and there
> were other girls my age and a bit older. All the boys were
> older and there were some men. We had to walk around a
> fire, which was scary. But Mummy guided me and so it was
> OK. Then Mummy started crying and said 'goodbye' and
> handed me to a strange woman. I cried and said I wanted to
> go home. But Mummy ran away and I didn't go home again
> for two years.

Manemma is now eleven and she sits forlornly, surrounded by
family members, on the floor of their two-roomed house. She is
telling me the story of her wedding day, five years earlier. 'When
I was getting married, I had no idea what was going on,' she continues. 'I was young and I loved getting all dressed up but when

they told me that I had to leave home, I cried and cried. I didn't want to leave my parents, my sisters and my brothers but they made me. As soon as I got to my husband's home, my mother-in-law made me work for her.'

Manemma's marriage ended in disaster. After two years, her twenty-year-old husband wanted a more sexually mature woman and sent her packing. 'How did your husband treat you?' I don't want to ask her directly whether he tried to have sex with her. Manemma is now eleven years old but looks much younger and she squirms with embarrassment and says, 'I don't want to talk about my husband.' Doctors report of the frequent rape of pre-pubescent girls in her situation. Of one thing Manemma is sure. She says she never wants to get married again.

I turn to her father and ask how he could have let such a thing happen to his daughter? Unembarrassed, he returns my stare, shrugs his shoulders and answers in a matter-of-fact tone, 'It's the way things happen here. I have five daughters and cannot afford to feed them all. Girls are married at a very young age. Older men usually like young girls and the girls are expected to accept the situation. It's the tradition.' He looks at his daughter accusingly and I wonder for how long she will be able to resist another wedding.

I want to scream when I hear him use the word 'tradition' by way of explanation. How many crimes are committed against women in the name of tradition the world over? Why, as human-kind grows better informed, globalized and apparently more knowledgeable, does the reverence for outdated and inexplicable tradition persist, flouting reason and even the law? How convenient for the aura of tradition to obscure misogyny and even legitimize criminal behaviour.

Child weddings are illegal in India. The Child Marriage Act, passed during British rule in 1929, specified that a girl must be fifteen and a boy eighteen before they can get married. After independence, in 1978, the Act was revised to raise these age limits to eighteen and twenty-one respectively. In 2006, the Prohibition of Child Marriage Act introduced the penalty of two years' imprisonment for males over the age of eighteen who marry underage girls or who officiate at a wedding involving a girl under eighteen.[1] Parents of girl brides can also be punished and the new law allows child brides and grooms to void their marriages on reaching adulthood.

Despite legal reforms over nine decades, the law has been widely ignored in this country of some 1.2 billion. The most recent figures available from India's National Crime Records reveal only forty persons were convicted of child marriage offences in 2012. And yet the latest figures from UNICEF claim that some 18 per cent of girls in India are being married under the age of fifteen and 30 per cent under the age of eighteen. Rajasthan is one of the states with the highest rates of child marriage. Just a few miles from some of the most popular tourist attractions in India, the cities of Jodhpur and Jaipur, little girls are being forced into illegal, underage marriage and subjected to child sex abuse.

In the government buildings in Jodhpur the Department of Child Welfare is reminiscent of the India of the last century and a far cry from the high-tech, IT-savvy, sending-rockets-into-space India of today. A ceiling fan whirls noisily over a handful of staff who sit in an untidy office, dusty files are piled high on a desk which boasts one telephone. It is the auspicious time of the year for weddings in May known as Akshaya Tritiya and the phone has been installed as a hotline so that informers can tip the officials off about illegal ceremonies. It remains silent.

The director of Child Welfare looks unperturbed. He explains that the wedding organizers are clever. 'They are always one jump ahead of us. They announce a wedding and then change the date or the venue. Rajasthan is a big place and the police cannot patrol the entire area. Maybe if they had enough cars, they could stop the weddings.' The other problem is that a lot of land in the state of Rajasthan is still owned by wealthy and politically well-connected landowners whose estates have special privileges.

The heat rises from the desert of Rajasthan and obscures the horizon. The car leaves us on the edge of a private estate where the driver says 'the police do not dare enter'. He assures us that it won't be hard to find the mass wedding and vaguely points out the direction. The problem is that, at 45 degrees, it is difficult for me and my local fixer, Farzana, to walk carrying the camera gear and the haze makes it impossible to see. After stumbling around for a few minutes, we hear the sound of drums and string instruments.

As we get closer, garishly coloured tents emerge from the dust. There are several hundred people, the women all brightly dressed in pinks and reds and the men in white dhotis and turbans. The older women sing as they carry the brides' dowries, wrapped in silk carpets, towards the grooms' enclosure. The scene is a riot of colour, drumbeats and excitement. With difficulty, Farzana and I duck through the crowd and head for the most splendidly decorated tent, looking for the brides.

We draw back the flap of the tent to find about fifteen young girls, dressed in crimson nylon dresses with garlands around their necks and decorated with strings of glass jewels which encircle their heads and end threaded into a nostril. None of them look more than sixteen years old. A child bride who can be no more than six years old, dressed like a doll in crimson and gold, stares with kohl-encircled eyes, uncomprehending as the events unfold around her.

The cacophony of sound suddenly increases, the musicians play with extra fervour and the women start singing. The brides are led out to where the priest is waiting beside the sacred fire. They see their husbands-to-be for the first time. Dressed in white, the youngest groom appears to be about twelve and there are a few in their twenties and thirties. The six-year-old stumbles as she carries out the wedding ritual of encircling the fire while the priest recites his mantras. She howls as her mother-in-law leads her away to her new home.

From the moment she is born, the girl child in India is seen as a supernumerary in the family, an extra mouth to feed and incapable of making a contribution to the family income. Indeed, the tradition of extravagant dowries in India means she can be a crippling economic burden. If the bride is young enough, the groom's family demands less. For the girl's family, therefore, the sooner she can be got rid of the better. This tradition is widely accepted among the rural communities of India. Although illegal, no one is going to call the police.

The dramatic consequences of inaction are seen in local hospitals. In the casualty department of the Mahatma Gandhi Hospital in Hyderabad, a fifteen-year-old is rushed into casualty. She is having convulsions and is writhing in pain. The gynaecologist on duty tells me, wearily, that 'she is a classic example of what can go wrong if you have a baby too young. She has high blood pressure and, because her body is not yet fully developed, her pelvic passage is too small and the baby will get stuck. We shall have to carry out a caesarean.'

According to a recent Indian government census, 300,000 girls in India have given birth, some for a second time by the time they are fifteen.[2] Dr Shailaja takes me through to the neo-natal ward and points to the undernourished, underdeveloped children there. She stops at a bed where a thirteen-year-old is cradling a tiny baby. The doctor says, 'Look what happens to these child brides.' She tells the girl to stick her tongue out. 'See, she's anaemic. Most of them are. And look at the baby, he's only four pounds in weight. He'll be lucky to survive. Fifty per cent of the babies born to children are more likely to die than those born to older mothers.' Fortunately, the young mother gazes with incomprehension at the English-speaking doctor.

The hospital reflects the paradox that is India today, the modern and the medieval existing side by side. Dr Shailaja, from a family of middle-class professionals in Bangalore, is confident, competent and clearly impatient as she surveys the rows of helpless women. She has all the tools of modern medicine at her disposal but is thwarted by the stubborn adherence to a barbaric tradition. She is also a compassionate woman and her eyes fill with tears as we move on to the gynaecological ward.

Here, women as young as twenty-three have hysterectomies. Their bodies, ravaged by multiple pregnancies, are already worn out. 'When they get home', Shailaja says, 'they will be unable to conceive and will be too weak to work in the fields. More often than not, their husbands will throw them out.' The grim reality in India today is that a girl can be married at the age of six, be a mother at twelve and find her body destroyed in her early twenties. And then there is the impact on her education.

A child bride will be withdrawn from primary school and denied a chance of secondary education. I meet two sisters, Anjali and Vinisha, aged eleven and thirteen at their home in Jaipur. Their mother and older sisters are massaging their limbs with a mixture of yogurt and turmeric. Their hands and feet have already been covered with swirling patterns of henna. The noise of the grooms' arrival can be heard outside; they are coming on horseback accompanied by a brass band. The tension in the girls' bedroom rises. 'Of course I'm nervous, wouldn't you be?' says Vinisha, the older girl. She is irritated and frightened at what is about to happen to her. 'We haven't even seen our husbands, let alone met them.'

She says she loves her home, her sisters and her school and now she is to lose them all. 'There will be no chance of going to school at my in-laws' place. I'll just cook, do the housework and please my husband. I shall have to cover my head with a veil and do whatever my mother-in-law says.' A young bride not only loses the social and intellectual stimulus of school but, without literacy skills, she is also excluded from public announcements and campaigns to promote health care, nutrition and contraception. Child marriage exacerbates all India's problems, social and economic.

There is another, more sinister reason for parents favouring child marriage in India today. In 2014, an Indian press agency published a story about a farmer and his wife from the northern Indian state of Haryana, who withdrew their fifteen-year-old daughter, Paru, from school in order to marry her off to a forty-year-old man. Nothing unusual in that. It is the reason that the mother, Basanti Rani, gives that is disturbing: 'In an increasingly insecure society, where rape and sexual abuse have become so common, marrying off my daughter is a wise move. Who will marry her had she been abused or raped? Now, at least, her husband can look after her.'[3]

The wonder is that this marriage took place in the northern state of Haryana, one of the more progressive in tackling child marriage. The local government have introduced a programme called 'My daughter, my wealth' by which parents get 2,500 rupees (£250) if, at the age of eighteen, their daughter is not married. But this was not incentive enough for the Rani family; the fear of rape is greater.

Haryana has had its share of this horrific crime. In 2015, a 28-year-old, mentally ill Nepalese woman was gang-raped and murdered in a field. The post-mortem showed she had been hit unconscious by a stone and that stones, blades and sticks were forced inside her during the attack. Eight men were arrested. A month later, a teenager in Haryana hanged herself from the ceiling fan in her bedroom. She was reportedly upset that the police had changed her case of gang-rape to rape. She wanted to name all four men who had raped her but the police said that they wanted her to identify only one of the rapists in her testimony.

In its report on the rape and murder of the woman in Haryana, BBC News online gives a brief outline of some of the rapes that have made the headlines in India recently.

> 16 December 2012: Student gang-raped on Delhi bus, sparking nationwide protests and outrage
>
> 30 April 2013: A five-year-old girl dies two weeks after being raped in Madhya Pradesh
>
> 4 June 2013: A thirty-year-old American woman gang-raped in Himachal Pradesh
>
> 17 September 2013: Five youths held in Assam for allegedly gang-raping a ten-year-old girl
>
> 15 January 2014: A Danish woman is allegedly gang-raped after losing her way near her hotel in Delhi
>
> 23 January 2014: Thirteen men held in West Bengal in connection with the gang-rape of a woman, allegedly on orders of village elders who objected to her relationship with a man
>
> 4 April 2014: A court sentences three men to hang for raping a 23-year-old photojournalist in Mumbai last year[4]

It was the first of these, the gang-rape and murder of 23-year-old Jyoti Singh on a Delhi bus on 16 December 2012 that led to mass demonstrations against rape in India, the like of which have never been seen before. Jyoti Singh was a medical student who had six months to go before qualifying. She had been studying hard all week and decided to treat herself to a movie at the weekend with a friend, Awindra Pandey, a software engineer who, like her, came from Uttar Pradesh. They watched *Life of Pi* at a popular shopping mall in Delhi and Awindra offered to accompany her back to the Delhi suburb where she lived.[5]

By now it was nine o'clock and dark. The tried to persuade a rickshaw to take them but all the drivers they asked said it was too far. They tried to flag down cars to no avail. They waited by a bus stop where a bus pulled up claiming to be going to their destination. They climbed in. What they did not know was that the bus was a school charter bus and was not licensed to pick up passengers in Delhi and that all six men in the bus had been drinking heavily. What happened next is scarcely believable.

The men locked the doors of the bus and started taunting the couple, asking Jyoti why she was out alone with a man who was not her husband so late at night. Awindra intervened, saying it was none of their business. He was stripped, badly beaten, knocked unconscious and thrown to the back of the bus. They decided that Jyoti needed to be taught a lesson. While the bus drove around Delhi for an hour and a half, all six men took turns in attacking her and raping her. She tried to fight back, biting her attackers. They used a rusted, L-shaped iron rod, the tool used as a car jack, to insert in her vagina. She suffered severe injury to her genitals, abdomen and intestines. One of the attackers reached into her body and pulled out part of her intestines.

One of the gang said, 'She's dead, she's dead. We must get rid of her.' The bus pulled up and threw Jyoti and Awindra, both naked, onto the verge. When he saw Jyoti move, the bus driver tried to reverse the bus to crush her. Awindra moved her out of the way and the bus drove away. Frantically, he tried to persuade rickshaws and cars to stop to help them. None did. Finally, a cyclist stopped to help. He looked at Jyoti and later said, 'She looked like a cow looks after giving birth. There was blood everywhere.' He called the police who arrived and spent valuable time asking what had happened while Jyoti, writhing in agony, lost blood and consciousness on the side of the road. Finally, they called an ambulance.

The vicious assault, said the attackers, was Jyoti's fault. 'When being raped, she shouldn't fight back. She should be silent and allow the rape. Then they'd have dropped her off after doing her and they'd only have hit the boy.' Mukesh Singh, one of the attackers, makes this astonishing statement in an interview recorded while he was in jail awaiting trial.[6] Sitting on a stool in his cell, with a neatly trimmed moustache and freshly laundered checked cotton shirt, he speaks with confidence and complete lack of remorse. He claims to have been driving throughout the attack, a claim that is denied by the fellow accused who say he took part in the gang rape.

Mukesh Singh reflects the opinion of too many men in India today when, throughout the interview, he insists that the girl is to blame. 'A girl is far more responsible for rape than a boy,' he says. 'A decent girl wouldn't roam around at nine o'clock at night. Housework and housekeeping is for girls, not roaming in discos and bars at night doing wrong things, wearing wrong clothes.' The wrong clothes are an incitement; the men are victims of wanton provocation.

Doctors were astonished that Jyoti survived the attack. The first surgeon to inspect her injuries said, 'I have been practising for twenty years and I have never seen such a case. We do not know which parts to join. We do not understand how she is alive.' The case became a cause célèbre in India, the government intervened and Jyoti was transferred to the Mount Elizabeth Hospital in Singapore, which specializes in organ transplants. She suffered a cardiac arrest in the plane that took her there and died of multiple organ failure thirteen days after the attack on 29 December. Her mother, Asha Devi, was by her side. 'Jyoti turned to me and said, "Sorry, Mummy, that I gave you so much trouble,"' Asha Devi recalls; 'the sound of her breathing stopped and the lines on the monitor faded.'

Up until the attack, Jyoti Singh's life had been the stuff of an

Indian fairy tale. Her name means 'light' and her parents rejoiced at her birth. 'We were given the gift of light when she was born. People don't rejoice as much when a girl is born. We did. We gave out sweets and everyone said, 'You're celebrating as if it's a boy!'

Her father, Badrinath Singh, wanted to be a teacher as a child but his family was too poor to allow him to stay at school after his eleventh birthday. He vowed that he would educate all his children, the two boys and his daughter. 'It never entered our hearts to ever discriminate,' he says. 'How could I be happy if my son is happy and my daughter isn't? It was impossible to refuse a little girl who loved going to school.' Jyoti wanted to be a doctor. Singh sold family land and worked double shifts as a loader at Delhi airport to realize her dream.

A tutor at college remembers Jyoti's feminist beliefs and her determination. 'The differences between a girl and a boy are created in people's mind at birth,' he recalls her saying. 'In fact, a girl can do anything.' She worked at a call centre, 8.00 p.m. to 4.00 a.m., to help pay her fees, sleeping only three or four hours at night before resuming her studies in the early morning. Her dream was to build a hospital back in the village where she was born. She was excited at the thought of finishing her medical exams and of being able to help her parents. Her mother remembers her saying, 'Mum, Dad, now you don't have to worry any more. Your little girl is a doctor. Everything will be fine.'

The reaction to Jyoti's death reveals India at its best and at its worst. The police reacted swiftly. They identified the bus from CCTV footage and they rounded up the six rapists and murderers with the help of the sketches made by Awindra Pandey and statements taken from Jyoti as she lay dying in a hospital bed. The five men and one juvenile, a seventeen-year-old, were arrested within twenty-four hours of the crime.

The horrific details of the attack spread through social media and demonstrations took place across the country. The first protests in Delhi took place outside the house of the city's chief minister, Sheila Dixit, who had previously angered young women by saying that a female journalist who had been murdered in 2008 had been 'adventurous' for being on the streets of the city at night.[7] Kavita Krishnan, secretary of the All India Progressive Women's Association, announced at the demonstration that 'women have every right to be adventurous. We will be adventurous. We will be reckless. We will be rash. Don't you dare tell us what to wear. Don't tell us what time of the day or night we may be out or how many escorts we need.'

Rape is commonplace in India. Police figures suggest that one takes place every twenty minutes but the case of Jyoti Singh captured the collective imagination.[8] This was not just another of India's regular rape and murder stories. It was the stuff of Greek tragedy. Hers was a family that was brave enough to challenge the norm. Her parents regarded her as an equal to her brothers. She rewarded them by achieving the best results at school and before, unheard of in her village, going on to university. But, to her misogynistic and brutal male attackers, she had overstepped the mark. She had flouted tradition and was made to pay with her life.

The violence of the attack, her poor background, her progressive parents, her feminism, her aspirations, the fact that she was 'adventurous' enough to go to the cinema of an evening with a male friend struck a chord with the expectations of the young women of India today. In the following days, tens of thousands of women gathered at the India Gate and outside the Indian Parliament building in Delhi. They shouted: 'We won't tolerate rape' and 'Freedom' and held banners which read: 'Enough is enough. Put rapists behind bars NOT women behind the bars of patriarchy'.

The police reacted with force. The media was excluded from the area where the demonstrations took place, nonetheless the few pictures available show the police using flame-throwers, water cannon, tear gas and lathis, police batons, to attack the young women protesters and the men who now joined the protest. Barriers were overthrown and cars torched. The prime minister, Manmohan Singh, made a statement appealing for calm, quoting Gandhi in saying that 'violence will serve no purpose' and promising change in the way rape cases are handled in the country.

MPs in the Lok Sabha, the Indian Parliament, talked of India's shame, called for rapists to be hanged and for urgent measures to ensure women's safety. Better street lighting and regular police patrols on public transport were promised. A judicial review was announced and the Verma Committee set up. Eighty thousand submissions were considered and the committee concluded its review by blaming the government and police for inaction in the majority of rape cases. In a bid to rid Delhi's reputation as the 'rape capital of India', six fast-track rape courts were set up in the city.

Four months after the attack one of the defendants, Ram Singh, was found hanged in his prison cell leaving just the juvenile and four adult men to be tried. In August 2013, the juvenile was sentenced to the maximum term possible, three years in a reform facility. A month later, the four surviving adult defendants were found guilty of the rape and murder of Jyoti Singh and the attempted murder of Awindra Pandey. As he sentenced them to death, Judge Yogesh Khana spoke of the case that had 'shocked the collective conscience of India'. Three years later, none of them have been hanged; they are still appealing against their sentences.

A year after the assault, research carried out for an opinion poll revealed that 90 per cent of the women asked said that they felt no safer on the streets of Delhi;[9] police figures showed that crimes against women had increased. It looked as if was Delhi was returning to business as usual and the outrage and promises made after Jyoti's rape and murder were forgotten.

Meanwhile, film director Leslee Udwin had been making a documentary about the brutal rape of Jyoti Singh, which was to be broadcast simultaneously in the UK and in India in March 2015.[10] India's politicians were alarmed by the pre-publicity given to the documentary which confirmed that antediluvian attitudes towards women in India are not just found among uneducated drunkards, like the accused, but among the professional classes as well. India's Parliamentary Affairs Minister Venkaiah Naidu claimed that the film was part of a conspiracy 'to defame India' and the broadcast was banned. But the film was shown on the BBC in the UK and the ugly highlights, the interview with the accused, Mukesh Singh, and with two defence lawyers, made their way on to social media and reignited the fury among the women of India.

M. L. Sharma, one of the defence lawyers in the trial says, in broken English, that 'in our society, we never allow our girls to come out from the house after 6.30 p.m. or 7.30 p.m. or 8.30 p.m. in the evening with any unknown person. They (Jyoti Singh and Awindra Pandey) left our Indian culture. They were influenced by the film culture in which they can do anything. You are talking about a man and woman as friends. Sorry. That doesn't have any place in our society. A woman . . . immediately put the sex in his eyes. In India, we have the best culture. In our culture, there is no place for a woman.'

Another lawyer who defended the six accused, A. P. Singh, takes the unacceptable argument even further. Referring to Jyoti's decision to go to the cinema with a male friend, he says a girl can go out 'but she should go with [her] family members like uncle, father, mother, grandfather, grandmother, etc. etc. She should not go in night hours with her boyfriend. If my daughter or sister engaged in pre-marital activities and disgraced herself and allowed herself to lose face and character by doing such things,

I would most certainly take this sort of sister or daughter to my farmhouse and, in front of my entire family, put petrol on her and set her alight.'

Just as one of the accused, Mukesh Singh, said, 'a girl is far more responsible for rape than a boy', the two lawyers, educated, professional men, both members of India's Bar Council reiterated the belief that rape is always a girl's fault. Women, enraged and perplexed by the endemic culture of routine rape in their country, responded furiously in social media. Journalist Nandini Krishnan wrote in her blog, 'I don't know, maybe they do it over and over again not because they don't realize it is wrong, but because they are addicted to the sense of power they have while they are doing it, and because – just a thought – they can *get away with it*, over and over and over again.'

Police statistics certainly confirm that they can get away with it. Only one of 706 rape cases filed in Delhi in 2012 ended in a conviction. A prison psychiatrist describes rapists as 'normal human beings with anti-social traits . . . So that whenever they feel there is a chance they could rape a woman, they do it. There are people in jail who have done 200 rapes. That is the number they can remember; it could be more. They say that it is a "man's right". They don't think of the other person as a human being. The negative, cultural values about women are very important in this type of act.'[11]

How did women get so denigrated in Indian society? After all, four of the 'top ten' Hindi gods are goddesses, Lakshmi, Durga, Kali and Saraswati, and are worshipped with enthusiasm by men and women alike. There have been a woman president and prime minister. But there appears to be a dangerous disconnect between the women who have made it to the top and the millions of women for whom India is the worst place to live on earth. Looking for answers, Indian sociologists and feminists blame the rural traditions among families that continue to influence the vast majority of Indians today, both those who remain in the villages and those newly arrived in the cities like the men who were found guilty in the Jyoti Singh case.

Boys can help till the land; girls are weak and useless. Boys are worth investing in and, if money is limited, only the boys will be sent to school. It is hardly surprising that in India today 82 per cent of men and only 65 per cent of women are literate.[12] From their earliest memories boys will note that they are given more food than their sisters, their mothers will always serve them first and the birth of their brothers is met with rejoicing. 'Many of our people grow up thinking that the girl is less important,' says a prominent woman politician, 'and because she is less important, you can do what you like with her.'[13]

In the interview with Mukesh Singh, he expands on the 'you can do what you like with her' philosophy. He speaks of how previous rape victims have had their eyes gouged out or were set alight. Most chilling of all, he says that because of the death sentence handed out to him and the three other accused in the Jyoti Singh case, women are now more at risk. 'The death sentence will make things even more dangerous for girls,' he says. 'Now when they rape, they won't leave the girl like we did. They will kill her. Before, they would rape and say, "Leave her, she won't tell anyone." Now when they rape, especially the criminal types, they will just kill the girl. Death.'

Death, the ultimate solution, is meted out to the women of India with abandon: to rape victims to ensure that they cannot testify; sati, the ceremony of burning a widow on her husband's funeral pyre, although banned in 1988, is still practised; 'dowry deaths', the murder of brides who default on wedding agreements, have been commonplace for centuries and now the girl is at risk even before she has a chance to emerge from the womb.

India is losing millions of girls a year. They are the victims of foeticide, the murder of foetuses in the womb, and of infanticide, the murder of girls between the ages of zero and four. The losses are having a dramatic effect on India's sex ratio. The number of girls born in relation to boys has fallen every year since 1991. The 2011 census showed there were 914 females per 1,000 males, the lowest ever recorded.[14] In some parts of the country, there are fewer than 800 girls for every 1,000 boys born. Advances in medical equipment has teamed up with the prejudice of a patriarchal society with devastating results.

Mobile sex selection clinics drive unchecked into almost every village or neighbourhood. The test costs only a few hundred rupees. Once a woman knows she is bearing a baby girl, she might call in the local practitioner. 'I crush the bark of the mango tree and marwa tree together into a paste-like substance,' a medicine man working in Rajasthan explains, 'I then mix it with other ingredients, including locally brewed wine and I add black magic and tell the woman she must take it first thing in the morning, on an empty stomach.'[15]

Other village midwives talk of inserting sticks and glass into the vagina to kill the foetus. No wonder thousands of women die every year from such practices. If the mother and baby survive against the odds, then the more traditional methods of infanticide are used. For centuries, baby girls have been drowned at birth or simply left to die through neglect, starved to death or fed with too much salt. Once again, today's scientific advances are there to help. Pesticide is used increasingly to kill babies of only a few days old.

By the late 1980s, most doctors' clinics in the towns of India had an ultrasound machine by which parents could learn the sex of the foetus and choose to have an abortion in situ straightaway. Abortion has been legal in India since 1971 with a wide remit. Abortion is allowed in cases of rape, danger to the health of mother and foetus and the failure of birth control devices used by the parents. It is up to the discretion of the medical practitioner. The number of baby girls killed in the uterus has now overtaken the number who are murdered by the more traditional methods of infanticide.

The ratio of girls born compared with boys began to fall in 1991. The Pre-Conception and Pre-Natal Diagnostic Techniques Act was passed in 1994 making it a criminal offence for a doctor to use gender as a reason for abortion.[16] However, due to India's preoccupation with population growth, abortion has never been effectively policed in India; ultrasound clinics are rarely investigated by health officials and the killings continue. In a majority of states in India, there have been no prosecutions under the law. In two states, there have been small fines, between 300 and 4,000 rupees, and only one case of two years' imprisonment.[17] It is hardly surprising that the law is not being implemented when the police, the doctors, and the families subscribe to the same mindset.

As Sriti Yadav, writing in the woman's magazine *Feminspire*, puts it, 'so essentially, raising a girl child is equivalent to investing in a failing business and raising a boy is an assurance to a lottery win. Who in their right minds would give birth to a female kid?' And a girl is always a risk. Like in so many cultures we have looked at, a girl's sole worth lies in her virginity. Yadav points out that 'a slight rebellion from the strict path and the girl is no longer worth a decent boy; that means no marriage and an unmarried girl is a curse for her entire family. When such strict social conditions are imposed upon a girl, she becomes a liability; most parents would chose to shy away from such a responsibility. The solution is: no female child in the family.'[18]

It is not just the illiterate farming communities who are killing their baby girls. The states with the lowest sex ratio in India include Haryana and Punjab, which are among the wealthiest states in India, judged by per capita income. Amrita Guha, an Indian academic from Calcutta, blames the combination of wealth that gives access to modern medical technology and the persistence of cultural conservatism. 'My view is that relative affluence, without any accompanying progressive attitudes towards women, have exacerbated the trend towards female feticide' among the middle classes of India.[19]

So why do even more affluent parents prefer boys? In most cases, a woman severs all relationships with her family when she marries. Her birth family resent money spent on her maintenance and education because a girl's life will thereafter belong to her husband and her in-laws. The identity of the girl is lost to her birth family and her main duty to her new family is to carry on the family name by producing a son. If a family has aspirations in the new consumer-driven India, they won't want numerous children. Their preference will be a boy.

Amita lives in a middle-class area of Delhi. She reminds me of the lead character in the prize-winning Indian film *The Lunchbox*, in which Nimrat Kaur plays the dutiful, lonely wife who has a sadness and wistfulness about her as she prepares her husband's lunch in metal containers every day. Amita gets up at dawn to start cooking in her tiny kitchen with two gas rings. The fan whirrs overhead as she carefully rolls out the paranthas and checks the chili content in the chicken biryani. She prepares four lunchboxes: one for her husband and one each for her two daughters, in their twenties, and a nineteen-year-old son, all of whom are college students.

She tells me that she still mourns the daughters she lost. Between giving birth to her daughters and the birth of her son, she had two pregnancies. The ultrasound confirmed that they were girls and each time she was forced by her husband's family to abort the foetus. She breaks down in tears as she remembers the first abortion. 'The baby was nearly six months old. I miss her.' When the ultrasound showed that she was pregnant again with a girl, Amita says the family again forced her to abort. 'I said that girls have as much right to live as boys, but my mother-in-law told me I was stupid.'

After the law was introduced against gender selection in abortion clinics, it took eleven years for the first conviction in 2006.

The doctor was imprisoned for two years. 'Our main anxiety is that existing strategies are not working,' says Dr Puneet Bedi, a Delhi-based gynaecologist, who has been a passionate campaigner against sex selection abortions.[20] The problem he believes is that the doctor is motivated by money and the woman is coerced by family and social pressure and the deed takes place behind closed doors. It is hardly surprising that medical practitioners show no interest in putting their house in order and inspections by health authorities are random and few.

And then there are the social consequences of foeticide, which could offer another explanation for the Jyoti Singh case. With so few women in some areas of India and high numbers of unemployed, unmarried men, we need look no further for the reason for the increase in rape, argues Amrita Guha. 'As men see women as the vulnerable group who are becoming numerically smaller and the prospect of marriage recedes, the incidence of gang rape can only rise.' A common proverb in northern India has it that 'the lord of a woman is a man; a man's lord is his livelihood'. If a man has neither woman nor a job, he is a social outcast and likely to turn into a very frustrated, angry and dangerous person. But if he has money and cannot find a partner for life within his community, he can buy one.

The relatively wealthy state of Haryana has the worst sex ratio in India, with 861 girls born to every 1,000 boys.[21] The young men of Jind, a prosperous, farming district in Haryana, are in panic. In 2009, their leader, Pawan Kumar, set up the Unmarried Youth Organization and, in India's 2014 elections, launched the *bahu-dilao-vote lo* (brides for votes) slogan, demanding that their politicians should find them brides in exchange for their votes. They received short shrift from the Congress Party candidate, 'Why do people not think about brides when they resort to female foeticide? Brides are not a commodity which can be arranged from the market. Nobody will accept such an unusual, absurd demand.'[22]

Disappointed by their politicians, the young men of Haryana contact the people traffickers to find them brides. 'They are forced to buy brides,' says Sunil Jaglau, a village head in Haryana. 'This has turned into a big business around here. Agents and middlemen are flourishing.' The brides come from the most poverty-ridden areas of India, from Orissa, Bengal, Assam and Bihar, the kind of areas in India where we hear of farmers who regularly commit suicide, unable to pay the high cost of fertilizers and unable to cope with large families and debt. The families are only too happy to sell a daughter or two. The going rate for girls aged between ten and eighteen, is 500–1,000 rupees (£6–£12) each.

By the time they have travelled several thousand miles across India, they are sold in Haryana for anything between 4,000 and 30,000 rupees (£40–£300), making it well worth the trouble for the traffickers. They call them '*paros*', these traumatized girls who arrive in a state where they don't speak the language and have no cultural references. Local women already living in extended families are reluctant to accept them. Arriving without dowries or family, they are usually denied a traditional, legal wedding which leaves their married status ambiguous. They are alienated, not allowed to keep in touch with their families back home and given the hardest work. Rumours of abuse and worse abound in the villages of Haryana like the one of the woman who, they say, was beheaded for refusing to sleep with her owner's brothers.

There are said to be tens of thousands of *paros* living in the villages of Haryana. A local government minister, Randeep Singh Surjewala, says that they act if they get complaints about their treatment and at the same time they are stepping up their campaign against foeticide. 'We are trying to educate people socially and address the sex ratio problem. We want to make our people appreciate and cherish the girls of our community.' There are banners over the main streets in Haryana which say: 'Save Our

Girls'. At least these have replaced the ones which the abortion clinics put up before which read: 'Pay Now, Save Later'.

Dowries were banned in India in 1961 but, like so many laws designed to protect women, the ban has been widely ignored. Traditionally, in rural India the dowry would consist of clothes, jewellery, a modest sum of money or a parcel of land. In modern India, the consumer society has produced a groom with more ambitious demands – a colour TV, music systems, kitchen equipment, motorbikes and cars. It has become a social evil in which the father of several daughters can easily be bankrupted by the process. In desperation, he asks to pay in instalments, sometimes well after the wedding has taken place. During this period, if the items do not arrive on time, the new bride might be beaten by the family, imprisoned in her new home or killed.

The latest figures from India's National Crime Records Bureau reveal 8,233 dowry deaths for 2012.[23] The favoured method is burning. The husband's family will ensure that the wife is wearing an inflammable nylon sari and the 'accident' will invariably take place in the kitchen. The female wards in hospital burn units in India are always full of what the doctors call 'kitchen killings'. Alarmed by the increase in these horrific deaths in the 1980s, the dowry laws were modified to treat every death by burning within the first seven years of marriage as a dowry death.

The laws are there but the courts in India are notoriously unsympathetic to cases involving violence against women. In 2014, judges sitting in the Supreme Court claimed that the dowry death laws were being used as a 'weapon by disgruntled wives. The simplest way to harass is to get the husband and his relatives arrested under this provision.' Recently, the police have been instructed to be much more demanding in their investigation of such cases, making it harder for the woman, who may be lying close to death in a hospital bed, to get her voice heard. Nearly 200,000 suspects were arrested for dowry deaths in 2012; only 15 per cent were convicted.

In India, a woman is killed in a 'dowry death' every hour[24] and a baby girl is aborted every twelve seconds.[25] The murder of women has reached epidemic proportions in a country which boasts the world's tenth richest economy. The secretariat of the G20 group of nations, which includes India, has declared India the worst place on earth to be born a woman, even worse than Saudi Arabia. A few years ago, the UN's Department of Economic and Social Affairs declared India the most dangerous place in the world to be born a girl, with females almost twice as likely to die before reaching the age of five as boys.[26]

India has spent £60 million on sending a spacecraft to orbit Mars while girls remain uneducated and at risk. The protection of girls in India, as in so many countries, is not a priority. Shemeer Padinzjharedil, who runs an NGO that documents crimes against women, says, 'It's a miracle a woman survives in India. Even before she is born, she is at risk of being aborted due to our obsession for sons. As a child, she faces abuse, rape and early marriage and even when she marries, she is killed for her dowry. If she survives all of this, as a widow she is discriminated against and given no rights over inheritance or property.'[27]

India's leading woman novelist, Anita Desai, has been criticized for writing about the women of India as helpless beings, with no control over their lives. 'But I try,' she says, 'as every writer tries to do, even in fiction, to get at the truth, to write the truth.'[28] In her novel *Voices in the City*, one of the principal characters, Monisha from Calcutta, says,

I think of generations of Bengali women, hidden behind the barred windows of half dark rooms, spending centuries washing clothes. Kneading dough and murmuring aloud verses from the 'Bhagavad Gita' in the dim light of sooty lamps.

Lives spent in waiting for nothing, waiting on men who

are self-centred and indifferent, hungry and demanding and critical, waiting for death and dying misunderstood.[29]

In despair of ever escaping the male-dominated, restricting environment in which she lives, Monisha kills herself. Desai, who chooses to live in America, is reluctant to comment on modern India, observing that 'India is a curious place that still preserves the past, religions, and its history. No matter how modern India becomes, it is still very much an old country.'[30] Outraged by the increase in violent rapes, however, she has recently said, 'Men still don't accept women as human beings who must live their lives. It may take generations before there is any real change.'[31]

Is there any sign of change? Since Prime Minister Narendra Modi came to power in 2014, he has promoted a pro-woman image. He has spoken out against sexual violence, female foeticide and has accused parents of not raising their sons correctly.

The women of India might have had reason for optimism until the prime minister's real feelings on the subject emerged in June 2015. In a state visit to Dhaka University, he made an extraordinarily tactless and revealing reference to the Bangladeshi prime minister and women in general by saying, 'I am happy that the Bangladesh Prime Minister, despite being a woman, has declared zero tolerance for terrorism.'[32]

Modi's bigoted remarks led to an outpouring of outrage from the women of India under the hashtag #DespiteBeingAWoman: 'Despite being a woman, I managed to figure out how to use a car and drive with it.' And 'Despite being a woman, I can breathe, eat, crap and exist. Must be an achievement!' Just as after the Jyoti Singh rape case, the women of India fought back with indignation and fury. But with such sentiments being expressed by the leader of the world's largest democracy, it could be some time yet before India loses its unenviable reputation as 'the worst place on earth to be born a woman'.

I I

RAPE AS A WEAPON OF WAR

Bosnia and the Democratic Republic of the Congo

I was trying to sleep but there was hardly room to lie down. There were hundreds of us there and the stench from the buckets we used as toilets was overwhelming. They came at night with torches. My twelve- and fourteen-year-old daughters were lying alongside me. One of the soldiers, a tall bearded man, shone the torch on Esma, my fourteen-year-old, and said, 'I'll have her.' I said, 'No, no, please take me.' Esma started screaming hysterically. I was calm and I think he thought it would be less trouble to take me.

They kept me for fourteen days. At first it was just the bearded one, his name was Dusko. I could smell the alcohol on his breath as he raped me. But, after a couple of days, he gave me to anyone who wanted me. Sometimes it was two a day and sometimes ten. At first I fought them with my nails and teeth but they beat me and then I just let them get on with it. I was bleeding and I was in a bad way so they took me back to the hall. I asked the women there, 'Where are my daughters?' They said, 'They came to take them.' I never saw them again.

I am sitting listening to Ivanka's story in Posušje, eastern Croatia, in a disused railway carriage being used to accommodate families who have fled the fighting. It is October 1993, the height of the Bosnian War. Ivanka pours out the coffee she has prepared in the Turkish style with a trembling hand. She is forty-two but her hair is grey and she looks like a woman in her sixties. She has lost everything – mother, husband, her two daughters and ten-year-old son. When the experts added up the figures at the end of the war, they reckon that some 50,000 women and girls were raped in this conflict between 1992 and 1995. Ivanka is just one of them.[1]

Other women come to the door of the railway carriage and listen in as she talks. Ivanka is embarrassed and upset and gets up to shut the door. I am grateful she is talking to me. I have already approached a number of other women the workers at the refugee camp tell me have been raped but Ivanka is the first to actually use the word. Some of the women shake their heads and say they cannot talk about what happened, 'It is too shameful.' Others just say 'it' when describing the assault on their bodies and the event that has ruined their lives. I feel guilty probing them and move on. Ivanka is the only one who will tell me the full story.

Serb soldiers arrived in her village near Doboj, in northern Bosnia in May 1992. Their aim was to 'ethnically cleanse' the area, to rid it of the Muslim population while enjoying the spoils of war. 'The Chetniks came into my house, took what they wanted and trashed the rest. They did that to all the houses belonging to Muslims. They took my husband and son away and put me and my daughters in a truck and drove us to a local school and put us into the sports room there, the gym. It was so crowded. When the soldiers came in to throw us pieces of bread or to take us away, they would step on us as they walked around.'

Ivanka was released from what is now known as one of the notorious 'rape camps' of the Bosnian War when the Muslim government forces recaptured Doboj in October 1995. Of the 2,000 or so women who once slept in the hall, only a few hundred were there when the buses came to drive them to safety. She has no idea what happened to her daughters. Many of the younger rape victims, and some were as young as ten, were raped to death. Their underdeveloped bodies couldn't stand the repeated abuse.

Ivanka is desperate to find the men in her family, her husband, brother and son. If she finds her husband, she is anxious that he does not find out that she was raped. If he were to find out he'd be likely to reject her. She thanks God that she is beyond child-bearing age because a number of the rape victims in the refugee camp are pregnant. 'They say that they will kill their babies as soon as they are born,' says Ivanka. 'How can they love the children of Serbian rapists and murderers?' She has heard that somewhere the International Red Cross is compiling lists of prisoners but she does not know how to access them. If it was not for the friendship of the women she shares her railway carriage with, she says, she would have killed herself months ago. I hold her hand and try to reassure her, saying that surely the war will be over soon, but what do I know?

Children who survived the massacres play outside. A heart-breakingly beautiful blonde-haired and blue-eyed little girl sits on the steps of the carriage and stares vacantly. 'She doesn't speak after what happened. She saw them kill her father,' Ivanka explains. A small boy called Eman builds houses out of twigs and bits of cardboard. 'This is my house,' he says proudly and, pointing to a smaller structure alongside, says, 'Look, this is where my father keeps the car.'

The boredom of refugee life is broken only by the daily food delivery by the charity workers who look after their needs and the occasional arrival of parcels of clothes from the richer countries of Europe. The women pick through the discarded coats, dresses, suits and shoes put together by well-meaning women in London,

Paris and Berlin. Ivanka complains, 'Why do they send so many clothes for men? Don't they know that we don't have any?' Six-year-old Eman wanders over to look into the boxes. 'Why don't they send toys? Clothes are boring,' he says.

I feel guilty. I am one of those well-meaning women who tried to do my bit. Like so many of us, I watched in horror as some 90,000 Serb troops mobilized and attacked Bosnia-Herzegovina after its people voted for independence in March 1992. As the war progressed and created the biggest humanitarian crisis since the Second World War, I raised money for the refugees. In 1993, I held a charity ball, 'Bop for Bosnia' in Studio One at the BBC. Tony Blair, then Shadow Home Secretary, and several hundred others came. We raised enough money to send convoys of food and clothes for refugees escaping the war in Bosnia. 'Damn!' I thought as I looked at the disappointed six-year-old. 'Why didn't I think of toys?'[2]

As a journalist, I covered the war from the beginning, scarcely believing that it took just over two hours to fly from London and into the mire of chaos, destruction and death. The closest I have ever come to being killed in my work was when I joined a convoy taking relief through Croatia to the besieged Muslim town of Jablanica in Bosnia. I was in the lead truck while we were driving through a gorge at night when the driver made a stupid mistake. He stopped on an illuminated bridge to read a map, exposing the convoy to attack. Artillery fire rained down on us from Serb-held positions in the surrounding mountains. After the initial shock, I picked up my camera and filmed. It wasn't the first time that I dis-covered the comfort of the camera in such situations – it distances you, watching events through a lens makes you think you're just a movie-watching spectator, it helps you cope. We were lucky. Only one of the trucks received a direct hit and the two occupants escaped with an eye injury and another with shrapnel in his leg. We limped into Jablanica to a grateful welcome from the hungry

Muslim residents and a furious rebuke from the commander of the Spanish UN peacekeeping forces who were camped close to the town. He had lost two men on the same road the previous week and rightly accused us of being irresponsible and foolhardy.

I remember Sarajevo after a bombardment from Serbian troops based in Pale, in the hills above the Muslim city. The image of an apartment block missing an entire external wall is one I shall never forget – shattered concrete revealing unmade beds, half-finished meals and children's games scattered. Daily life violently interrupted and personal effects crudely exposed for all to see. The former inhabitants cowered in basement bunkers where they were to spend most of the rest of the war. I remember filming in the village of Srebrenica, a few weeks before its people suffered the most brutal massacre of the war. Thousands of Muslims had taken refuge there from the surrounding area after the UN declared the village 'a safe area'. As I was filming families camping in hot and unsanitary conditions in a school hall, a woman came up to me and yelled, 'Why do you just bring your cameras here to entertain the outside world? Why don't you do something?'

That woman's voice still haunts me, both because it cruelly sums up the work of a TV journalist and because of what almost certainly happened to her next. The UN peacekeepers, a battalion of Dutch soldiers, stood by as the Serbian army, under the command of General Ratko Mladić, entered the village in July 1995 and took away 8,000 boys and men to be slaughtered. Gazing at the thousands of terrified Muslim men, Mladić promised his men a 'feast of blood'. As for the women, the general said to them, 'Beautiful. Keep the good ones over there. Enjoy them!'[3]

A Dutch medical orderly later gave evidence to the war crimes tribunal: 'The soldier was lying on the girl, with his pants off. She was lying on the ground, on some kind of mattress. There was blood on the mattress, she was covered with blood. She had bruises on her legs. There was even blood coming down her legs.

She was in total shock. She went totally crazy.'[4] In another testimony, a 43-year-old rape victim recalled that 'he forced me to
take off my clothes. I cried and begged him not to. He seemed to
me like he was twenty years old. I was telling him: "I am an old
woman; I could be your mother." He said: "I have been in the field
for a month, I have no woman, I want to and I can."'[5]

What effect did rape have on the tens of thousands of women?
The American feminist Andrea Dworkin writes that a person's
'struggle for dignity and self-determination is rooted in the
struggle for actual control of one's own body, especially control
over physical access to one's own body'.[6] Bosnian rape victims
repeatedly talk of feeling defiled, dirty and humiliated. Sadeta, a
22-year-old, who had been raped by Serbian troops in her village
of Rizvanovici, throws a terrible insight into rape as an act of war:
'Killing them isn't interesting enough for them any more. It's a lot
more fun to torture us, especially if they get a woman pregnant.
They want to humiliate us . . . and they've done it, too. Not just
in my case, either, all the women and girls will feel humiliated,
defiled, dirty in some way for the rest of their lives . . . I feel dirty
myself somehow. And I feel as though everybody can see it when
they pass me in the street.'[7]

We have to take into account the background of the Muslim
woman in Bosnia to understand the extent of her suffering.
Before Yugoslavia became a communist state in the aftermath
of the Second World War, Muslims adhered to the patriarchal
traditions of a strict Islamic society. A Muslim woman wore the
veil and her domain was the house and her business was rearing
children. The communist regime did its best to do away with
these traditions but when President Tito died in 1980 there was a
revival of the old-fashioned way. 'Returning to the old traditions
was thought to be a national prerequisite for a national renais-
sance,' explains Azra Zalihic-Kaurin in her essay on the subject.[8]
Among other restrictions, premarital sex was forbidden, rape was

like death. Rape is devastating for any woman but for the Muslim woman it is surely worse. Too often she is blamed. Rape victims in Pakistan and Afghanistan are routinely condemned to death. Bosnian Muslim women were often disbelieved and excluded. Many young survivors feared that they would never enjoy lives as wives and mothers. 'Everyone does not believe we were forced,' said eighteen-year-old Sevlata in a refuge in Tuzla, 'and they think that we are going to go with [the Serbs] again. We can't imagine marriage as a normal thing. We know that the man will always be suspicious.'

Rape in the context of war is not 'just' sexual violence. It is an act of hate and an exercise of power. Most of the women who were brave enough to tell their stories during and after this war speak of rape accompanied by brutal physical attacks: 'He nearly choked me to death', 'After they raped me, they thrust a broken bottle into me'. In war, rapists tend to depersonalize their victims; rape is simply one of the acts of violence and a right of war. Many victims were astonished to recognize their abusers as former neighbours. A teenage survivor who testified at the trial of Zoran Vuković, convicted rapist and torturer, said he laughed while he was raping her: 'I had the feeling that he was doing this precisely because he knew me, to inflict even more evil on me.'[9]

'Murder, pillage and rape' have always been a by-product of war, or 'collateral damage' to use the more modern term popularized by coalition forces during the 1991 Gulf War. At the 'Rape of Nanking' in 1937, tens of thousands of Chinese women were raped and murdered by troops of the Japanese Imperial Army.[10] There was widespread rape of German women as angry, vengeful Soviet troops made their way west across Germany in 1944. Hundreds of thousands of women were raped in the Berlin area after the city fell in 1945.[11] The twentieth century does not have a monopoly on the barbarous practice. The armies of Genghis Khan and conquering Roman legions behaved in an equally abusive manner. The difference in the Bosnian War is that rape was a weapon of war with a specific goal defined by the commanders. It was part of the programme of ethnic cleansing and genocide.

When Slobodan Milošević ordered the invasion of Bosnia-Herzegovina in 1992, Muslims represented 43 per cent of the population, Serbs 33 per cent and Croats 17 per cent. The Serbs wanted two-thirds of the territory and the Muslims and Croats had to be cleared out. The Croatian journalist and author Seada Vranić says that the rape of non-Serb women was part of the 'Greater-Serbian expansionist policy'. 'Behind it all lay just one idea: to expel the population of other nationalities from a given territory. So they dreamed up a monstrous plan: they went into the houses of non-Serbs and raped them. Rape is a very effective means for that purpose: if three or four women arrived in a village (with reports of how the soldiers were raping all non-Serbs), all the villagers would take flight.'[12]

Many women were raped in public in order to encourage the flight. Rape humiliates the men in the family; it tears communities apart. In collecting her testimony, Vranić heard from victims and eye-witnesses of how men were incapacitated, often tied to trees, and women were raped in front of their husbands and children, their breasts were cut off and their wombs torn open. Vranić wrote her book *Breaking the Wall of Silence* in haste during the war, to try to alert the international community to what was going on. No wonder she says that: 'All that testimony really crushed me. I was on the brink of physical and psychological collapse.'[13]

By 1993, the European Community investigators, who included Simone Veil, asserted that rape was 'perpetrated with the conscious intention of demoralizing and terrorizing communities, driving them from their home regions and demonstrating the power of the invading forces.'[14] Soldiers in subsequent war crime trials have admitted that they were ordered to rape in order to boost Serbian army morale. Rape of the female body, they were told, was part of the conquering process. A rape victim who survived the notorious Trnopolje internment camp in northern Bosnia, 24-year-old Hatiza says, 'They did it to humiliate us. They were showing us their power. They stuck their guns in our mouths. They tore our clothes. They showed the "Turkish women" they were superior.'[15] One survivor who says she was raped every night that she was held asked one of her abusers why he did it. He replied: 'because you are Muslims and there are too many of you.'[16]

Many survivors tell of how their abusers would boast about the Serbian babies they were making, they were not interested in women who were already pregnant when they were captured. There was talk of 'inferior Muslim wombs' being conquered by Serbian sperm and, because of the inferiority of the Muslim the result would be pure Serb. Hatred of 'the Turk' was a recurring theme. In the ethnic cleansing of the Foča area in eastern Bosnia, 22-year-old Azra was held in a prison and raped by her Serbian neighbour, Dragan, who was the local policeman. 'They said we were at war now, there wasn't any law and order any more. They shouted curses "Fuck your Turkish mother" or "Death to all Turkish sperm".'[17]

The Serbs have notoriously long memories. Their preoccupation with the Turk was instilled by their history as part of the Ottoman Empire when many former Christians converted to Islam for preferential treatment and better job prospects under Turkish rule. They became Bosnia's Muslims. Just as hatred was whipped up against the Jews in Germany in the 1930s because of their supposed wealth and intelligence, so the Bosnian Muslims were hated for their alleged self-interested collaboration with the Turks. Islamophobia was a phenomenon here in Europe well before it was whipped up by the right-wing parties of EU countries in the twenty-first century.

One of my more shameful memories as a journalist is the night I spent as a dinner guest with General Ratko Mladić, currently on trial in The Hague on charges of mass murder and inciting his men to sexual violence. In an interview with me that afternoon, he had spoken of the 'barbarians at the gate'. 'Why don't the other European governments support us?' he asked. 'Do they not realize that my army is fighting to prevent the Turks from once again threatening the gates of Vienna?' referring to the siege of Vienna in 1683. I nodded sympathetically and I agreed to sup with the devil, in the person of General Ratko Mladić, when he invited me to stay at his headquarters that night.

I have always believed the ends justify the means and, before I left the next morning, I had persuaded him to give me a pass to get through Serb lines and to film in the besieged village of Srebrenica the next day. But before I left, the supreme commander of Serb forces left me in no doubt that the aim of his war was genocidal. An estimated 40,000 civilians died in the war, twice as many combatants killed. The majority of civilian deaths were Muslim. The women who survived were often the unwilling carriers of the future generation of Serbs for whom, in the eyes of men like Ratko Mladić, the war had been fought.[18]

In the rape camp in the school in Doboj, Ifeta was taken to a classroom where she was raped by three men. 'And while they were doing it they said that I was going to have a baby by them and that it'd be an honor for a Muslim woman to give birth to a Serbian kid.'[19] Another inmate at the Doboj camp, Kadira, remembers that, 'Women who got pregnant, they had to stay there for seven or eight months so they could give birth to a Serbian kid. They had their gynecologists there to examine the women. The pregnant ones were separated off from us and had special privileges; they got meals, they were better off, they were protected. Only when a woman's in her seventh month, when she can't do anything about it any more, then she's released. Then they usually take these women to Serbia . . . They beat the women who didn't get pregnant, especially the younger women; they were supposed to confess what contraceptives they were using.'[20]

Little is known about what happened to the women taken to Serbia. Maybe, as bearers of Serbian children, they continued to get special privileges. During the Second World War, the Nazis organized the Lebensborn programme to breed pure, Aryan children to compensate for Germany's war casualties. Perhaps the Serb leaders were thinking along the same lines as they ordered these rapes and protected the subsequent pregnancies in order to repopulate a 'Greater Serbia'. We may never know if there was a deliberate breeding programme. The questioning of suspects in The Hague has concentrated on the circumstances of the sexual assault and not on what happened to the survivors. We cannot ask the chief architect of this genocidal war, Slobodan Milošević, who died of a heart attack in his prison cell in The Hague while on trial in 2006.

And there was another plan for pregnant Muslim women. Other 'pregnant ones' relate that, in the latter stages of pregnancy, they were driven to the border and were made to walk across to one of the diminishing number of territories still controlled by the Muslim Bosnians. As these women staggered across the line, their bellies swollen, the message was clear: the next generation born on these contested lands would be Serb. Thirty-year-old Jasmina was one of them. When she returned to Tuzla, she said, 'I was so ashamed. I wore a loose dress for fear of meeting a member of my family or a friend. As it turned out, they were all dead. All I had left as family was the enemy in my womb.'

Another survivor, Saneda, was one of eleven pregnant women who were taken to Sarajevo. 'I knew it wasn't my kid. I knew what I went through. It wasn't a child born of love or from a respectable marriage. If anyone had tried to show it to me after it was born, I'd have strangled them and the baby too . . . If I'd ever had any chance to kill the kid inside me, I'd have done it.'[21] The German journalist, Alexandra Stiglmayer, spoke to Saneda's doctors who said they sedated her to stop her committing infanticide. After she gave birth the baby was taken to England and adopted.[22] Pregnant women who managed to get to more sophisticated women's clinics in the towns of Bosnia Herzegovina and Croatia were given more options.

In January 1993, a UN investigation by a team of five people interviewing doctors and checking medical records in hospitals in Zagreb, Sarajevo, Zenića and Belgrade found that of 119 pregnant rape victims 88 received abortions. In Zenića, sixteen women between the ages of seventeen and twenty-two were more than twenty weeks pregnant and, therefore, could not receive abortions.[23] Doctors admit to taking a flexible view of the old Yugoslav law that only permitted abortions within the first trimester. Women who found themselves in the Catholic parts of Croatia had a harder time. Pope John Paul's warning to women to 'accept the enemy into them' was met with incredulity by doctors and counsellors like Mubera Zdralovic, who helped women in the Croatian capital, Zagreb. 'Does the Pope not understand? The foetus growing inside the woman is a living reminder of the horror she has suffered, like a wound that keeps on growing.'[24]

The number of rapes perpetrated during the Bosnian War, guessed at up to 50,000,[25] can never be confirmed. Some women would have quietly dealt with the problem themselves, with the help of local doctors and midwives, and would have been too ashamed to tell anyone. Serbian and Croatian women were raped too, but Bosnian women make up the vast majority of rapes recorded. After all, they were a deliberate target in the war of genocide. Just as the Bosnian War was different in this respect, so was the justice meted out in the aftermath of the conflict.

When it was set up in 1993 the International Criminal Tribunal for the former Yugoslavia (ICTY) was the first international criminal tribunal to enter convictions for rape as a form of torture and for sexual enslavement as crime against humanity. The first convictions came in the so-called 'rape camp case' against three Serbs in 2001. Dragoljub Kunarac was sentenced to twenty-eight years, Radomir Kovač to twenty years and Zoran Vuković to twelve years for the crimes of 'rape, torture, enslavement and outrages upon personal dignity' committed in the Foča area of Bosnia between 1992 and 1993. There was complete silence in the court as Judge Florence Mumba delivered her powerful and emotional summing up.

> The three accused were not just following orders, if there were such orders, to rape Muslim women. The evidence shows free will on their part. Of the women and girls so detained, one was a child of only twelve years at the time. She has not been heard of since she was sold by one of the accused. The women and girls were either lent or 'rented out' to other soldiers for the sole purpose of being ravaged and abused. Some of the women and girls were kept in servitude for months on end. The three accused are not ordinary soldiers, whose morals were merely loosened by the hardships of war. These are men with no known criminal past. However, they thrived in the dark atmosphere of the dehumanization of those believed to be enemies.[26]

Judge Mumba then told the three men in the dock to stand and she sentenced them.

By 2011, the ICTY had indicted seventy-eight men for crimes related to sexual violence; as of February 2014, thirty have been convicted.[27] That is a fraction of the men responsible for some 50,000 rapes but it is a start and better than the country that holds the current record for sexual violence in war. In the Democratic Republic of the Congo (DRC), it is estimated that forty-eight women are raped every hour.[28] If we calculate the number of rapes that could have taken place in the DRC since the war began in 1996, it adds up to 7,989,120 rapes. Between July 2011 and December 2013, the UNJHRO registered 187 convictions by military jurisdictions for sexual violence. Sentences range from ten months to twenty years in prison.[29]

I shall not attempt to explain the confusion of militias, foreign-backed armies and government troops whose activities have branded the conflict in the DRC as 'Africa's First World War'.[30] Suffice it to say that it is a vast, landlocked country which has been used to fight a proxy war in the aftermath of the genocide in neighbouring Rwanda. Government forces have been supported by Angola, Namibia and Zimbabwe while rebels have been backed by Uganda and Rwanda. In 2009, Rwandan troops swapped sides and backed the government. There are dozens of ethnic groups and private militias, fuelled by the huge reserves of diamonds, gold, coltan and cassiterite in the country, which give cause for further conflict. Whatever the number and nature of the armies and whoever is backing them, they are all guilty of rape.

Nearly 7 million people have been killed in the war so far. Joseph Kabila was re-elected president in 2011, promising to restore law and order, but his government still faces rebellious militias in the east of the country. The DRC has been the subject of numerous reports on the so-called 'epidemic' of rape. The authors of a report by Human Rights Watch entitled 'Soldiers Who Rape, Commanders Who Condone' say that rape victims claim that the war is being fought 'on their bodies' and they conclude that the scale of sexual violence in the eastern Congo make the area the most dangerous place on earth to be a woman.[31]

Seventy-nine per cent of women interviewed in one survey in the eastern province of South Kivu said that they had been gang-raped.[32] Between attacks, the women reported that they would be 'cleaned' by guns wrapped in cloth being inserted in their vaginas. Seventy per cent of rape victims said they had been tortured during or after the rape and many victims were murdered. Others reported that family members were forced to have sex with one another. The *Economist* wrote after an investigation in 2008 that women were killed 'by bullets fired from a gun barrel shoved into their vagina.'[33]

Those who survive suffer; there are physical and psychological effects and a high chance that families might reject a woman or girl after the abuse. Many of the victims are only children who are forced by their pregnancy to leave school. Others face the daunting task of raising a child, the result of rape, without family support. Up to 60 per cent of the combatants involved are said to be HIV positive[34] and rape victims run a high risk of being affected. Some rapes are so violent that they result in fistula, when the walls between the vagina, rectum and/or bladder are destroyed leading to chronic incontinence and the further likelihood of exclusion from their communities.

So what makes the DRC such a brutal, murderous nightmare for a woman? I met Faith in the offices of the NGO Freedom From Torture, in London. She is a rape survivor who, fortunately for her, had links with an NGO in Kinshasa, which helped her escape the country. She has been repeatedly raped over several years and is, she says, extremely grateful and happy to be in the UK. I was mightily relieved to hear that even our asylum-seeker-wary Home Office believed her story and has given her permission to settle here. She is smartly dressed, has neatly bobbed hair and is articulate in telling her story. As she goes through the catalogue of abuse she has suffered, I am struck by how often she uses the expression 'women are not valued in the Congo'. Is this what it is all about? The dozens of reports into why the DRC has earned its unenviable reputation have come up with a myriad of theories but it is Faith's simple explanation that rings true and seems to form the basis of all other theories. Human Rights Watch (HRW) investigators have concluded that rape as 'a weapon of war is used by all sides to deliberately terrorize civilians, to exert control over them, or to punish them for perceived collaboration with the enemy.'[35] As in Bosnia, women are abused to punish the community and undermine the morale of their menfolk. The HRW report blames the lack of chain of command that allows soldiers to run amok and cites an incident involving thousands of soldiers sent to Kabare in August 2008.[36]

No provision was made for food or accommodation for men who had not been paid for weeks. It is hardly surprising that 'this period was characterized by widespread looting and abuses against civilians'. Any woman or girl seen with food was an obvious target in the circumstances. A seventeen-year-old told HRW, 'I had gone to the fields to find potatoes. I was returning to the house. Then I saw soldiers coming toward me. They asked what I was doing in the fields. They said I could choose: give them food or become their wife. I said to take the food. They refused and [raped] me, then they took the food anyway.'[37]

In her paper 'Rape as a Weapon of War in the DRC', Carly Brown argues that it is the status of women in the country that has made her so vulnerable and that the 'subjugation of women creates a clear pathway for men to exploit and abuse women . . . women are seen as objects, forced to bear the brutalization of men's frustrations.'[38] Another academic, Jonathan Gottschall, in a paper entitled 'Explaining Wartime Rape' takes this idea further. 'Rape in war is deemed as a result of a conspiracy, not necessarily conscious but still systematic, of men to dominate and oppress women. While men may fight on different sides and for different reasons, in one sense they are all warriors on behalf of their gender – to oppress women.'[39]

Faith, the asylum seeker who never finished secondary school, has learned from experience what the academics conclude in their flowery language and she could be speaking for many more women than just the Congolese when she says women are not valued by men. She says of the men who raped her: 'For them rape is a pleasure. For them it is normal. They can do it as many times as they like because no one and nothing is stopping them.' Faith got into trouble because she tried to do something to stop it. She had been living on the streets with her younger brother in Kinshasa when, at the age of fifteen, she was picked up by a charity, 'L'association de secours pour les enfants de rue', and she stayed and worked for them. As one of the few effective NGOs in the country, it started to attract women rape victims who had fled the fighting in the east of the country and Faith became aware of the extent of the problem. By this time she was twenty, married with two children and had been promoted to be vice chairman of the charity. She heard how the women had appealed to soldiers from rival armies, to the police and even to family members but no one would help them.

'They told me that even young children were being raped and so I called a meeting in a church hall. I criticized the president for not doing anything. There were spies at the meeting who called the police and they took me to a police station. I was detained for one month in a container.' She was kept with twenty other prisoners in the container without enough food or water, with a bucket in the corner that served as a toilet and where the police came in daily to beat them. 'There were men and women kept there together. I was raped by a fellow detainee. All the women were raped.' She did not learn her lesson. She was hospitalized after the detention suffering from severe malnutrition and dehydration. When she recovered, Faith called another meeting to draw attention to the plight of children caught up in the conflict zones. This time she was sent to prison for two months, 'they beat me badly, using sticks and their boots. Three times I was raped by prison guards.' When she got back home, her husband criticized her for her involvement in anti-government activities and tried to stop her leaving the house. 'But I went back to what I was doing with the charity because people trusted me there and I didn't want to let them down. I knew I had to help people.'

Her third and last protest was the most ambitious. 'Women kept coming to us and telling us about rape. Women have no respect and rape is a by-product of this lack of respect and yet the government does nothing. So we marched down the streets with banners and slogans saying, "Kabila, we are tired of you because you don't protect us."' To her surprise the demonstrators were allowed to disperse and she went back home, but not for long. 'They came at five in the morning. I heard a loud knocking at the door and they said that they were looking for the person who had defamed the president. I came to the door and they said, "We are looking for you."' They put Faith in the police car and positioned her in the car in such a way that she could watch what happened next.

They beat my children and one of them raped my twelve-year-old niece. 'We are doing this in front of you,' they said, 'to show that you can't mess with our government.' My niece was screaming. I was screaming. They threatened to kill me there and then. My children were watching and neighbours began to gather but no one dared do anything. I can't describe the pain I felt when they raped the little girl. I was powerless. I couldn't do anything. If I knew that this would be the outcome of all that I had done, I would have stopped my campaign.

They took me to a prison on the border with Angola where I was raped so many times by the prison guards that I lost count. They said that they were doing it to me to punish me for insulting the president and that I was unlikely to leave the prison alive. It became a daily routine: I was abused, beaten, raped, abused, beaten, raped. I thought I would die.

After three months, the NGO she had been working for managed to bribe the jailers to release her and Faith flew to the UK.

'Women in my country get no respect or care from government officials. In the DRC, men don't value women,' Faith repeats for the third time during the course of the interview. Women are routinely raped, she says, and yet the rape victim will carry a stigma for the rest of her life. 'Men worry that she will be HIV positive or carry another sexual disease.' What will happen to her niece, I ask? 'If the community gets to know,' she says, 'she has no chance of getting married. She will be an outcast. But, if the family manage to keep it a secret, who knows?' Faith has kept control of her emotions throughout this account of her terrible ordeal but, at this point, she cries.

In November 2012, several hundred Congolese troops poured into the town of Minova in the north of the DRC. They had been defeated in battle and were drunk and angry. With the approval of their officers, they took out their rage and humiliation on the women of the town on the edge of Lake Kivu. Their commanders allegedly ordered their men to 'Go and get women'. The subsequent mass rape of over a hundred women and girls was described as a horrific and shameful atrocity by the UN[40] and was followed by calls for the men and those in charge to be held accountable. In the subsequent proceedings, which became known as the Minova trial, lawyers claimed that the prosecution received orders from the government and the trial became a farce. Government agents were able to use pressure for urgent action from the international community as an excuse to rush through the evidence in a way that would not stand up in court. No commanding officer was prosecuted and, of the thirty-nine men charged, only two junior soldiers were convicted of rape.[41]

Meanwhile, the women in Minova are suffering for daring to testify in court against their rapists. According to Masika Katsuva, who runs a refuge for the rape victims of Minova, of the fifty-six women who dared to appear in court with hoods over their heads to protect their identities, fifty say they have been threatened.* 'They keep attacking us, we have no protection, no support,' she says.[42] Masika herself has been raped twice; once by twelve men. She says that she has received a letter with death threats and that they spend nights hiding in the bush. 'We gave everything to the trial. We trusted them,' she says, 'How could they leave us like this?'[43]

The astonishing thing is that the rape trial of Minova, with its comparatively small number of victims by the standards of the DRC, became an international cause célèbre, publicized by an unlikely celebrity couple – Angelina Jolie and the then British Foreign Secretary, William Hague. The duo travelled out to the DRC and emoted conspicuously in front of dozens of photographers as they visited the Heal Africa Hospital in Goma which cares for thousands of rape victims a year. It was their presence and their condemnation of sexual violence in the DRC that gave the ongoing trial such prominence. And the dynamic duo did even more. They met a year later in London for a global summit designed to tackle sexual violence in conflict zones. To resounding applause, Hague proclaimed that: 'We owe it to future generations to end one of the greatest injustices of our time.'[44] The 1,700 delegates greeted his words with ecstatic applause. None of the women from Minova were invited to the summit and none have received the £15,000 that was recommended as compensation to each woman for her suffering.[45]

The three-day summit in London cost £5.2 million. Somehow the phrase 'they don't value women' springs to mind.

---

* Sadly, Masika died suddenly on 2 February 2016.

12

SEX INEQUALITY IN THE UK

The Pay Gap

I start work at 7.30. I wash and dress the mainly elderly patients, lifting them out of bed to remove incontinence pads and then I give them a good scrub down. I like helping people, otherwise I wouldn't be in the job. Trouble is, there's no time just to sit and chat with them over a cup of tea these days. It's all work, work, work. We have to deal with family members as well, who can sometimes get quite abusive. We do the best we can but you can't help but feel undervalued and underpaid. I've worked twenty years and never had Christmas Day off. I would never go on strike. How could I just walk out on them? But my back hurts and my neck hurts after all the heavy lifting. I'm on the scrapheap and I know I wouldn't get a job anywhere else.

I meet forty-nine-year-old Alison in a pub just outside Dudley, in the West Midlands. She's a good-looking, friendly brunette who nurses a pint of lager as we chat. She's brought along two work colleagues, Jackie who is fifty-six and Val who is ten years older. They all work as care assistants for a local council rehabilitation home where they look after patients who have just been released from hospital or elderly people who can no longer live alone and are admitted to the home while the council looks for a long-term solution.

No one who becomes a care assistant can expect a bed of roses. It is one of the lowest paid of manual jobs in the UK. It pays £9 an hour and the work is gruelling. The women first took on the job because of the hours. They start early and can be back home in time to see the children return from school. With cuts in local government spending, the work has got harder but it is not the work that the women have met to complain to me about. It is the blatant inequality.

In 1997, the new Labour government under Tony Blair promised to create greater equality in the labour market with a new assessment of the work done by, say, a care worker and a bin man, in order to introduce a fairer pay structure. The evaluation process was supposed to be completed by the end of that year. Dudley Council produced its findings in 2012. Alison hands me over the evaluation sheets with furious indignation. The assessments look at twelve different aspects of a manual worker's work.

'Look at these!' she says. Under the category 'Responsibility for People', the care assistant scores the same points as a waste collector. She goes on:

> The bin man might have to say 'good morning' to a passer-by while we are responsible for the health and well-being of vulnerable people. That's what we do, we're responsible for people. How can they say we're the same? And look at the scores for 'Physical Demands'. The bin man gets 5 and we get 2. I've watched them at work. These days, they only have to push the wheelies out to the truck and then the bin is picked up mechanically to tip the rubbish in. We have to collect all the soiled rubbish, put it in bags we can hardly lift and carry them outside in all weathers. And we have to lift patients as well – it is all physically demanding and yet we get a low score.

And then there is the category 'Mental Demands'. The Care Assistant scores 2 and the Waste Collector scores 3. 'What is this about?' asks Jackie. 'We are the ones who have to deal with confused and scared old people, we are the ones who have to reassure their families and even cope with bereavements. It is a nonsense. I remember the council chappie coming with a clipboard to do the evaluations. He asked us a few questions and did not bother to stay long enough to watch us at work. I tell you it is the men all sticking together to get the best deals for the men.'

The women are right to be suspicious. When the inspectors started comparing wages between men and women in 1997, they came across a scandalous combination of trade union and employer protectionism and discrimination in local council practices in the West Midlands. Paul Savage, a former shop steward and equal pay campaigner who is advising a couple of hundred women in Dudley says, 'They found that bin men, gravediggers and road sweepers on £15,000 a year were getting £30,000 because of bonuses for just showing up, so-called attendance allowances. It was not a case of jobs for the boys; it was bonuses for the boys and only the boys.' Such bonuses were unheard of for women on comparable pay.

In the spirit of new fairness promised by the new Labour government, the women were promised compensation for this glaring disparity in pay. In many cases, trade unions negotiated with the council behind the scenes and, as ever, the women were short-changed. 'I've worked for them for twenty years and the council first offered me £9,000,' says Jackie, 'but I smelled a rat because I heard of others who got much higher offers for the same amount of work. It seemed so random, as if they were trying it on so I refused. They then offered me £11,200 and I refused again. I finally accepted £16,000. I got no help from my union, UNISON. The union rep kept saying that I should settle because the council was running out of money and could withdraw the offer at any time.'

Sixty-six-year-old Val looks embarrassed. 'I've worked for the council for twenty-five years and I accepted £9,000 and later learned that it should have been £25,000. You know what it's like. Christmas was coming up, I wanted to get presents for the grandkids and it sounded like a lot of money.' What is especially galling for the women sitting with me in the pub is that it is now known women who got lawyers to fight for their compensation payments on a 'no-win no-fee basis' received payments of more than £100,000. What would Val have done if she had got the £100,000 to which she was probably entitled? Without a moment's hesitation she says, 'I would have bought myself a bungalow and retired. Look at me. I am sixty-six and still working. I have been so tired sometimes that I have gone to bed crying. I've been ill with tiredness.'

They feel they have been part of a male conspiracy, from both sides – from the employers and the male-dominated unions who should have represented them. 'We see the bin men in the pub at midday. They get paid eight hours for a five-hour day. The men always get the best deals from the bosses,' Alison says, bitterly. As for the compensation offers, 'They should have told us not to take the offer. I remember a meeting with our local union rep when he started shouting at me and said, "You shouldn't have taken the offer." I told him to stop shouting at me and asked him where he was when we needed advice? They just didn't want to know. I've just heard that they have a woman local trade union official at another union, UNITE, so I'm changing.'

There is even a woman head of the Trades Union Congress (TUC) . . .

That is the last thing Mum wrote. I don't know what she wanted to say next. The woman head of the TUC is of course Frances

O'Grady, the TUC's first female General Secretary and a big campaigner for equal pay. But what was she going to say about her? That's just one of the infinite number of unasked questions I now have for Mum.

Fortunately, before she died, Mum left summaries of each chapter. The previous chapters she managed to finish, but not this one. Here is what she wanted to say in this chapter:

> How is it that a country that gave us Emily Pankhurst and Margaret Thatcher is currently number twenty-eight in the list of countries offering equal pay – behind Bulgaria and Burundi? For every £1 earned by a man, a woman earns 85p. We are all aware of the heart-warming story of the female Dagenham workers who fought for equal pay in the 1960s. It is still happening. Why does a man working in the warehouse at Asda today earn more than a woman at the checkout, whose skills require numeracy and customer relations? Why do women earn, on average, 21 per cent less than men at corporate, managerial level? Why are there so few women at this level? There are mandatory quotas in France, Italy, Spain, the Netherlands and Germany. Why is the UK so far behind? Institutionalized misogyny say the Fawcett Society, the campaigning group on equal pay. But, looking back at my own career and the regrets I have about family life, I ask whether women can and should try and compete.

In front of me, I've got a mess of notes, telephone numbers, scribbled ideas and articles. Finishing this chapter is a really hard task. Every time I read through her notes I want to ask Mum what she wanted to say and I can't. So I'm continually reminded of her absence and it stings. The fact that the chapter Mum didn't finish is the one where she wants to talk about her regrets about family life makes this all the more complicated. As her daughter I'm left to examine her feelings about being a mother. Yes, Mum, I wish I could tell you what a wonderful mother you were and how proud your son, George, and I are of you. Please don't feel regret. As previous chapters show, you did manage to do what so many women feel they can't do, you had an exceptional career that changed the lives of thousands of people AND you brought up two children. I'll go on to explain as best I can why Mum's regrets about family life are unfounded but first let's look at the questions she wanted to answer at the start.

According to TUC analysis, women working full time still earn almost £5,000 a year less than men, though the pay gap in some jobs is three times bigger.

The research shows one of the biggest pay gaps is between male and female health professionals. It's been calculated at 27 per cent, which works out as the difference between £18.50 an hour and £25.33.[1] The TUC says a key reason for the size of the pay gap in health is the earnings of the best-paid professionals. Top male professionals in health earn nearly £50 an hour, almost twice as much as top-earning women who earn £24.90 an hour.

The TUC has found women working in manufacturing occupations experience the next biggest pay gap at 22 per cent less than men. Women working as managers, directors and senior officials experience the next biggest pay gap at 21 per cent, which works out at men getting £26.80 an hour whilst women get just £21.

The union says women earn less than men in thirty-two of the thirty-five major occupations classified by the Office for National Statistics. The three major occupations where women earn more than men – transport drivers, electricians and agricultural workers – are all male dominated. Fewer than 50,000 women are employed in these sectors, compared to 1.5 million men. The gender pay gap across the private sector is 19.9 per cent, far higher than the 13.6 per cent pay gap in the public sector. The research shows the gender pay gap is even bigger for women working part-time, who earn 35 per cent less per hour than men working full-time.[2]

Here are some examples of occupations with the biggest gender pay gaps:

Occupation: Health professionals
Hourly Pay, Men: £26.54
Hourly Pay, Women: £18.32
Gender Pay Gap (per cent): 31.0
Gender Pay Gap (per hour): £8.22
Gender Pay Gap (per year): £16,029

Occupation: Culture, media and sports occupations
Hourly pay, men £18.62
Hourly pay, women £13.50
Gender pay gap (per cent) 27.5
Gender pay gap (per hour) £5.12
Gender pay gap (per year) £9,984

Occupation: Corporate managers and directors
Hourly pay, men £27.51
Hourly pay, women £21.78
Gender pay gap (per cent) 20.8
Gender pay gap (per hour) £5.73
Gender pay gap (per year) £11,174

Occupation: Skilled trades occupations
Hourly pay, men £12.03
Hourly pay, women £10.00
Gender pay gap (per cent) 16.9
Gender pay gap (per hour) £2.03
Gender pay gap (per year) £3,959[3]

But why is there such disparity between what women earn and what men earn in the same job across multiple industries?

The law when it comes to equal pay says women have been entitled to equal pay for equal work ever since 1970 when the Equal Pay Act was introduced, but since 2010 the law on equal pay has been set out in the 'equality of terms' provisions of the Equality Act 2010. The right to equal pay means that there should be no difference in the contractual terms of a woman and a man doing equal work, who both work for the same employer.

The Fawcett Society says there are four main causes of the gender pay gap. They are:

Discrimination

It's illegal but some women are still paid less than men for the same work – this can happen when a man and a woman are doing exactly the same role and receiving different pay, or where work of equivalent value carried out by women is underpaid.

Recent research shows that unfair treatment of women remains common, especially around maternity. The Equality and Human Rights Commission has found 54,000 women are forced to leave their job early every year as a result of poor treatment after they have a baby.[4]

Unequal Caring Responsibilities

Women continue to play a greater role in caring for children as well as for sick or elderly relatives. As a result more women work part time, and these jobs are typically lower paid with fewer progression opportunities.

The pay gap opens up significantly once women hit their forties. Often as they return from a break to raise children women find that their male contemporaries are being promoted ahead of them.

A Divided Labour Market

Women are still more likely to be in low-paid and low-skilled jobs, affecting labour market segregation. Eighty per cent of those working in the low-paid care and leisure sector are women, while only 10 per cent of those in the better-paid skilled trades are women.

Feminized sectors tend to be less valued and less well paid – women make up 60 per cent of those earning less than the living wage.

Men in the Most Senior Roles

Men continue to make up the majority of those in the highest paid and most senior roles – for example, there are just six female chief executives in the FTSE 100.

The law should be protecting women from unequal pay and we may now be seeing some change. New regulations coming into force in 2016 will require large companies to publish their gender pay gaps for the first time.

The TUC believes that as four decades of equal pay legislation have only halved – rather than eradicated – the gender pay gap, a tougher approach is needed to stop millions of workers losing out on pay and career opportunities, simply because of their sex.

The union says more senior level part-time jobs are needed to help women continue their careers after having children. Too many women are forced to trade down their jobs and abandon their careers just to find working hours that can fit around their childcare arrangements. The TUC wants the government to boost the availability of more senior part-time jobs by encouraging employers to advertise all jobs on a flexible basis where possible.

They say ministers could take the initiative by making it a require-
ment for all public-sector job vacancies.

The TUC and the Fawcett Society believe the government
should also strengthen the right to request flexible working
by removing the six-month qualifying period and making it
available to employees on the day they start a new job. They
did say one of the reasons for the gender pay gap was the lack
of transparency in pay systems that allow companies to pay
female employees less than their male colleagues, without staff
even being aware of it. The TUC called for tighter regulations
when it comes to transparency. They believe publishing annual
gender pay gap information and conducting regular pay audits
would enable companies to identify any gender pay gaps, and
take action to close them.

Dr Eva Neitzert, deputy chief executive of the Fawcett Society
campaign group, says:

It is disgraceful that in 2014 women in the UK still effectively
work for free for nearly two months of the year relative to
men and deeply concerning that last year the gap widened
again for the first time in five years.

The UK is fast sliding down the rankings of gender equal
societies and we need to take action now. We urgently need
action to tackle low pay, with the majority of those paid
below the Living Wage being female.

Our research shows that lifting the national minimum wage
to the Living Wage would reduce the gap by 0.8 per cent – this
compares to a historic slow pace of change that has seen the
gap fall by just 6.2 per cent over the past sixteen years.

We also need to make sure that having children does not
spell the end of a woman's career progression by ensuring
that part-time and flexible work opportunities are available at more senior levels. The public sector should lead by

example and advertise all vacancies on a flexible basis, unless there is a clear business case not to.

In July 2015, Prime Minister David Cameron pledged to end the gender pay gap within a generation. In October of the same year, along with Women and Equalities Minister Nicky Morgan, he announced new measures to eradicate gender pay inequality. It appears the government did listen to the TUC's campaign to make companies more transparent about their employees' salaries. The new steps include forcing larger employers to publish information about their bonuses for men and women, extending plans for gender pay gap reporting beyond private and voluntary sector employers to include the public sector and working with business to eliminate all-male boards in the FTSE 350.

The government's words are promising. The prime minister has said, 'You can't have true opportunity without equality. There is no place for a pay gap in today's society and we are delivering on our promises to address it.'

Nicky Morgan says,

As a government we are committed to seeing every person in our nation realize their potential. Greater gender equality will help us to achieve this so tackling the gender pay gap is an absolute priority. That is why in our manifesto we made a commitment to require companies with more than 250 employees to publish the difference between the average pay of their male and female employees.

Closing the gender pay gap is not only the right thing to do, it is essential for improving our productivity as a nation. Ensuring that women achieve their full potential will have a significant impact on our economy.

She's promised to make sure children in schools know their rights. She says it's important to tackle the gender pay gap from a young age. The way to do this is making sure all children believe they can do any career regardless of their sex. Schools must encourage girls to think about working in often male-dominated careers like technology and engineering.

Other schemes such as shared parental leave and pay have also been introduced by this government. It remains to be seen whether David Cameron's pledge to end the gender pay gap within a generation will be realized. It seems like there's a long way to go.

Perhaps one reason women earn less than men is something to do with their confidence. It could be argued that years of patriarchy have led women to believe they are not worthy of being paid the same as men and therefore they don't ask for more money in the same way as men do. As an A-list Hollywood actress, I appreciate her money worries don't compare with most women in the world but I think Jennifer Lawrence's point about her earnings rings true for many women who feel unable to negotiate for themselves. In a recent essay she explains that the main reason she couldn't negotiate a better salary was because of a need to be liked.

She writes, 'I failed as a negotiator because I gave up early . . . But if I'm honest with myself, I would be lying if I didn't say there was an element of wanting to be liked that influenced my decision to close the deal without a real fight.'[5]

Lawrence goes on to wonder if one reason women continue to earn less than men is because they're often asking men for the increase in salary and women don't want to seem difficult or offend or scare men. I believe that this need to be liked is an ingrained female trait, that from very early on, girls are taught to be people-pleasers and therefore don't have the confidence in themselves to ask for more money.

In her book *Everyday Sexism*, feminist campaigner and founder of the Everyday Sexism Project Laura Bates says the argument that women's caring responsibilities is a barrier to earning more money starts with the sexist premise that women are the carers in the first place.

She writes: 'the . . . problem with the idea of women "making sacrifices" for family is the very notion that having children will necessarily impact on a woman's career but not on a man's. This reality, compounded by inflexible working hours and a lack of shared parental leave, is often quoted as if it were an immutable fact that women must accept, rather than a long-existing prejudice that could and should be altered.'

The long and hard way around this is to keep challenging the idea that women are the principle carers in a family. There is no reason a father can't take a career break and look after children. It is society's expectation that women will stop work when they have babies that means this continues to be the norm. The question 'Can men have it all?' is rarely asked, it's more often than not mothers making sacrifices.

As long as society continues to believe that mothers are the best carers of their children, we are denying women the same opportunities as men. As long as girls are given dolls and plastic ovens to play with and boys are given spaceships and railways, both boys and girls will grow up to believe their roles are already defined for them and their careers and choices around parenting are predetermined.

Known often as 'the motherhood trap', one reason women are earning less than men is they take time out of their careers to have children and then upon returning can't compete with the men who have built up their careers and salaries. Helen Lewis, deputy editor of the *New Statesman*, writes, 'The "motherhood trap" exposes one of capitalism's most uncomfortable secrets – the way it relies on so much unpaid labour, often from women, to sustain itself. This labour comes at the expense of career opportunities, and their lifetime earning power: the pay gap between men and women in their twenties is all but eradicated, but a "maternity gap" still exists, and women's wages never recover from the time devoted to childbearing . . .'[6]

Somehow Mum managed not to fall into the 'motherhood trap'. She brought up two children without compromising her work. I know she had regrets about family life because of what she said she wanted to write about in this chapter: 'But, looking back at my own career and the regrets I have about family life, I ask whether women can and should try and compete.'

As the daughter of someone who never let being a woman hold her back in her career and, in fact, used her sex to her advantage, for me the answer to the question 'should women compete', is yes.

Mum did have regrets about not spending more time with us. There were many times when she was working abroad when we were children, but actually she managed to have long periods at home between assignments and I don't look back on my childhood wishing we spent more time together. She often asked me if I'd rather have a mother at home and at the school gate. I always said no. I was so proud of what she was doing. I am sure being able to do work that fulfilled her intellectually and not feeling restrained by motherhood made her a better mother because she wasn't frustrated and resentful at being with us. If she had stayed at home with us, then I'm sure she would have been driven mad with boredom and resorted to taking it out on us. Would she have been a better mother if she'd sacrificed her career to be with us? No. Our lives were enriched by her and who she was. I wish I was able to ease any guilt she felt but perhaps women who work will always feel like that no matter how much their children tell them it's OK.

Whilst trying to finish this chapter and reading Mum's notes about this book, I came across this quotation from Kathleen

McGinn, professor of business administration at Harvard: 'Having a working mother is good for you.' I decided to Google Kathleen McGinn and have a look at her research in the context of Mum's worries about family life.

McGinn says, 'Women whose mothers worked outside the home are more likely to have jobs themselves, are more likely to hold supervisory responsibility at those jobs, and earn higher wages than women whose mothers stayed home full time.'

She goes on to say working women are not only good role models for their daughters but for their sons too: 'Men raised by working mothers are more likely to contribute to household chores and spend more time caring for family members.'

According to McGinn: 'There's a lot of parental guilt about having both parents working outside the home . . . But what this research says to us is that not only are you helping your family economically – and helping yourself professionally and emotionally if you have a job you love – but you're also helping your kids.'[7] This was echoed in a piece written for the *Guardian* by the journalist Anne Perkins about the memorial service we held for Mum. She said that my brother and I are testament to the fact that Mum did manage to do what so many women believe they can't do. She had an extraordinary career and had us. She wrote:

[Sue and I] were the same generation, and I watched her career as it grew from conventional success, on the *News at Ten*, to something dauntingly intrepid. She was annoyingly, tiresomely, enviably, admirable. Daughters, listen, please. She never acknowledged the apparent limitations that many of the rest of us allowed to constrain us. She was brave and determined and clear-sighted right from the start. She never appeared to doubt herself, or sit about moaning about what she couldn't do.[8]

I believe my mother was an exceptional person. Her energy was boundless. As children we would be left with a nanny while she was away but she was always on the end of the phone. She would bounce back off a plane, having just escaped from some hovel in a far-flung corner of the earth and she would throw everything at being a wonderful, kind and caring mother. We also were lucky enough to travel with her to places most children our age wouldn't have dreamed of seeing and through her work we met so many fascinating people. The stark contrast between the horrors she saw abroad and the relatively comfortable home life we had in North London meant as children we were always reminded how lucky we were and it gave us a good understanding of what it means to be grateful for the privileged lives we have.

As a thirty-something woman myself, married and thinking about starting my own family, I feel incredibly lucky to have my mother's example of motherhood to follow. Far from feeling deprived of attention, watching her travel the world and exposing injustices only made me feel empowered that I can achieve anything. I'm reminded of what Mum wrote in her chapter on women in Saudi Arabia. She says: 'Daughters take their lead from their mothers. I lose count of the number of times I told my daughter that women are equal to men and that she can achieve anything in life.' I've never felt that being a woman has held me back because she showed me that it doesn't. So, Mum, there's no need to feel regret. I have nothing but pride in you and what you achieved, as both a journalist and a mother. Thank you. And in answer to your question, yes, women should try and compete; you've shown us that it's possible to win.

CONCLUSION

by Lyse Doucet

It's not possible to write a real conclusion to this book. This war of 'Brave Ones Who Fight Back' still goes on with all too many battles still being waged on all too many fronts. I put 'Women's Rights 2016' into an Internet search engine and up pops an article in the *Huffington Post* which starts 'Cows are given more rights than women in many parts of the world'.

There are reverses, and advances. Many more women and men are now finding the courage, as well the force of stronger legal and political backing, to fight back. But the decades-long campaign of one of its most tenacious fighters, armed with a camcorder, a critical eye and a compassionate heart, has drawn to a terribly sad and sudden close.

'She believed the whole world needed to know,' reflects her husband and fellow journalist Nick Guthrie when we meet for lunch on a grey winter's day in London to discuss how to write this conclusion to Sue's powerful book. Her illness stole the time she would have used to write this last chapter herself.

The quiet, unassuming restaurant where Sue and Nick often met reminds me of Sue in a way. Properly folded white linen napkins evoke the crisply pressed shirts she wore on television, matched by the neat, straight lines of her bobbed brown hair.

There's a correct way to do things. That's very Sue.

I also remember my very first meeting with Nick. I had gone to see him in the early 1990s – his then role was Planning Editor for BBC *Breakfast News* – with a possible story about women in Afghanistan. 'Tell us something we don't know about Afghan women,' he advised me, in his gruff 'get to the point' way, punctuated by an encouraging smile.

That's exactly what Sue strived for, all her working life.

This book is a testament to her dogged determination to tell the most compelling stories of women's lives that needed to be told. This is an everywoman book: her chronicles of injustice and abuse cover countries as distant as Egypt and Argentina and cultures as different as India and Ireland.

It shocks. Abducted women like Patricia are drugged and thrown out of planes by the junta in Argentina's 'Dirty Wars' after they give birth and their child is given away to a military family. Luljeta, a fourteen-year-girl from Kosovo is raped 'all the time' by members of an international peacekeeping force. Girls and young women endure 'horrible horrible pain' because their external female genitalia have been partially cut or completely removed.

And yet, it inspires too. Women like Maimouna flee Gambia so she can stop her family's traditional role in the village genital 'cutting' ceremonies. French journalist Célhia de Lavarène and American Kathy Bolkovac dedicate themselves to doing whatever they possibly can to stop the sex-trafficking trade in Bosnia. Ultimately, even the most persistent cannot prevail over such deeply rooted misogyny and traditional belief, as well as systemic corruption. But they do make a difference.

Everyone knows this is a long war.

'Sue's rage against wrong was her main weapon in her fight for the oppressed,' recalls Ian O'Reilly, a mutual friend, who worked with Sue for more than twenty years as a producer and cameraperson. Together they slipped surreptitiously across borders, usually travelling incognito to shine a bright light into the world's hidden corners.

'As well as expose, she wanted to humiliate the wrongdoers,' he explains as we occupy a semicircle of dull green plush chairs in a hotel lounge that feels stuffed with upholstered furniture and empty of people. Ian has dubbed this room 'Granny's Parlour'. It's tucked away down a side street a few blocks from the BBC's London headquarters. Friends, colleagues and 'co-conspirators' Sue and Ian would sometimes escape to this quiet space for a coffee or a drink, a bit of gossip, and some plotting of another film.

This is how Sue explains her journalism in the book *Practising Videojournalism*, written by Vivien Morgan, her former Channel 4 colleague and a TV videojournalist herself. 'It mattered to me that so many people were suffering and living under appalling regimes and in difficult environments where I knew TV could maybe accelerate or change world reaction by showing what it was like.'

Ask a journalist why they take so many risks, pelt headlong towards danger when others anxiously pull back, ask so many questions and create such a stir. You will often hear the same matter-of-fact reply: 'It's what we do.'

But there was something else in Sue's distinctive signature. Watching her fearless work over the years, sometimes travelling and filming on her own, I found myself constantly asking another question: 'How did she do it?'

How did she keep calm when she crossed army lines in Syria in 2011 with a fake Syrian identity card, pretending to be her driver's deaf-mute sister, to become the first Western journalist to film opposition protests at the very start of an unprecedented uprising? How did she keep her nerve in 1994 when she posed as an amateur ornithologist and secretly filmed a story in southern China on how prisoners were being shot to order for their organs. Her report on how organs were sold to wealthy patients awaiting transplants in Hong Kong shocked many around the world. It earned Sue a seven-year prison sentence in absentia in China – but even that didn't stop her from going back.

How did Sue keep returning, time and time again, to the same places, without ever getting caught? Deploying various passports and nationalities, she went back and forth to countries like Burma, Nepal, Romania and Zimbabwe and, in the early years, Russia. She repeatedly raised issues like female genital mutilation, forced marriages, honour killings, trafficking of every possible kind.

'My heart still quivers when I think of it,' Ian recalls of their undercover filming inside military headquarters in Burma in 1997. It was a time when hardly any outsiders were allowed to enter the closed authoritarian state, much less penetrate the deepest darkest corridors of power.

Sometimes she posed as an amateur historian, other times a wide-eyed tourist, or a frustrated female traveller in male-dominated worlds.

'She would go to countries where women were completely insignificant so the authorities would never suspect she was capable of exposing them,' explains her proud daughter Sarah. 'She carried around photos of my brother George and I and she would bring them out and say she was just a mother of two on holiday.'

During one trip to Romania, Sue pretended to be a buyer and arranged to purchase a different baby every day to prove it could be done. 'She cried a lot on that trip,' admits Ian. Nerves of steel were wired to a soft heart.

'She was unapologetic about being a campaigning journalist,' is how Tony Jolliffe explains what drove her. One of the BBC's most creative camerapersons, Tony teamed up with Sue from 2010 to 2014. Their successful double act kicked off when Sue secured rare access to North Korea and they produced an extraordinary film which won them a prestigious Emmy award in the United States. Memorable scenes include Sue's straight-faced questioning of squirming officials, and her light-footed dancing with delighted children to the lilting tune of a state-sponsored refrain. Their work evolved into a succession of films which informed some of the most compelling stories in this book, including a series on female genital mutilation (FGM) set in the Middle East, Africa, and Europe.

Sue managed to find ways to raise her voice, and give voice to those who had none, within the editorial parameters of a public broadcaster like the BBC. The power of her storytelling came from her armoury of restrained language, a telltale expression, a curt reply, blunt question, even that occasional mischievous smile.

'She could be very good at being understated,' says Tony. 'But, on the ground, there was no doubt she saw it as black and white, goodies and baddies. She wanted to team with up with the good to go after the bad.'

Her single-minded focus, which sometimes blurred the nuances and almost always broke some rules occasionally, upset BBC colleagues based in the countries in question who would have to contend with the wrath of officialdom once her undercover filming, and their secrets, were revealed.

But it was for this sort of bold journalism that Tony Hall – Lord Hall of Birkenhead – her friend from Oxford University days who is now the BBC's director general, poached her from ITN in 1992. He brought her into the BBC when he was running the News Department. 'I wanted some of that sort of journalism in our stable,' he told the BBC Radio 4 programme *Last Word* shortly after Sue passed away in October 2015.

At the poignant memorial service for Sue on 1 December 2015 in a packed All Souls Church adjacent to the BBC in central London, he recalls Sue's 'inauspicious beginnings' as a journalist at ITN where she realized that women were 'limited to subjects like the Royals or the Chelsea Flower Show'. He quotes Sue saying, 'I remember thinking at a very early stage if you were interested in what I was doing – campaigning journalism and human rights – three burly men with a large camera and a big fluffy phallic microphone is not the most tactful way to interview, for example, a rape victim in a war situation.'

By the late eighties 'Sue and technology came together' when she realized that Sony's new Hi8 video camcorder, which had just emerged, could be her secret weapon. It was compact enough to conceal, and was the same nondescript unthreatening camera tourists were starting to use. It also brought a significant improvement in quality over the grainy images of earlier models. When it came to secret filming, it was a game changer. Stories that were only being told in print could now be captured on camera, in quality good enough to broadcast.

'I knew that as a VJ [videojournalist] I had the power to help change things or at least to get things moving,' Sue explains in the 'Videojournalist Pioneers' chapter of Vivien Morgan's book. Sue and Vivien made their first trip with a Hi8 camera to Romania in the late eighties, before and after the revolution, and travelled together on some reporting trips for several years after. There was an explosion of news and revelations across Eastern Europe after the Berlin Wall came down in 1989 – perfect territory for enterprising videojournalists equipped with the new improved cameras.

Increasingly smaller tapes also made a difference. 'My notoriety in TV news is how I put tapes in my knickers to get them through customs and it was true!' admits Sue in Vivien's book.

In focusing on an unjust world, Sue's eye often fixed on the plight of women, although she didn't see herself solely as a female campaigner on gender issues. Women's rights, or their glaring absence, just stood out everywhere she went, where so many wrongs had to be put to right.

'Sue never defined herself as a feminist, unlike many of us,' agrees Vivien, who became one of Sue's closest friends over thirty-five years. 'She always felt her story should stand on its merits and her being a woman attached to it was not relevant.'

Her other strongly held belief was that no country could take the moral high ground when it came to human rights abuses, including the treatment of women. In Sue's world, there is no 'us and them'.

'It was the Ireland story that prompted her to write this book,' says Ian O'Reilly of 'Ireland's Fallen Women' which forms chapter 3 of this book. 'She exclaimed "This is an EU country and even here it's being swept under the carpet. I am shocked!"'

As always, the impact of journalism spanning so many years and continents is hard to measure precisely. The list of Sue's BBC films runs to twenty-two pages. And there was more than a decade of reporting at ITN before that. You can begin to judge its merit in the countless broadcasting and human rights awards won by Sue and her teams, the commentary and conversation they provoked and, most important of all, the real change they achieved towards the ultimate goal of ending the abuse and impunity.

Most journalists dare to hope their reporting can make a difference. We're often disappointed. In Sue's case, her singular focus on certain issues did play a significant role in what could only be a long, slow process of raising awareness, and empowering others to speak out, and eventually take action. But there are other examples where change in someone's life, and the laws which bind, was immediate and inspiring.

Such is the case of Min Min Lama from Nepal, a teenage girl raped at the age of fourteen and sentenced to twelve years in prison for having an abortion.

In 1999, when Sue visits Min Min in prison, she writes how 'this tiny and fragile girl has become a symbol for those campaigning in Nepal to change the abortion law'. Then sixteen years of age, Min Min is the youngest prisoner, but not the only such victim.

'Nearly one hundred women, or a fifth of the female prisoners in Nepal are serving time on abortion-related charges and many of them, like Min Min Lama, have been raped by a male relation.'

As Sue puts it, she goes on a 'three-day trek to confront the woman who had induced the abortion'. Min Min's step-sister-in-law, who insists her brother could never have done such a thing, tricked Min Min into taking a drug to induce an abortion. Sue manages to extract a confession on camera which leads to Min Min's release.

Even more, Nepalese law was changed to allow abortions in the cases of rape and under-age sex abuse.

Another film that brought about legal change focused on the illegal trade in human organs. In their 2001 report, Sue and Ian documented how donors came from Moldova, operations were performed in Turkey, and those seeking transplants were largely from Israel. In Judaism, it's believed the body should go to its grave whole, which meant there was a limited availability of organs for transplant. Their documentary led to the passage of a law that partly restricted medical insurance companies from funding overseas transplants.

In other cases, Sue's work helped bring the plight of an entire country out of the shadows and into a global spotlight. Burma, or Myanmar as it's now known, stands out in this regard.

In the late nineties Sue and Ian focused on how large Western companies were doing business with the ruling generals. Journalists couldn't get visas so they set up a fake business. Enter a casual-wear clothing company with all the required paraphernalia: telephone and fax numbers, email addresses, business cards. They somehow managed to secure a rare business visa, and even meetings with senior Burmese army officers.

Ian recounts how, before their crucial visit to the embassy in London, 'Sue said we should appear wealthy as doors open for wealthy people. Sue got all dressed up, had her hair done and borrowed some large flashy jewellery from her mother-in-law. With the help of my mate Jonathon I too put together a similarly affluent-looking costume. We were ready.'

Their undercover filming exposed how Western labels were being manufactured in Burmese factories controlled by the military junta. As a result, companies like Burton in the UK and Dunnes Stores in Ireland stopped their operations.

Sue and Ian, with the help of the equally determined Burma activist known as Ms Faith, also succeeded in secretly recording and smuggling out an interview with Aung San Suu Kyi. At that time, the renowned pro-democracy campaigner was living under her strictest period of house arrest. Her words, broadcast on the BBC, resonated far and wide.

Burma is now a more open, less repressive place, after a long, hard and halting period of transition. Aung San Suu Kyi's National League for Democracy recently swept to power in the country's first national vote after a half century of military rule finally came to end in 2011.

When news reached Burma of Sue's passing, Suu Kyi wrote how Sue had 'showed great courage and commitment in reporting from Burma during some of our darkest days, and exemplified my belief that the best journalists are also the nicest'.

And Sue counts among the most persistent. By the late nineties she was turning her steely gaze on issues of forced marriage and what are called 'honour killings' in conservative Muslim communities in countries such as Pakistan and Jordan.

'She did these stories of honour killings and forced marriages in Pakistan much earlier than anyone else,' says writer and activist Yasmin Alibhai-Brown who was also Sue's friend.

Yasmin, a feisty campaigner herself, speaks of the 'terrible uproar' when Sue, working again with Ian, then turned their cameras on families of Pakistani heritage living in Britain.

'She was fighting a second battle against these forces of secrecy and protectionism,' Yasmin tells me in an impassioned telephone conversation. 'Sue really did break through these walls of silence.'

As those walls starting crumbling, some of those verbal bricks fell on Yasmin too, a Ugandan-born British Muslim with Pakistani ancestry. 'Community leaders, conservative Muslims and preachers would say to me "How can you know this woman who is a racist and a colonialist?"' Her response, in conversations and her newspaper columns, was to insist: 'It would be racist if she didn't do it because she would be saying other lives don't matter as much as white lives.'

And that is what informed Sue, and Tony Jolliffe's approach, when in 2012 they began working on their powerful series on female genital mutilation, now referred to as FGM. 'We both knew our films couldn't end this practice but we wanted to bring it to the front of conversation,' he tells me.

Tony and I meet for coffee in his London neighbourhood after he asks for a bit of time to reflect on Sue's legacy. As with all us of us who knew Sue, it's also an affectionate reflection on a remarkable person he still can't believe is gone. During four years of making films with Sue, in sixteen different and often difficult countries, he says, 'I can't remember a day when she was anything other than cheerful good company.' That's a huge compliment in the pressure-cooker world of journalism.

Their FGM reports, filmed in five countries, received solid editorial backing from the BBC's *Newsnight* programme, and in particular two deputy editors – Shaminder Nahal, now at Channel 4, and Liz Gibbons who commissioned the first FGM film and others after it. It contrasted starkly with the reticence in some other media, including even other BBC departments, at the time.

'There was a view in some places that FGM was a little exotic and a little disgusting,' remarks *Newsnight* producer James Clayton who also worked on some of the films. Earlier, as a freelance journalist, he tried to interest a Sunday newspaper in running a piece on this practice. He was told 'senior editors would never put stories about vaginas being cut in the paper'.

True to form, when Sue tackled it she got straight to the point, so to speak.

Tony tells me an anecdote about filming an operation of 'female genital reconstruction' in a French hospital. 'Tony! Have you got it?' Sue whispered tersely through her surgical mask.

'Got what?' he queried through his mask.

'The clitoris!' she declared.

'Yes!'

He says the *Newsnight* report from France, which contrasted French and British approaches to tackling FGM, caused a stir, including articles in the press. No one was being prosecuted in Britain, where families were often sending their daughters back to other countries to be 'cut', while France was taking a tougher line with prosecutions and inspections, including medical examinations of young girls once they returned to France.

'Why have we failed so lamentably here compared to the French and their one hundred convictions?' Sue asks in her opening chapter 'The Cruellest Cut'. The answer, she points out, lies in the way '[w]e respect tolerance and accept cultural differences, but it allows abuse to take place behind closed doors'.

The driving passion of Sue Lloyd-Roberts was to fling open the doors, kick them down if she had to, or wiggle in through the windows. Former *Newsnight* deputy editor Liz Gibbons remembers when she first shared a statistic with Sue in 2012 that suggested that 90 per cent of Egyptian women had undergone some form of FGM.

She says: 'I could have told any reporter my half-baked statistic about FGM in Egypt, and my interest in commissioning a film and got absolutely nothing back. But what Sue delivered was not just an amazing film but a whole series of follow-up reports which I genuinely think led to a real change in attitudes and policy, in the

UK at least.' Sue had again 'turned an issue into a cause'. Liz calls their close collaboration on the films 'one of the things I'm most proud of from *Newsnight*'.

By 2013, reports about FGM were appearing everywhere in the British media. By 2014, the government hosted a 'Girl Summit' aimed at mobilizing local and international efforts to end FGM, as well as forced and child marriages, within a generation.

While looking at Sue's impact on highlighting FGM, one of the most inspiring conversations I had was with Muna Hassan, a young student campaigner in the British city of Bristol who featured in one of Sue's films. Born of Somali parents in Sweden, Muna had moved to Britain at the age of eight. She became involved in the local charity Integrate Bristol when she was just a teenager and soon started speaking out against FGM.

'Sue came to Bristol and let us speak from the heart,' Muna recounts when we find time to speak on the telephone in between the demands of finishing her university degree and carrying on her fight for many causes. 'She pushed us and said, "If you have something to say, say it now."' I imagine Sue saying that, in her no-nonsense way.

Muna's palpable enthusiasm cuts through the distance of a telephone call. For her, and her colleagues who feature in this book's first chapter, the BBC films amplified their voices and catapulted what had been a local community issue into a national and international one.

Suddenly, the language changed. Muna explains how Sue spoke of a 'form of abuse' not a 'cultural practice'. What had been viewed as something 'happening halfway across the world' became a British issue, a topic to tackle even in Parliament.

And it didn't stop with FGM. Muna tells me it 'opened a can of worms'. The debates on FGM spiralled into greater community engagement on a wider range of issues including growing radicalization among Muslim youth.

'We'll never forget her,' she says quietly before our call ends. 'But we still have a long, long battle ahead.'

Many won't forget Sue – for her films, and for the fact her work didn't stop with the films. Sue joined campaign groups for Burma, and also Tibet, another of her major concerns. She was also a tireless fundraiser – in the style of a woman who, for all her intensity on serious issues, was also fabulously fun company with her love of a little bit of mischief and, wherever possible, a lot of dance.

'There was Bop for Bosnia which provided trucks full of equipment, Rock for Romania raised money for Aids orphans, Tango for Tibetan refugees, and then we did the Bushmen's Ball for Survival,' lists Vivien Morgan who, like all Sue's close friends, struggles to come to terms with the loss of a fellow traveller.

'We were planning an FGM event,' adds Vivien, 'but it didn't happen.'

Sue never let go of stories, nor the people in them.

Behind the public eye, noticed only by a few, there were the countless acts of kindness: a bit of money from her own pocket pressed into poor families' hands; advice for Tibetans seeking asylum; financial help for school fees in Romania, a place in London to eat and sleep.

As her daughter Sarah reminisces in her introduction to this book, the doors of their lovely home in North London were opened to 'government ministers, journalists, activists, or victims fleeing persecution from one war-torn country or another'.

The exiled Tibetan leader the Dalai Lama called her 'London Sue'. Young journalists now following in her footsteps call her an inspiration. Those who travelled in her time speak of her pioneering place in videojournalism, the secret undercover filming in investigative journalism that became her professional signature.

Then there's this book. Sue's husband Nick tells me she was also thinking about a novel which would have focused on women's stories.

But then, suddenly, she had her own personal battle to wage against myeloid leukaemia – albeit in Sue-style. On 27 July, she wrote in her hospital blog: 'Have been in for almost a week now and the chemo has been quite gentle. I am managing to work on my book every morning, Nick and I go for a walk in Regent's Park or out to lunch at midday and then the chemo starts at 2.00 and lasts about six hours.'

Ian O'Reilly remembers how 'her last conscious weeks were a frenzy of emails and text messages between us as she demanded to know this detail or that from some of our stories she was including in the book.'

Sue, and those who knew her well, could only believe – we'll get through this. Until, finally, the brave journalist who had somehow managed to escape from every possible situation for so long, was forced to leave this story unfinished.

'I told her "Let's leave the book for a few days and concentrate on the stem cell transplant,"' reflects Nick. 'After that, all hell broke loose and she got the virus which went to the brain, from which she never really recovered.'

When Sue passed away, some newspapers got in touch with Tony Jolliffe to ask for photographs of Sue in war zones. 'She wasn't a war correspondent,' he told them. They still insisted that was what they wanted to see.

Sue wanted us to see different wars of our time, the many everyday battles being waged day in, day out, many of them being fought by, and against, women and young girls.

She fought with them, and for them, until the very end.

Lyse Doucet
BBC Chief International Correspondent

NOTES

I THE CRUELLEST CUT

1   As reported in 'UK regrets The Gambia's withdrawal from Commonwealth', BBC News, 3 October 2013; http://www.bbc.co.uk/news/uk-24376127

2   Elizabeth Cady Stanton, *The Woman's Bible* (Dover Publications, 2002).

3   Charles Darwin, 'Journal' as quoted in *Charles Darwin: Destroyer of Myths* by Andrew Norman (Pen & Sword Books, 2013), p.61.

4   Gustave Le Bon, 'The Crowd' as quoted in *The Darwin Effect* by Jerry Bergman (Master Books, 2014), p.235.

5   Mernissi (1987: 42).

6   Natalie Angier, *Woman: An Intimate Geography* (London, Virago, 2014), p.58.

7   http://www.who.int/mediacentre/factsheets/fs241/en/

8   United Nations Children's Fund, Female Genital Mutilation/Cutting: A statistical overview and exploration of the dynamics of change (New York: UNICEF, 2013); http://www.childinfo.org/files/FGCM_Lo_res.pdf

9   http://www.medindia.net/news/Egyptian-Clerics-Say-Female-Circumcision-UnIslamic-23055-1.htm

10   Nawal El Saadawi, 'Nawal El Saadawi: "I am going to carry on this fight for ever"', *Independent*, 22 July 2014; http://www.independent.co.uk/news/people/profiles/nawal-el-saadawi-i-am-going-to-carry-on-this-fight-for-ever-2371378.html

11   Nawal El Saadawi, *The Hidden Face of Eve* (London, Zed Books, 2007), p.40.

12   http://www.who.int/mediacentre/factsheets/fs241/en/

13   Leyla Hussein, 'Efua Dorkenoo obituary', *Guardian*, 22 October 2014; http://www.theguardian.com/society/2014/oct/22/efua-dorkenoo

14   http://www.trustforlondon.org.uk/wp-content/uploads/2015/07/FGM-statistics-final-report-21-07-15-released-text.pdf

15   Paul Peachey, 'FGM trial: CPS accused of "show trial" as UK's first female genital mutilation case collapses', *Independent*, 4 February 2015; http://www.independent.co.uk/news/uk/home-news/fgm-trial-cps-accused-of-show-trial-as-uks-first-female-genital-mutilation-case-collapses-10024487.html

16 ibid.
17 https://www.gov.uk/government/speeches/girl-summit-2014-david-camerons-speech
18 Naana Otoo-Oyortey, 'Nawal El Saadawi: "I am going to carry on this fight for ever"', *Independent*, 22 July 2014; http://www.independent.co.uk/news/people/profiles/nawal-el-saadawi-i-am-going-to-carry-on-this-fight-for-ever-2371378.html
19 http://www.legislation.gov.uk/ukpga/2003/31/pdfs/ukpga_20030031_en.pdf

2   THE GRANDMOTHERS OF THE PLAZA DE MAYO

1 'Argentina's grim past', BBC News (14 June 2005). http://news.bbc.co.uk/1/hi/world/americas/4173895.stm
2 Jonathan Mann, 'Macabre new details emerge about Argentina's "dirty war"', CNN (23 March 1996); http://edition.cnn.com/WORLD/9603/argentina.war/index.html
3 Paul Vallely, *Pope Francis: Untying the Knots: The Struggle for the Soul of Catholicism* (Bloomsbury, 2015).
4 'World in Brief: Argentina: Bishops Apologize for Civil War Crimes', *Los Angeles Times*, 18 April 1996.

3   IRELAND'S FALLEN WOMEN

1 St Jerome c.342–420.
2 Edward Andrew Reno, 'The Authoritative Text: Raymond of Penyafort's Editing of the "Decretals of Gregory IX" (1234)', Columbia University Academic Commons, 2011; http://academiccommons.columbia.edu/catalog/ac%3A132233
3 Anne Isba, *Gladstone and Women* (Hambledon Continuum, 2006).
4 ibid.
5 James M. Smith, *Ireland's Magdalen Laundries and the Nation's Architecture of Containment* (Manchester University Press, 2008), p.xv.
6 Patricia Burke Brogan, *Memoir with Grykes and Turloughs* (Wordsonthestreet, 2014).
7 http://www.sistersofcharity.com
8 Patricia Burke Brogan, *Memoir with Grykes and Turloughs* (Wordsonthestreet, 2014).
9 This is the bishop who, in 1992, was discovered to have a love child as a result of an affair with an American divorcee. Eamonn Casey, Bishop of Kerry, resigned and left Ireland.
10 Quoted in the documentary *Mothers Against the Odds*, by Anne Daly and Ronan Tynan (Esperanza Productions, 2012).

11 ibid.

12 Pope Paul VI, Humanae Vitae, 25 July 1968.

13 Quoted in the documentary *Mothers Against the Odds* by Anne Daly and Ronan Tynan (Esperanza Productions, 2012)

14 ibid.

15 ibid.

16 ibid.

17 Senator Martin McAleese, 'Report of the Inter-Departmental Committee to establish the facts of State involvement with the Magdalen Laundries', 2013; www.justice.ie/en/JELR/Pages/MagdalenRpt2013, p.iv.

18 Catherine Shoard, 'Philomena Lee on meeting the Pope: "Those nuns would be jealous now"', *Guardian*, 6 February 2014.

19 Senator Martin McAleese, 'Report of the Inter-Departmental Committee to establish the facts of State involvement with the Magdalen Laundries', p.vii.

20 'Bruce Arnold: McAleese Report flies in the face of painful evidence of laundry victims', *Irish Independent*, 18 February 2013.

21 Colm O'Gorman as reported in 'Ireland: Proposed "mother and baby homes" investigation welcome, but a missed opportunity to address Magdalenes', Amnesty International, 9 January 2015.

22 Simon McGarr, 'McAleese report leaves questions unanswered', *Irish Examiner*, 19 February 2014.

23 Senator Martin McAleese, 'Report of the Inter-Departmental Committee', p.vii.

24 Joan Burton as reported in 'Demanding justice for women and children abused by Irish nuns', BBC News, 24 September 2015; http://www.bbc.co.uk/news/magazine-29307705

25 'Church in Ireland needs "reality check" after gay marriage vote', BBC News, 24 May 2015; http://www.bbc.co.uk/news/world-europe-32862824

26 ibid.

27 'Fewer than one in five attends Sunday Mass in Dublin', *Irish Times*, 30 May 2011; http://www.irishtimes.com/news/fewer-than-one-in-five-attend-sunday-mass-in-dublin-1.585731

28 M. E. Collins, *Ireland, 1868–1966: History in the Making* (Ireland, Edco, 1993), p.431.

29 'An unfortunate amendment on abortion', *The Tablet*, 17 September 1983; http://archive.thetablet.co.uk/article/17th-september-1983/3/an-unfortunate-amendment-on-abortion

4 SAUDI ARABIA

1 http://reemasaad.blogspot.co.uk/2009/08/lingerie-campaign.html

2 'Men banned from selling Lingerie in Saudi Arabia', *Telegraph*, 5 January 2012;

http://www.telegraph.co.uk/news/worldnews/middleeast/saudiarabia/
8993690/Men-banned-from-selling-lingerie-in-Saudi-Arabia.html

3 Shamim Aleem, *'Mothers of Believers', Prophet Muhammad(s) and His Family: A Sociological Perspective* (AuthorHouse, 2007).

4 David Commins, *The Wahhabi Mission and Saudi Arabia* (London, I. B. Tauris & Co., 2006).

5 ibid.

6 'Saudi police "stopped" fire rescue', BBC News (15 March 2002). http://news.bbc.co.uk/1/hi/world/middle_east/1874471.stm

7 'Saudi Sheikh warns women that driving could affect ovaries and pelvis', Riyadh Connect, 28 September 2013.

8 David Leigh, 'US put pressure on Saudi Arabia to let women drive, leaked cables reveal', *Guardian*, 27 May 2011.

9 Joshua Muravchik, *Trailblazers of the Arab Spring: Voices of Democracy in the Middle East* (Encounter Books, 2013), p.27.

10 Suad Abu-Dayyeh, 'Saudi Women Activists Jailed for Trying to Help Starving Woman', 9 July 2013; http://www.huffingtonpost.co.uk/suad-abudayyeh/saudi-women-activists-jai_b_3565568.html

11 Olga Khazan, ' "Negative Physiological Impacts"? Why Saudi Women Aren't Allowed to Drive', The Atlantic, 7 October 2013.

12 Cassandra Jardine, 'There's such ignorance about us', *Telegraph*, 12 December 2005; http://www.telegraph.co.uk/culture/3648711/Theres-such-ignorance-about-us.html

13 'Wajeha al-Huwaider – Woman of Action', A Celebration of Women.org, 1 June 2013; http://acelebrationofwomen.org/2013/06/wajeha-al-huwaidar-woman-of-action/

14 Rajaa Alsanea, *Girls of Riyadh* (Fig Tree, 2007).

15 Gallup.com, 'Saudi Arabia: Majorities Support Women's Rights', 21 December 2007; http://www.gallup.com/poll/103441/saudi-arabia-majorities-support-womens-rights.aspx

16 Ahmed Abdel-Raheem, 'Word to the West: many Saudi women oppose lifting the driving ban', *Guardian*, 2 November 2013.

17 Gallup.com, 'Saudi Arabia: Majorities Support Women's Rights', 21 December, 2007; http://www.gallup.com/poll/103441/saudi-arabia-majorities-support-womens-rights.aspx

18 https://en.wikipedia.org/wiki/Women%27s_rights_in_Saudi_Arabia

19 https://en.wikipedia.org/wiki/Women%27s_rights_in_Saudi_Arabia

20 'Saudi Arabia's king appoints women to Shura Council', BBC, 11 January 2013; http://www.bbc.co.uk/news/world-middle-east-20986428

21 Sabria Jawhar, 'Saudi Women Owe Voting Rights to Arab Spring', The World Post, 26 September 2011.

22 Sherard Cowper-Coles, *Ever the Diplomat: Confessions of a Foreign Office Mandarin* (HarperCollins, 2014).

23   http://www.raifbadawi.org

24   Ian Black, 'Saudi Arabian security forces quell "day of rage" protests', *Guardian*, 11 March 2011.

25   Rania Abouzeid, 'Saudi Arabia's "Day of Rage" Passes Quietly', *Time*, 11 March 2011; http://content.time.com/time/world/article/0,8599,2058486,00.html

5   EGYPT

1   For a general overview see 'The dynamics of democracy in the Middle East', The Economist Unit, March 2005, pp.14–15; http://graphics.eiu.com/files/ad_pdfs/MidEast_special.pdf

2   Ahdaf Soueif, 'Image of unknown woman beaten by Egypt's military echoes around world', *Guardian*, 18 December 2011; http://www.theguardian.com/commentisfree/2011/dec/18/egypt-military-beating-female-protester-tahrir-square

3   ibid.

4   Scott Pelley, 'Lara Logan breaks silence on Cairo assault', CBS, 1 May 2011; http://www.cbsnews.com/news/lara-logan-breaks-silence-on-cairo-assault/

5   ibid.

6   Brian Stelter, 'CBS Reporter recounts a merciless assault', *New York Times*, 28 April 2011; http://www.nytimes.com/2011/04/29/business/media/29logan.html

7   ibid.

8   Caroline Davies, 'Tahrir Square women's march marred by rival protest', *Guardian*, 8 March 2011; http://www.theguardian.com/world/2011/mar/08/rival-protesters-clash-women-tahrir

9   ' "The Future of Egyptian women is in danger" – Samira Ibrahim speaks out', *Guardian*, 13 March 2012; http://www.theguardian.com/lifeandstyle/2012/mar/13/women-samira-ibrahim-egypt-virginity-tests

10 Mohsen Habiba, 'What made her go there? Samira Ibrahim and Egypt's virginity test trial', Aljeezera, 16 March 2012; http://www.aljazeera.com/indepth/opinion/2012/03/20123161333129201850.html

11 Isobel Coleman, ' "Blue bra girl" rallies Egypt's women vs. oppression', CNN, 22 December 2011; http://edition.cnn.com/2011/12/22/opinion/coleman-women-egypt-protest/

12 'Egypt's Islamist parties win elections to parliament', BBC 21 January 2012; http://www.bbc.co.uk/news/world-middle-east-16665748

13 Mariz Tadros, 'To politically empower women on a global scale we need more than quotas', *Guardian*, 8 March 2012; http://www.theguardian.com/global-development/poverty-matters/2012/mar/08/political-empower-women-egypt

14 http://www.indexmundi.com/egypt/demographics_profile.html

15 Al-Masry Al-Youm, 'Shura Council committee says female protesters should take

responsibility, if harassed', *Egypt Independent*, 11 February 2013; http://www.egyptindependent.com/news/shura-council-committee-says-female-protesters-should-take-responsibility-if-harassed

16 Elisabeth Jaquette, Muftah, 'The Heroes of Tahrir: Operation Anti-Sexual Harassment', 4 February 2013; http://muftah.org/heroes-of-tahrir/#.Vw4DVGNU 20M

17 OpAnitSH Facebook, 'Press Release: Mob sexual assaults reported to OpAntiSH during June 30th demonstrations hit catastrophic skies', 3 July 2013.

18 Dana Hughes, Molly Hunter, 'President Morsi Ousted: First Democratically Elected Leader Under House Arrest', ABC News, 3 July 2013; http://abcnews.go.com/International/president-morsi-ousted-democratically-elected-leader-house-arrest/story?id=19568447

19 Ahdaf Soueif, 'Egypt's revolution won't be undone: the people still have the will', *Guardian*, 30 May 2014; http://www.theguardian.com/commentisfree/2014/may/30/egypt-revolution-wont-be-undone-sisi-young-activists

20 Anthony Bond, Lucy Thornton, 'Shaima al-Sabbagh: Heartbreaking picture shows moments of panic after leading Egyptian female protester dies after being "shot by police"', *Mirror*, 25 January 2015; http://www.mirror.co.uk/news/world-news/shaima-al-sabbagh-heartbreaking-picture-shows-5039047

7   BOYS WILL BE BOYS

1 Robert Capps: 'Sex-slave whistle-blowers vindicated', Salon.com, 6 August 2002; http://www.salon.com/2002/08/06/dyncorp/[Retrieved 13.2.2013]

2 STOP, 2015, figures available from: http://www.stoptraffickingofpeople.org/ [Retrieved 13.2.2016]

3 'Bosnia sex trade shames UN', *Scotsman*, 9 February 2003.

4 North Atlantic Treaty Organization, 'NATO's role in Kosovo', updated 30 November 2015; http://www.nato.int/cps/en/natolive/topics_48818.htm [Retrieved 13.2.2016]

5 'Young West African Girls Face Perils of Prostitution, Trafficking', Voice of America, 27 October 2009; http://www.voanews.com/content/a-13-young-west-african-girls-face-perils-of-prostitution-and-trafficking-66383792/547929.html

8   FORCED MARRIAGE

1 IRIN, 'Forced marriages: In Kashmir, old habits die hard', *Express Tribune*, 25 November, 2013 http://tribune.com.pk/story/636425/forced-marriages-in-kashmir-old-habits-die-hard/ [retrieved: 20.2.2016]

2 Christina Julios, *Forced Marriage and 'Honour' Killings in Britain: Private Lives, Community Crimes and Public Policy Perspectives* (Routledge, 2015), pp.106–10.

3 BBC Politics 97, 'Immigration Rules Relaxed'; http://www.bbc.co.uk/news/special/politics97/news/06/0605/straw.shtml [retrieved: 20.02.2016]

4 'Huge rise in forced marriages for women', Independent.ie, 20 July 1998; 'MPs told: Don't aid forced marriages', *Independent*, 7 August 1998.

5 BBC 'MP calls for English tests for immigrants', 13 July 2001; http://news.bbc.co.uk/1/hi/uk/1436867.stm [retrieved:20.2.2016]

6 Helen Pidd: 'Rotherham report "reduced me to tears", says MP who exposed abuse decade ago', *Observer*, 14 August 2014.

7 Yasmin Alibhai-Brown: 'I'm no Tory, but we should all be thanking David Cameron for ending forced marriages', *Independent*, 14 June 2015.

8 ibid.

9 HONOUR KILLINGS

1 Aurangzeb Qureshi, 'Defending Pakistani women against honour killings', Aljazeera, 7 March 2016.

2 'Pregnant Pakistani Woman Stoned to Death', *Guardian*, 28 May 2014.

3 http://www.liquisearch.com/pakistani_diaspora_in_the_united_kingdom/health_and_social_issues/forced_marriage

4 IRIN, ' "Honour" killings pose serious challenge to rule of law' (UNOCHA 2007); http://www.irinnews.org/report/74591/jordan-%E2%80%9Chonour%E2%80%9D-killings-pose-serious-challenge-rule-law [retrieved 28.02.16]

5 Manuel Eisner, 'Belief that honour killings are "justified" still prevalent among next generation, study shows', Cambridge University, 20 June 2013; http://www.cam.ac.uk/research/news/belief-that-honour-killings-are-justified-still-prevalent-among-jordans-next-generation-study-shows

6 Dan Bilefsky, 'How to avoid honor killing in Turkey? Honor Suicides', *New York Times*, 16 July 2006.

7 IPCC, November 2008, https://www.ipcc.gov.uk/sites/default/files/Documents/investigation_commissioner_reports/banaz_mahmod_executive_summary_nov_08_v7.pdf

8 BBC, ' "Honour" attack numbers revealed by UK police forces', 3 December 2011; http://www.bbc.com/news/uk-16014368 [retrieved 8/03/16]

9 Jerome Taylor, Mark Hughes, 'Mystery of Bradford's Missing Children: were they forced into marriages abroad?', *Independent*, 4 February 2008.

10 ibid.

10 INDIA

1   Ministry of Law and Justice, New Delhi, 11 January 2007, 1Pausa21, 1928 (Saka).

2   Ministry of Law and Justice, New Delhi, 11 January, 2007, 1Pausa21, 1928 (Saka).

3   Neeta Lal, 'India: Home to One in Three Child Brides', Inter Press Service News Agency, 20 August 2014.

4   'India police arrest eight for "brutal" Haryana rape and murder', BBC News, 9 February 2015.

5   The details of the rape and murder of Jyoti Singh come from contemporary newspaper accounts and the documentary *India's Daughter*, directed by Leslee Udwin (Assassin Films, March 2015).

6   Quoted in *India's Daughter*, directed by Leslee Udwin (Assassin Films, March 2015).

7   'Soumya murder: CM remark has city fuming', *The Times of India*, 3 October 2008.

8   India's National Crime Records Bureau (NCRB), Crime against Women, 2013; http://ncrb.nic.in/StatPublications/CII/CII2013/Chapters/5-Crime%20against%20Women.pdf

9   'Indians See Rape as a Major National Problem: Majorities Say Law and Law Enforcement Are Inadequate', Pew Research Center, 22 April 2014.

10 Quoted in *India's Daughter*, by Leslee Udwin (Assassin Films, March 2015).

11 Quoted in *India's Daughter*, by Leslee Udwin (Assassin Films, March 2015).

12 http://www.censusindia.gov.in/2011-common/census_2011.html

13 Quoted in *India's Daughter*, by Leslee Udwin (Assassin Films, March 2015).

14 http://www.censusindia.gov.in/2011-common/census_2011.html

15 George Thomas, 'Disappearing Daughters: India's Female Feticide', CBN World News, 6 July 2012; http://www.cbn.com/cbnnews/world/2012/june/disappearing-daughters-indias-female-feticide/?mobile=false

16 http://www.ncpcr.gov.in/view_file.php?fid=434

17 'Doctor sentenced to 2 years imprisonment for violating PCPNDT', Business Standard, 12 February 2013; http://www.business-standard.com/article/pti-stories/doctor-sentenced-to-2-years-imprisonment-for-violating-pcpndt-113021200833_1.html

18 Sriti Yadav, 'Female Feticide in India: The Plight of Being Born a Woman', Feminspire, 5 April 2013

19 Amrita Guha, 'Disappearing Daughters: Female Feticide in India', Seneca International, 20 January 2014; http://www.seneca-international.org/2014/01/20/disappearing-daughters-female-feticide-in-india/

20 As quoted in 'Challenges in implementing the ban on sex selection' by Sandhya Srinivasan, Info Change India; http://infochangeindia.org/women/analysis/challenges-in-implementing-the-ban-on-sex-selection.html

21 http://www.censusindia.gov.in/2011-common/census_2011.html

22 Manjeet Sehgal, 'Voters in Haryana village demand brides for votes', *India Today*, 25 September 2014

23 India's National Crime Records Bureau (NCRB) Crime against Women, 2012. http://ncrb.nic.in/StatPublications/CII/CII2012/cii-2012/Chapter%205.pdf

24 Dean Nelson, 'Women killed over dowry "every hour' in India", *Telegraph*, 2 September 2013.

25 George Thomas, 'Disappearing Daughters: India's Female Feticide', CBN World News, 6 July 2012; http://www.cbn.com/cbnnews/world/2012/june/disappearing-daughters-indias-female-feticide/?mobile=false

26 Dean Nelson, 'India "most dangerous place in world to be born a girl"', *Telegraph*, 1 February 2012; http://www.telegraph.co.uk/news/worldnews/asia/india/9054429/India-most-dangerous-place-in-world-to-be-born-a-girl.html

27 *Express Tribune*, 12 April 2016; http://tribune.com.pk/story/393034/india-advances-but-many-women-still-trapped-in-dark-ages/

28 *Anita Desai: A Life in Literature*, BBC HARDtalk, 21 January 2005.

29 Anita Desai, *Voices in the City* (Orient Longman India, 2001).

30 Neeru Tandon, *Anita Desai and her Fictional World* (Atlantic Publisher & Distributors, 2007), p.204.

31 Joshua Barnes, '"You Turn Yourself into an Outsider": An interview with Anita Desai', Sampsonia Way, 14 January 2014.

32 Rama Lakshmi, 'India's Modi just delivered the world's worst compliment', *Washington Post*, 8 June 2015.

11   RAPE AS A WEAPON OF WAR

1 Elisabeth J. Wood, 'Multiple perpetrator rape during war', in Miranda A. H. Horvath & Jessica Woodhams (eds.), *Handbook on the Study of Multiple Perpetrator Rape: A multidisciplinary response to an international problem* (Routledge), p.140. See also Wikipedia: https://en.wikipedia.org/wiki/Rape_during_the_Bosnian_War

2 Held at BBC's TV Studios in White City, Bop for Bosnia raised more than £60,000 and was instrumental in launching War Child, a charity dedicated to supporting children affected by conflict.

3 R. Gutman, 'General Mladic Directly Involved in "Cleansing", Witnesses Say', *Moscow Times*, 9 August 1995; http://www.themoscowtimes.com/ (9th August 1995)

4 Lance Corporal David Vaasen (then private first class) T.1429-30, cited in: Judgement, Prosecutor vs Krstic, Case no. IT-98-33-T, T, ChI, 2 August 2001 Klip/Sluiter (eds.), ALC-VII-575.

5 Albina Sorguc, 'Srebrenica Anniversary: The Rape Victims' Testimonies', Balkan Insight, 11 July 2014; http://www.balkaninsight.com/ [retrieved: 12 Feb. 16]

6 Andrea Dworkin, *Pornography: Men Possessing Women* (New York, Dutton, 1989), p.243.

7 Alexandra Stiglmayer, 'The Rapes in Bosnia-Herzegovina' in Alexandra Stiglmayer (ed.), *Mass Rape: The War Against Women in Bosnia-Herzegovina* (University of Nebraska, 1994), p.96.

8 A. Zalihic-Kaurin, 'The Muslim Woman' in A. Stiglmayer (ed.), *Mass Rape: The War Against Women in Bosnia-Herzegovina* (University of Nebraska, 1994), p.173.

9 Witness 50, 29 March 2000, cited in: Transcript 30, p.1270, Kunarac et al. (IT-96-23 & 23/1) 'Foča' [Retrieved 12.02.2016]

10 Paragraph 2, p.1012, Judgment International Military Tribunal for the Far East; http://www.ibiblio.org/ [retrieved 12.02.2016]

11 Tilman Remme, BBC History: World Wars: 'The Battle for Berlin in World War Two; http://www.bbc.co.uk/history/worldwars/wwtwo/berlin_01.shtml [Retrieved 12.02.2016]

12 Seada Vranić, *Breaking the Wall of Silence: The Voices of Raped Bosnia* (Izdanja Antiabarbarus, 1996).

13 ibid.

14 Alan Riding, 'European Inquiry says Serbs' Forces have Raped 20,000', *New York Times*, 9 January 1993.

15 Alexandra Stiglmayer, 'The Rapes in Bosnia-Herzegovina' in Alexandra Stiglmayer (ed.), *Mass Rape: The War Against Women in Bosnia-Herzegovina* (University of Nebraska, 1994), p.92.

16 Lindsey Crider, 'Rape as a War Crime and Crime against Humanity: The Effect of Rape in Bosnia-Herzegovina and Rwanda on International Law', p.19; http://www.cla.auburn.edu/alapsa/assets/file/4ccrider.pdf

17 Alexandra Stiglmayer, 'The Rapes in Bosnia-Herzegovina' in Alexandra Stiglmayer (ed.), *Mass Rape: The War Against Women in Bosnia-Herzegovina* (University of Nebraska, 1994), p.109.

18 Figures for the number of civilians who died in the war vary. See the Centre for Justice and Accountability; http://www.cja.org/article.php?id=247; https://en.wikipedia.org/wiki/Bosnian_War#Casualties

19 Alexandra Stiglmayer, 'The Rapes in Bosnia Herzegovina' in Alexandra Stiglmayer (ed.), *Mass Rape: The War Against Women in Bosnia-Herzegovina* (University of Nebraska, 1994), p.118.

20 Alexandra Stiglmayer, p.119.

21 Alexandra Stiglmayer, p.133.

22 Alexandra Stiglmayer, p.133.

23 Todd A. Salzman, 'Rape Camps as a Means of Ethnic Cleansing: Religious, Cultural, and Ethical Responses to Rape Victims in the Former Yugoslavia', *Human Rights Quarterly*, Vol. 20, No.2 (May 1998), pp.361–2.

24 Angela Robson, 'Weapon of War', *New Internationalist*, issue 244 (June 1993).

25 David M. Crowe, *War Crimes, Genocide, and Justice: A Global History* (Palgrave Macmillan, 2013).

26 Press statement by International Criminal Tribunal for the former Yugoslavia: Judgement of Trial Chamber II In the Kunarac, Kovac and Vukovic case,

22 February 2001; http://www.icty.org/en/press/judgement-trial-chamber-i
i-kunarac-kovac-and-vukovic-case [retrieved: 13.02.2016]

27 International Criminal Tribunal for the former Yugoslavia, 2014 'Crimes of
Sexual Violence in Numbers'; http://www.icty.org/en/in-focus/crimes-sexual-
violence/in-numbers [retrieved 13.02.16]

28 Jo Adetunji, 'Forty-eight women raped every hour in Congo, study finds',
Guardian, 12 May 2011

29 'DRC: Some progress in the fight against impunity but rape still widespread and
largely unpunished – UN report'; http://www.ohchr.org/EN/NewsEvents/
Pages/DisplayNews.aspx?NewsID=14489&

30 Chris McGreal, 'The roots of war in eastern Congo', *Guardian*, 16 May 2008.

31 Human Rights Watch, 'Soldiers who Rape, Commanders who Condone:
Sexual Violence and Military Reform in the Democratic Republic of
Congo', 16 July 2009; https://www.hrw.org/report/2009/07/16/soldiers-who-
rape-commanders-who-condone/sexual-violence-and-military-reform

32 M. Ohambe, J. Muhigwa, B. Mamba: 'Women's Bodies as a Battleground: Sexual
Violence Against Women and Girls During the War in the Democratic Republic
of Congo' (International Alert 2005), p.30.

33 'Atrocities Beyond Words: A Barbarous Campaign of Rape', *Economist*, 1 May
2008; http://www.economist.com/node/11294767

34 Timothy Docking, United States Institute of Peace, 'Special Report: AIDS and
Violent Conflict in Africa', 15 October 2001; http://www.usip.org/publications/
aids-and-violent-conflict-in-africa

35 Human Rights Watch: 'Soldiers Who Rape, Commanders Who Condone:
Sexual Violence and Military Reform in the Democratic Republic of Congo',
16 July 2009; https://www.hrw.org/report/2009/07/16/soldiers-who-rape-
commanders-who-condone/sexual-violence-and-military-reform

36 Human Rights Watch, 'Soldiers Who Rape, Commanders Who Condone: Sexual
Violence and Military Reform in the Democratic Republic of Congo', 16 July 2009;
https://www.hrw.org/report/2009/07/16/soldiers-who-rape-commanders-
who-condone/sexual-violence-and-military-reform [retrieved:13.02.16]

37 Human Rights Watch interview with eighteen-year-old victim, Sake, 29 March
2009, ibid.

38 Carly Brown, 'Rape as a Weapon of War in the Democratic Republic of the Congo',
Torture, Vol. 22, No. 1, 2012; http://www.corteidh.or.cr/tablas/r29631.pdf

39 Jonathan Gottschall, 'Explaining Wartime Rape'; *The Journal of Sex Research*, Vol.
41: issue 2 (2004).

40 Mark Townsend, 'Revealed: how the world turned its back on rape victims of
Congo', *Guardian*, 13 June 2015.

41 Human Rights Watch 2015, 'Justice on Trial: Lessons from the Minova Rape
Case in the Democratic Republic of Congo'; https://www.hrw.org/report/
2015/10/01/justice-trial/lessons-minova-rape-case-democratic-republic-congo
[Retrieved: 13.2.2016]

42 Mark Townsend, 'Revealed: how the world turned its back on rape victims of Congo', *Guardian*, 13 June 2015.

43 ibid.

44 William Hague, End Sexual Violence in Conflict Global Summit 2014; https://www.gov.uk/government/uploads/system/uploads/attachment_data/file/319958/Global_Summit_to_End_Sexual_Violence_Statement_of_Action__1_.pdf

45 Mark Townsend, 'Revealed: how the world turned its back on rape victims of Congo', *Guardian*, 13 June 2015.

12 SEX INEQUALITY IN THE UK

1 ONS 2015, Annual Survey of Hours and Earnings 2015 Provisional Results, Table 2.6a (hourly pay excluding overtime); http://www.ons.gov.uk/employmentandlabourmarket/peopleinwork/earningsandworkinghours/datasets/occupation2digitsocashetable2

2 https://www.tuc.org.uk/equality-issues/gender-equality/equal-pay/women-still-earn-%C2%A35000-year-less-men

3 Source: Annual Survey of Hours and Earnings 2012. The gender pay gap for all 35 major occupations is available from the TUC press office. All gender pay gap figures have been calculated using mean hourly pay, excluding overtime. The annual figures have been calculated by multiplying the hourly pay gap by 37.5 (average weekly hours for a full-time worker) and then again by 52.

4 Ehrc 2015, Pregnancy and Maternity-Related Discrimination and Disadvantage First findings: Surveys of Employers and Mothers; http://www.equalityhumanrights.com/publication/pregnancy-and-maternity-related-discrimination-and-disadvantage-first-findings-surveys-employers-and-0

5 http://us11.campaign-archive1.com/?u=a5b04a26aae05a24bc4efb63e&id=64e6f35176&e=1ba99d671e#wage

6 http://www.newstatesman.com/politics/2015/07/motherhood-trap

7 http://hbswk.hbs.edu/item/kids-benefit-from-having-a-working-mom

8 http://www.theguardian.com/commentisfree/2015/dec/02/sue-lloyd-roberts-memorial-service

INDEX

SUE LLOYD-ROBERTS

Sue Lloyd-Roberts was a freelance video-journalist and television reporter who worked for both ITN and the BBC. After graduating from Oxford, she joined ITN in 1973 as a news trainee and went on to become the UK's first woman video-journalist, reporting as a one-person crew from many bleak outposts of the former Soviet Union and in China. Sue joined Channel 4 News and Channel 4 documentaries in 1981 and eleven years later moved to the BBC. She specialized in human rights and the environment and won praise for her undercover reporting from countries such as China, Burma and Zimbabwe. Sue was also the first video-journalist to get to Damascus and Homs at the start of the Syrian uprising in 2011. For over twenty years Sue reported for the BBC's *Newsnight* programme and for the last ten she also made documentaries for the BBC Our World documentary strand. Sue appeared regularly as a reporter and commentator on BBC Radio 4 programmes.

In the 1980s, Sue made a number of film reports on the history and the aftermath of Britain's atomic bomb trials and co-authored a book on the subject, *Fields of Thunder, Testing Britain's Bomb* (1985). Sue won many awards, including the British Environment and Media Award in 1993 and in 1995 the Royal Television Society International News Award and the Amnesty International's

Television News Award for her reports from the gulags of China.

In 1996, she was awarded European Woman of Achievement by the European Union of Women for her outstanding work investigating abuses of human rights. In 1998, Sue won the Television News Category at the One World Awards for an undercover report from Burma. In June 2000, she again won the Television News Category at the Amnesty International Awards for her film on the abuse of women in Nepal. In April 2001, Sue won the Actual International Award at Newsworld 2000 Barcelona for her investigation into the sex-trafficking business and Television News, One World Award for her report on the Masai people in Tanzania. In 2002, she won the Documentary Category at the One World Awards for a film on working children in India. In 2011 she won an Emmy in New York for her film, *Inside the North Korean Bubble*. In 2012, she was named as International Reporter of the Year at the One World Awards and won the Television News, Amnesty International Award for her reports from Syria. In 2014, she won the United Nations Women on the Move award for her report on FGM in the Gambia.

In 2002, Sue Lloyd-Roberts was appointed an MBE and, in 2013, a CBE for services to journalism. When not travelling the world, Sue lived in Mallorca and London with her husband, Nick. Sue is survived by her son, George, and her daughter, Sarah.

Sue Lloyd-Roberts Scholarship

This scholarship aims to further Sue's deep commitment to international affairs, reporting and human rights issues, and provide support each year for a student who would otherwise struggle to afford the fees to take up a place at Cardiff University, on either a Journalism MA or an International Journalism MA.

To apply for the scholarship, applicants must provide a statement of up to 1,000 words demonstrating their interest in women's rights and international journalism, as well as evidence that they require a scholarship in order to be able to undertake the course. During the course, the successful applicant will be expected to write their MA dissertation on a topic relevant to international affairs or human rights. Candidates will be shortlisted by Cardiff University journalism staff and the final selection will be made by Sue's children, Sarah Morris and George Morris. This is likely to involve a face-to-face or Skype interview.

The scholarship amount will cover the full cost of the tuition fees or £9,000, whichever is greater.

If you've been affected by Sue's work in this book and would like to support journalism like hers for future generations, please find out more about how you can donate to the fund using the website below.

http://www.jomec.co.uk/blog/sue-lloyd-roberts-scholarship/

Cardiff University is a registered charity, registration no. 1136855.

PICTURE CREDITS